BOOK
of
OLD TESTAMENT BIBLE
LITERACY

THE ESSENTIAL
COMPANION IN THE
QUEST FOR
Old Testament BIBLE
KNOWLEDGE

Books by Author

Travel Through Ephesians (2013)

Travel Through The Old Testament Vol. 1 (2016)

Travel Through The Old Testament Vol. 2 (2017)

God's Armor Against Satan's Weapons (2018)
(Tom Hiegel Bible Study Series, #1)

BOOK
of
OLD
TESTAMENT
BIBLE
LITERACY

THE ESSENTIAL
COMPANION IN THE
QUEST FOR
Old Testament BIBLE
KNOWLEDGE

Thomas L. Hiegel

Book of Old Testament Bible Literacy
Copyright © 2018 by Thomas L. Hiegel
TLH CREATIONS, Dayton OH

All rights reserved. No part of this publication may be reproduced, stored in a retrieval system, or transmitted in any form or by any means-electronic, mechanical, photocopy, recording, or any other—except for brief quotations in printed reviews, without the prior permission of the copyright owner.

All Scripture quotations are taken from the NEW AMERICAN STANDARD BIBLE®, Copyright © 1960, 1962, 1963, 1968, 1971, 1972, 1973, 1975, 1977, 1995 by The Lockman Foundation. Used by permission. (www.Lockman.org).

ISBN 978-0-9982861-3-6

Printed in the United States of America.

Table of Contents

ABBREVIATIONS 8
PREFACE 9
CHAPTER ONE. Keys to Each Old Testament Book of the Bible
.... 11
   The Hebrew Scripture Structure 12
   Old Testament Structure used by Christians 12
   Other Books Not Accepted in the Canon of Scripture 12
   G E N E S I S 15
   E X O D U S 20
   L E V I T I C U S 24
   N U M B E R S 27
   D E U T E R O N O M Y 31
   J O S H U A 35
   J U D G E S 38
   R U T H 42
   1 S A M U E L 45
   2 S A M U E L 49
   1 K I N G S 53
   2 K I N G S 57
   1 C H R O N I C L E S 61
   2 C H R O N I C L E S 65
   E Z R A 69
   N E H E M I A H 73
   E S T H E R 76
   J O B 79

PSALMS	83
PROVERBS	86
ECCLESIASTES	89
SONG OF SOLOMON	92
ISAIAH	95
JEREMIAH	99
LAMENTATIONS	103
EZEKIEL	106
DANIEL	109
HOSEA	112
JOEL	115
AMOS	116
OBADIAH	120
JONAH	122
MICAH	125
NAHUM	128
HABAKKUK	131
ZEPHANIAH	134
HAGGAI	137
ZECHARIAH	140
MALACHI	143

CHAPTER TWO. COLLECTION/DICTIONARY of People, Titles, Positions, and Nations Concerning The Old Testament Scriptures 146

CHAPTER THREE. COLLECTION/DICTIONARY of Places in the Old Testament or in Bible History 189

CHAPTER FOUR. COLLECTION/DICTIONARY of Old Testament-Related Words 208

CHAPTER FIVE. Bible Theology Terminology 224

CHAPTER SIX. Additional Detailed Descriptions of Key Old Testament Words and Helps to Aid in Study 242

INDEX 309

Abbreviations

OLD TESTAMENT ABBREVIATIONS

Gen	Genesis	SofS	Song of Songs (Solomon)
Ex	Exodus	Isa	Isaiah
Lev	Leviticus	Jer	Jeremiah
Num	Numbers	Lam	Lamentations
Deut	Deuteronomy	Ezek	Ezekiel
Josh	Joshua	Dan	Daniel
Judg	Judges	Hos	Hosea
Ruth	Ruth	Joel	Joel
1, 2 Sam	Samuel	Amos	Amos
1, 2 Kings	Kings	Oba	Obadiah
1, 2 Chron	Chronicles	Jon	Jonah
Ezra	Ezra	Mic	Micah
Neh	Nehemiah	Nah	Nahum
Est	Esther	Hab	Habakkuk
Job	Job	Zeph	Zephaniah
Ps	Psalms	Hag	Haggai
Pro	Proverbs	Zech	Zechariah
Eccl	Ecclesiastes	Mal	Malachi

GENERAL ABBREVIATIONS

BCE or B.C.E.	Before the Common Era (B.C.)
CE or C.E.	Common Era (A.D.)
cp, cps	Chapter, chapters
i.e.	"that is"
e.g.	"for example"
NT	New Testament
OT	Old Testament
vol	In this Volume
v, vv	Verse (s)

PREFACE

The Bible is a vital document to be read and understood. Therefore, the Bible student must be able to have references, which identify the persons, places, events, etc. contained in its pages. Let's face it; many times the name or place is passed over by the student, because of not having the reference tools to quickly retrieve the information.

The purpose of this Bible Literacy Guide is to place in your hands, a single reference book that contains most of the names, locations, and Bible book data needed to assist in Old Testament study. It is a collection of materials gathered during my study of the Bible, over many years, which makes it unique. To read through the collection of names, or of locations, is an education in itself. It is not the intent of this volume, to detail every person or location in the entire Bible. Rather, I have included what I consider a thorough work on most of the needed details. The section of Theology Terminology is a little deeper than the original intent of this book. However, I have collected these during many years of study, and have included many of the terms beneficial in your education.

Chapter 1 includes a valuable overview and keys to each of the thirty-nine books in the Old Testament of the Bible. Many of the Keys may serve as a Bible study (e. g. The names of God in a particular Bible Book are a great way to learn about God and His fullness). Other chapters in this work include separate collections/glossaries on (Chapter 2) People, Names and Nations of the Bible; (Chapter 3) Places in the Bible or in Bible History; (Chapter 4) Bible Words and Phrases; (Chapter 5) Theology Terminology; (Chapter 6) Detail expositions on over 125 words and phrases ("Land of Ancient Israel"; "Mesopotamia"; "Patriarchs"; "Philistines"; "Plagues of Egypt"; "Satan").

An extensive Index includes many helps to assist the Bible student in locating persons, places, scriptures, and words for personal study.

Acknowledgments

The following are many of the sources of information used in addition to my personal accumulated dictionaries and notes. These sources are given full appreciation for their contributions, many used with permission. Footnotes are included for additional recognition. The author owes a debt of gratitude to the following works:

Comfort, Philip, Elwell, Walter A., *The Complete Book of Who's Who in the Bible,* Castle Books, New York, 2014

The Complete Bible Companion, Barbour Publishing, Inc., Uhrichsville, Ohio, 2014

Dockrey, Kzren; Godwin, Johnnie & Phyllis, *The Student Bible Dictionary,* Barbour Books, Uhrichsville, Ohio, 2000

Easley, Kendell H. *Ultimate Bible Guide,* Holman Bible Publishers, Nashville, 1998

Harris, Katharine, *Nelson's Foundational Bible Dictionary,* World Publishing, 2004

Hiegel, Thomas L., *Travel Through the Old Testament, Vols. 1 & 2,* TLH Creations, Dayton, Ohio, 2017, 2018

Hudson, Christopher D., *The Barbour Bible Study Companion,* Barbour Publishing, Inc., Uhrichsville, Ohio, 2013

Taylor, Mark D., *The Complete Book of Bible Literacy,* Tyndale House Publishers, Inc, Wheaton, 1992

ONE

Keys to Each Old Testament Book of the Bible

THE HEBREW SCRIPTURE STRUCTURE

The Torah or Law (5) The Pentateuch	The Prophets		The Writings (11)
	Former (4)	Latter (4)	
Genesis	Joshua	Isaiah	Psalms
Exodus	Judges	Jeremiah	Proverbs
Leviticus	Samuel	Ezekiel	Job
Numbers	Kings	12 Minor	Ruth
Deuteronomy			Song of Songs
			Lamentations
			Ecclesiastes
			Esther
			Daniel
			Ezra-Nehemiah
			Chronicles

OLD TESTAMENT STRUCTURE USED BY CHRISTIANS TODAY

LAW (5)	HISTORY (12)	WISDOM (5)	MAJOR PROPHETS (5)	MINOR PROPHETS (12)
Genesis	Joshua	Job	Isaiah	Hosea
Exodus	Judges	Psalms	Jeremiah	Joel
Leviticus	Ruth	Proverbs	Lamentations	Amos
Numbers	1 Samuel	Ecclesiastes	Ezekiel	Obadiah
Deuteronomy	2 Samuel	Song of Solomon	Daniel	Jonah
	1 Kings			Micah
	2 Kings			Nahum
	1 Chronicles			Habakkuk
	2 Chronicles			Zephaniah
	Ezra			Haggai
	Nehemiah			Zechariah
	Esther			Malachi

OTHER BOOKS, NOT ACCEPTED IN THE CANON OF SCRIPTURE; the Apocrypha (including Deutrocanonical and Pseudepigraphical books) were of questionable high spiritual character, and did not receive universal approval throughout the church.

Name of Book	Accepted Source	Date of Events	Date Written
1 Esdras	Roman Catholic, Deutrocanonical	c.640-539 BCE	150-100 BCE

Non-Canon Books

2 Esdras	Roman Catholic, Deutrocanonical		95 CE
1 Maccabees	Roman Catholic, OT Apocrypha	175-135 BCE	c.103-63 BCE
2 Maccabees	Roman Catholic, OT Apocrypha	191-162 BCE	c.500 CE
3 Maccabees	Pseudepigraphical writings	c.100 BCE	300 BCE-300 CE
4 Maccabees	Pseudepigraphical writings		300 BCE-300 CE
Acts of Andrew, The	New Testament Apocrypha		
Acts of John, The	New Testament Apocrypha		
Acts of Paul, The	New Testament Apocrypha		
Acts of Peter, The	New Testament Apocrypha		
Acts of Thomas, The	New Testament Apocrypha		
Apocalypse of Abraham, The	Pseudepigraphical writings		300 BCE-300 CE
Azariah and the Three Young Men, The Prayer of	New Testament Apocrypha	An addition to the book of Daniel	150 BCE
Baruch	Roman Catholic, OT Apocrypha	Written in Babylon during the exile; 585 BCE	150-60 BCE
Bel and the Dragon	Roman Catholic, OT Apocrypha	Addition to the book of Daniel	50 BCE
Book of Enoch, The	Pseudepigraphical writings		300 BCE-300 CE
Book of Jubilees, The	Pseudepigraphical writings		300 BCE-300 CE
Ecclesiasticus or The Wisdom of Jesus, Son of Sirach	Roman Catholic, OT Apocrypha		190 BCE
Esther (Greek) -	Apocrypha	Six passages added to Esther	100 BCE
Judith	Roman Catholic, OT Apocrypha	594 BCE	c.150-63 BCE
Ladder of Jacob, The	Pseudepigraphical writings		300 BCE-300 CE
Epistle of Jeremiah, The	Pseudepigraphical writings		c.400-300 BCE
Gospel of Bartholomew, The	New Testament Apocrypha		
Gospel of Judas, The	New Testament Apocrypha		
Gospel According to Mary, The	New Testament Apocrypha		

BOOK OF OLD TESTAMENT BIBLE LITERACY

Gospel of Peter, The	New Testament Apocrypha		
Gospel of The Twelve, The	New Testament Apocrypha		
Gospel of Thomas, The	New Testament Apocrypha		
Life of Adam and Eve, The	Pseudepigraphical writings		300 BCE-300 CE
Prayer of Manasseh, The	Roman Catholic, Deutrocanonical	Addition to the book of 2 Chr.	
Protevangelium of James	New Testament Apocrypha		
Psalms of Solomon, The	Pseudepigraphical writings		300 BCE-300 CE
Sirach	Roman Catholic, OT Apocrypha		
History of Susanna	Apocrypha	Addition to the Book of Daniel	
Testament (Assumption) of Moses, The	Pseudepigraphical writings		300 BCE-300 CE
Testament of Solomon, The	Pseudepigraphical writings		300 BCE-300 CE
Testament of the Twelve Patriarchs, The	Pseudepigraphical writings		300 BCE-300 CE
Tobit (Tobias) -	Roman Catholic, OT Apocrypha	c.722-580 BCE	200 BCE
Wisdom of Solomon, The	Roman Catholic, OT Apocrypha	Era of Solomon; 970-931 BCE	100 BCE

GENESIS

Overview and Basic Outline

The book of Genesis reveals the beginnings of everything. The human race, sin, God's plan of redemption, family, nations, His chosen Jewish people, law, and Judgment (see below). Genesis lays the historical and theological foundation for the rest of the Bible. Genesis spans more time than all the remaining books in the entire Bible.

The first eleven chapters of Genesis focus on four great events of early world history: Creation, Fall, Flood, and Babel. The spread of sin culminates with a worldwide flood. Chapters twelve through fifty records the history of four great men we refer to as the Patriarchs, and their families: Abraham, Isaac, Jacob, and Joseph. God's promises of a great nation in a great land are happening.

His plan seems to have been delayed by various events; however, He has always been in control and will bring it to completion.

Genesis is the book of beginnings:
- The beginning of the world
- The beginning of the Human race
- The beginning of sin
- The beginning of redemption
- The Family
- Nations
- The beginning of the Hebrew Nation
- Government
- Law
- Sin
- Judgment

1. Four Great Events, Cps 1-11
    a. Creation 1:1-2:25
    b. Fall 3:1-5:32
    c. Flood 6:1-10:32
    d. Babel 11:1-9
2. Four Great Men, Cps 12-50
    a. Abraham 11:10-25:18
    b. Isaac 25:19-26:35
    c. Jacob 27:1-36:43
    d. Joseph 37:1-50:26

Thoughts About God in Genesis:

God is revealed as Creator. His names in Genesis include:
- Yahweh, LORD (First appearance)
- El Elohim, God (First appearance)
- Ruach Elohim, the Spirit of God (First appearance)
- El Elyon, God Most High (First appearance)
- Adonay, Lord (First appearance)
- El Shaddai, God Almighty (First appearance)
- El Olam, the Everlasting God (First appearance)
- El Roi, The God Who Sees Me (First appearance)
- Yahweh Yireh, the Lord Will Provide (First appearance)

His commands are righteous and He judges when humankind disobeys Him.

The Father makes covenant to redeem a people in Gen 15, the Son is promised in Gen 3:15, and the Spirit is mentioned in Gen 1:2 and 6:3.

Jesus Christ in Genesis:

The Seed. Our accepted seed has provided the fruit of life for us. Genesis traces the line of Christ, *the seed* from Abraham through Isaac, Jacob, and Joseph. Genesis shows us how God had a plan to eventually deal a deathblow to the head of Satan. It is through Abraham's seed, God would reach out to save His people.

We also note that Jesus did not begin as this seed of Genesis. His entrance into humanity was planned from before history, prehistory, or even time. Christ is the agent of creation (Col 1:16). He is the Redeemer as first promised in Gen 3:15, and it is through this seed that any person may accept His redemption.

Genesis reveals God's continual protection over the earliest people in Christ's lineage.

Literary Form of Genesis:[1]

Genesis is a preponderance of narrative, so the book becomes an anthology of stories. As the title "book of beginnings" hints, Genesis embodies foundational principles that range all the way from the nature of the world and humanity to the history of God's covenant dealings with the human race. The gallery of characters is large, but eight characters stand out: Adam and Eve, Noah, Abraham and Sarah, Isaac, Jacob, and Joseph.

In addition, Genesis includes a few passages of poetry (3:14-19). Its Hebrew style is like that of the other books in the Pentateuch. It is

---

[1] The Literary Form of each book includes a summary from the work of Leland Ryken, PhD. Additional thoughts are included from the author, Thomas Hiegel.

interesting to follow the geographical changes from section to section. The author (probably Moses) uses the word *toledot* meaning "records" indicating a structure of the book.

Highlights and Stories to Read in Genesis:
- The Creation Story, chapters 1,2
- Noah's Ark, chapter 6
- Abraham's Call, chapter 12
- The Offering of Isaac on an altar, chapter 22
- Jacob and his Father-in-Law, chapters 29-31
- Joseph's Dreams, chapter 37

Author
Actually, we do not know absolutely. The early church accepted Moses, as did the Jewish historian Josephus. Scripture records Lev 1:1-2; Neh 13:1; Matt 8:4; Acts 26:22, all as accepting Moses as the author of the first five books of the Bible.

An alternative theory, the JEDP theory, suggests four basic sources (authors) of the Pentateuch: (J) Those generally using the name *Yahweh;* (E) Those generally using the name *Elohim;* (D) An author of Deuteronomy; (P) Portions of the Pentateuch authored by postexilic priesthood. See the author's book *Travel Through the Old Testament, Vol. 1* for detailed explanation of JEDP sources of authorship.

When the Book was Written
The accepted date between 1491-1451 BCE.
The JEDP theory suggests four sources from the ninth to sixth centuries BCE.

When the Events Took Place
From creation until Joseph's death, about 1635 BCE.

Approximate Dates of Key Events	
Undatable	Pre-Adam World
4004 BCE	Re-Creation
4004	The Fall
2344	The Flood
2242	The Tower
1997	Abraham is born in Ur of the Chaldeans
1921	Abraham is called to set out for Canaan
1896	Isaac is born to Abraham and Sarah
1837	Jacob is born to Isaac and Rebekah
1821	Abraham dies in Canaan

1745	Joseph is born to Jacob and Rachel
1728	Joseph is sold into slavery
1716	Isaac dies in Canaan
1706	Jacob and his family move to Egypt
1689	Jacob dies in Egypt
1635	Joseph dies in Egypt

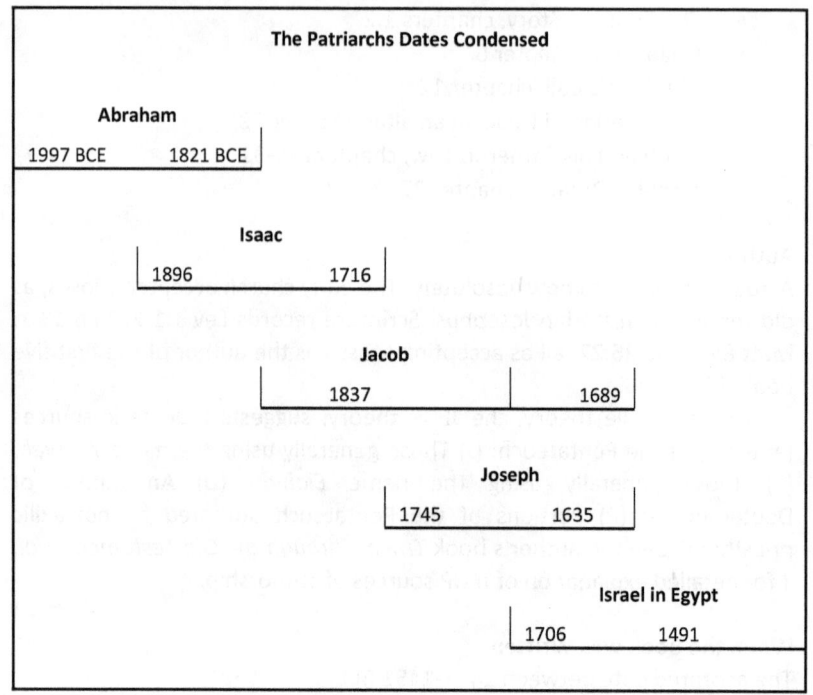

Keys to the Book

    Key Theme: God created all things including a plan for redemption.

    Key Word (s): *Create*

A rare Hebrew word in the Old Testament, "bara." It is always used of an act of God, and implying the act was "out of nothing." God alone has the power to create out of "nothing." No other individual in the Bible is said to "bara." The results of six days were accomplished only by *Elohim*. Another Hebrew word, used hundreds of times, meaning "made" could have been used, however He used *"bara."*

    Key Chapter: 15

Genesis

Key Verse (s):

*3:15 And I will put enmity
Between you and the woman,
And between your seed and her seed;
He shall bruise you on the head,
And you shall bruise him on the heel.*

*12:3 And I will bless those who bless you,
And the one who curses you I will curse.
And in you all the families of the earth will be blessed.*

50: 20 "As for you, you meant evil against me, but God meant it for good in order to bring about this present result, to preserve many people alive. 21 "So therefore, do not be afraid;

Key Characters

Adam and Eve-the original human beings (1:26-5:5).

Noah-the faithful builder of the ark (6:5-9:29).

Abraham and Sarah-the parents of a nation called God's chosen people (12:1-25:9).

Isaac and Rebekah-the original members of a new nation (21:1-35:29).

Jacob-the father of the twelve tribes of Israel (25:21-50:14).

Joseph-the preserver of his people and the nation of Egypt (30:22-50:26).

EXODUS

Overview and Basic Outline

The second part of the Pentateuch continues the story began in Genesis (Note that Exodus begins with "and" or "now"). Exodus picks up the story of the family of Israel in Egypt, and continues centuries later. It is the story of the birth of the nation of Israel. God visited His people and set them free from Egypt, His redemptive story in summary. When He redeemed His people, He entered a covenant relationship with them and instituted His dwelling with them, the tabernacle.

The book outlines the story of God's people the birth of Moses, through their deliverance from bondage, the giving of the law, and the construction of the tabernacle in the desert. The title of the book comes from the Greek word *exodus* meaning "going out" or "departure." The Hebrews refer to the book as "Now these are the names" from the first words. Exodus pictures the drama of God's redemption work. Here we meet the Redeemer of His people.

1. Captive in Egypt Cps 1-12
2. The Journey Towards Sinai Cps 13-18
3. Maturation At Sinai Cps 19-40

Thoughts About God in Exodus:

God is revealed as Redeemer. His names in Exodus include:
- Yahweh, LORD
- El, Elohim, God
- Ehyeh, I Am (First appearance)
- Adonay, Lord, Master
- El Shadday, God Almighty
- Yah, the LORD (First appearance)
- Yahweh Nissi, the LORD My Banner (First appearance)
- El Kanna, Jealous God (First appearance)
- Ruach Elohim, the Spirit of God
- Yahweh Ropheka, the Lord Who Heals (First appearance)

God loves His people and takes the initiative to save them from bondage. He also is shown as God who expects a redeemed people to live according to His covenant. Christ is the Passover Lamb and Spirit is the One who empowers for service.

Exodus

Jesus Christ in Exodus:
The Passover Lamb. The Hebrew word is derived from "that which one brings near to God." He is your perfect lamb, His blood—your passage to God.

Literary Form of Exodus:
The unifying motif is announced in the title: the departure of the Israelites from oppression in Egypt followed by a journey through the desert to the Promised Land. Three distinctly different genres appear—narrative (1-18 and 32-34), lawgiving (19-24), and architectural information about the building of the tabernacle (24-31 and 35-40). Each of these genres has its own focus—deliverance, covenant, and holiness, respectively. Moses is the unifying human hero.

Much of Exodus is historical narrative, while chapter fifteen is the first extensive use of poetry in the Bible

Highlights and Stories to Read in Exodus:
- The Birth of Moses, chapter 2
- A Burning Bush, chapter 3
- The Plagues on Egypt, chapters 7-12a
- The Exodus, chapter 12b, 14b
- The Ten Commandments and The Law, chapter 20

Author
Actually, we do not know absolutely. The early church accepted Moses, as did the Jewish historian Josephus. Scripture records Lev 1:1-2; Neh 13:1; Matt 8:4; Acts 26:22, all as accepting Moses as the author of the first five books of the Bible.

An alternative theory, the JEDP theory, suggests four basic sources of the Pentateuch: (J) Those generally using the name *Yahweh;* (E) Those generally using the name *Elohim;* (D) An author of Deuteronomy; (P) Portions of the Pentateuch authored by postexilic priesthood. See the author's book *Travel Through the Old Testament, Vol. 1* for detailed explanation of JEDP sources of authorship.

When the Book was Written
The accepted date between 1491-1451 BCE.
The JEDP theory suggests four sources from the ninth to sixth centuries BCE.

When the Events Took Place
1571-1451 BCE.

Approximate Dates of Key Events	
1571 BCE	Moses is born
1531	Moses flees Egypt for Midian
1491	Moses leads the Israelites out of Egypt; The Israelites cross the Red Sea
1491	The Law is given on Mount Sinai
1491-1451	Events in Numbers Wilderness wandering
1451	Moses Dies Israel enters the Promised Land

Keys to the Book

Key Theme: God hears, God delivers.

Key Word (s): *Delivered*

Found in 3:8; 5:18; 22:7, 10, 26. Its Hebrew meaning is quite clear and appropriate: "To strip away" or "to snatch away."

And that's what God did; he snatches away His people from Egypt, (displaying victory over their gods) to move them in to a land He had set aside for them. God is a God who delivers.

We see this word used when God is in action delivering or rescuing His people.

Also, consider Ps 18:4 *He delivers me from my enemies;* Ps 34:17 *the righteous cry and The Lord hears and delivers them out of all their troubles;* Job 36:15 *he delivers the afflicted in their affliction.* Your personal God will deliver you.

Key Chapter (s): 12-14

Key Verse (s):

6:6 Say, therefore, to the sons of Israel, 'I am the Lord, and I will bring you out from under the burdens of the Egyptians, and I will deliver you from their bondage. I will also redeem you with an outstretched arm and with great Judgments.

14:30-31 Thus the Lord saved Israel that day from the hand of the Egyptians, and Israel saw the Egyptians dead on the seashore. 31 When Israel saw the great power which the Lord had used against the Egyptians, the people feared the Lord, and they believed in the Lord and in His servant Moses.

19:5 'Now then, if you will indeed obey My voice and keep My covenant, then you shall be My own possession among all the peoples, for all the earth is Mine; 6 and you shall be to Me a kingdom of priests and a holy nation.' These are the words that you shall speak to the sons of Israel.

20:2 "I am the Lord your God, who brought you out of the land of Egypt, out of the house of slavery.

Key Characters

Moses-author of the Pentateuch and deliverer of Israel from Egyptian slavery (24:4).

Miriam-prophetess and older sister of Moses (2:7; 15:20, 21).
Pharaoh's daughter-the princess who rescued baby Moses from the water and adopted him (2:5-10).

Jethro-Midian shepherd who became Moses' father-in-law (3:1; 4:18; 18:1-12).

Joshua-assistant to Moses and military leader who led Israel into the Promised Land (17:9-14; 24:13; 32:17; 33:11).

LEVITICUS

Overview and Basic Outline

Leviticus is the third part of the Pentateuch. The final chapters of Exodus concerning the Tabernacle lead naturally to the opening of Leviticus. The title and the theme are revealed in the name, which means, "pertaining to the Levites" even though the tribe of Levites is not the focus. The book was written for the people with specific instructions to the priests.

Holiness, an attribute of God, is a central topic of interest. He expects His people to continue in fellowship with Him. Leviticus is a book of laws that kept the Hebrew people safe, healthy, and peaceful. Moses taught the ceremony called the Day of Atonement

The book is a teaching manual, or guidebook for God's newly formed nation, focusing on their worship and walk. Many do not understand how the ancient words of Leviticus are relevant to their lives today. However, His holiness is quite simply a moral living and being separated unto God for His use.

The Hebrews refer to the book as "and He called."

1. Offerings Cps 1-7
2. Priesthood Cps 8-10
3. Cleansing Cps 11-16
4. Holiness Cps 17-27

Thoughts About God in Leviticus:

God is revealed as Holiness. His names in Leviticus include:
- Yahweh, LORD
- Elohim, God
- Ha-shem, the Name (First appearance)

God, as the Supreme Holy One, exerts His right to instruct His people in what holiness demands. A sinful person has been given the right to approach God through the acceptable sacrifice. Christ is pictured as the only High Priest who is the atoning sacrifice.

Jesus Christ in Leviticus:

The High Priest. He is the only intercessor to God you need. Jesus presented Himself as the final sacrifice for every person. God instructed His people about offerings which pointed to Christ. The Old Testament offering had to be repeated time after time because it only "covered" sin.

Jesus then came and presented Himself a perfect, final sacrifice, "once and for all."

Literary Form of Leviticus:
The primary genre is the rulebook, which is at the same time a guidebook for living the religious and moral life that God intended for his people. The main literary principle at work is that literature uses particulars to embody universals; we look not only *at* the details of the text but *through* them to principles that apply today. The book is also a utopia that paints a picture of the good society and the institutions and practices that produce it. Realism abounds, including references to bodily functions.

Highlights and Stories to Read in Leviticus:
- Offerings to be Presented to God
- The Day of Atonement, chapter 16
- Hebrew Festivals, chapter 23

Author
Actually, we do not know absolutely. The early church accepted Moses, as did the Jewish historian Josephus. Scripture records Lev 1:1-2; Neh 13:1; Matt 8:4; Acts 26:22, all as accepting Moses as the author of the first five books of the Bible.

An alternative theory, the JEDP theory, suggests four basic sources of the Pentateuch: (J) Those generally using the name *Yahweh;* (E) Those generally using the name *Elohim;* (D) An author of Deuteronomy; (P) Portions of the Pentateuch authored by postexilic priesthood. See the author's book *Travel Through the Old Testament, Vol. 1* for detailed explanation of JEDP sources of authorship.

When the Book was Written
1451 BCE.
The JEDP theory suggests four sources from the ninth to sixth centuries BCE.

When the Events Took Place
1451 BCE.

Keys to the Book
    Key Theme: I am a holy God and to be worshipped.

    Key Word (s): *Blood*

Found in 1:5, 3:7, 4:7, and 8:15. We must understand the vital place of the shedding of *blood*. The connection or scarlet thread runs through the Old Testament. The word is related to the Hebrew word *adom*, which means "red."

From God shedding the first blood in Genesis, through each book, to the *"rising of the Son of Righteousness with healing it its wings"* in Malachi 4. Blood is always associated with life in the New Testament, always pointing to Christ (Heb 9:22).

Today, we do not follow the system of offerings in Leviticus. The New Testament makes it clear that from Pentecost forward, the church, the body of Christ is under the authority of the new covenant, not the old Hebrew's Covenant.

Key Chapter: 16

Key Verse (s):
11:45 For I am the Lord who brought you up from the land of Egypt to be your God; thus you shall be holy, for I am holy.

17:11 For the life of the flesh is in the blood, and I have given it to you on the altar to make atonement for your souls; for it is the blood by reason of the life that makes atonement.

Key Characters
Moses-Prophet and leader who acted as God's mouthpiece to explain His law to Israel (1:1; 4:1; 5:14; 6:1-27:34).

Aaron-Moses' brother and first high priest of Israel (1:7; 2:3; 10; 3:5, 8, 13; 6:9-24:9).

Nadab-son of Aaron, in training to become a priest, died because of disobedience to the Lord's commands (8:36; 10:1, 2).

Eleazar-son of Aaron who succeeded him as high priest of Israel (10:6-20).

Ithamar-son of Aaron who also became a priest (10:6-20).

NUMBERS

Overview and Basic Outline
The Hebrews call the fourth book of the Pentateuch "In the wilderness" a much more accurate title, for it explains what happened to the Israelites during the thirty-eight years they traveled through wilderness. The name "Numbers" (from the two censuses), originated in the Greek translation of the Septuagint followed by the Latin Vulgate.

The book traces the Israelites move from Sinai to the wilderness of Paran and finally to the plains of Moab. The book, as in Exodus and Leviticus, begins with the conjunction "and" showing the continuity of the Pentateuch.

It narrates the transition from the old generation that left Egypt and sinned in the desert to the new generation that stands of the brink of the Promised Land with new hope. It covers a history of thirty-nine years. We read of Israel's murmuring and rebellion against God when they were faced with the difficult realities of life. The book does not end in defeat, but with a people ready to enter the Promise Land.

Two censuses or numberings are recorded in the book. The challenge of understanding the large numbers used in Numbers, remains today. The author of this work does not believe that large numbers in the Bible always have an exact meaning. However, the large numbers in Numbers certainly demonstrate the greatness of God's providence and His miraculous supply.

1. At Sinai, Cps 1-10
2. Sinai to Kadesh, Cps 11-13
3. Wandering Around Kadesh, Cps 14-21
4. On the Banks of Jordan, Cps 22-36

Thoughts About God in Numbers:
God is revealed as Sovereign Power. His names in Numbers include:
- Yahweh, LORD
- El, Elohim, God
- Ruach, Spirit
- Adonay, Lord, Master
- Ruach Elohim, the Spirit of God
- Shaddai, Almighty
- Elyon, Highest

God is shown as faithful to His Covenant. He made covenant with Abraham and reminds His people in Num 32:11. The Spirit is present as the One enabling service and inspiring prophecy in 11:25 and 24:2.

Jesus Christ in Numbers:
A Pillar of fire by night, A Pillar of cloud by day. He is always with you, and will lead you each step of your journey in life.

Just as the Israelite people looked upon *the serpent lifted up by Moses* and were healed (a picture of Jesus on the cross), we have the privilege to lift up Jesus in our life and expect to be healed.

The *manna* illustrated Christ as the Bread of Life. The *rock* that brought water was also a type of Christ.

Each of these is mentioned in the New Testament as being examples of Christ.

Literary Form of Numbers:
Combination of narrative (in the form of a travel story) and lawgiving; the result is called a mixed-genre format. The overall story is twofold: forty years of wandering in the wilderness and preparation for settlement in the Promised Land. God and Moses are the leading characters. Through a combination of historical, theological, and literary writing, the book tells us both what *happened* and what *happens* (meaning that it embodies universal experiences and principles).

One new feature is the prophetic oracle, given by Balaam in cps 23, 24, written in poetic parallelism similar to Isaiah and Jeremiah.

Highlights and Stories to Read in Numbers:
- Spies Sent into the Promised Land, chapter 13
- Moses Strikes a Rock, chapter 20
- Boundaries of the Promised Land, chapter 34

Author
Actually, we do not know absolutely. The early church accepted Moses, as did the Jewish historian Josephus. Scripture records Lev 1:1-2; Neh 13:1; Matt 8:4; Acts 26:22, all as accepting Moses as the author of the first five books of the Bible.

An alternative theory, the JEDP theory, suggests four basic sources of the Pentateuch: (J) Those generally using the name *Yahweh;* (E) Those generally using the name *Elohim;* (D) An author of Deuteronomy; (P) Portions of the Pentateuch authored by postexilic priesthood. See the author's book *Travel Through the Old Testament, Vol. 1* for detailed explanation of JEDP sources of authorship.

Numbers

When the Book was Written
The accepted date is between 1491-1451 BCE.
The JEDP theory suggests four sources from the ninth to sixth centuries BCE. Numbers is a mixture of J, E, and P materials.

When the Events Took Place
1491-1451 BCE.

Keys to the Book
  Key Theme: A long delay because of sin.

  Key Word (s): *Wilderness, Anointed*
The first of two key words in Numbers is *wilderness*. It is a key because it is found forty-eight times in the book and always refers to a land of little vegetation and very little rain. Sometimes used for desert (Jer 25:24). Jeremiah uses it to describe the hostile environment that accompanies God's Judgment.

The second key word, *Anointed* is a verb that means, "To wet or dab a person with olive oil." Read it in 3:3, 6:15, 7:1, and 10. Priests and Prophets were anointed at the beginning of their service. It set one apart for God's special purposes. Even the tabernacle itself was anointed during the Exodus. The anointing oil was a very exquisite and expensive blend of oil and spices.
  In the New Testament, all who are believers in Christ are said to be anointed. See 2 Cor 1:21.

  Key Chapter: 14

  Key Verse (s):
14:22 "Surely all the men who have seen My glory and My signs which I performed in Egypt and in the wilderness, yet have put Me to the test these ten times and have not listened to My voice, 23 shall by no means see the land which I swore to their fathers, nor shall any of those who spurned Me see it

20:12 But the Lord said to Moses and Aaron, "Because you have not believed Me, to treat Me as holy in the sight of the sons of Israel, therefore you shall not bring this assembly into the land which I have given them."

  Key Characters

Moses-great Prophet and leader who acted as God's mouthpiece to explain His Law to Israel (1:1, 19, 48; 5:1, 4, 5, 11, and over two hundred other references).

Aaron-Moses' brother and first high priest of Israel (1:3, 17, 44; 2:1; 3:1-10; 12:1-5; 20:23-29).

Miriam-sister to Moses and Aaron, also songwriter and prophetess; stricken with leprosy because of jealousy toward Moses (12; 20:1; 26:59).

Joshua-Moses' successor as leader of Israel; one of the only two people to see both the Exodus from Egypt and the Promised Land (11:28; 13; 14; 26:65; 27:15-23; 32:11, 12, 28; 34:17).

Caleb-one of the men sent to scout Canaan; faithful to God in his desire to conquer the land; one of the only two people to see both the Exodus from Egypt and the Promised Land (13-14; 26:65; 32:12; 34:19).

Korah-Levite who assisted in the Tabernacle; killed because of his rebellion against the Lord (16:1-40; 26:9).

Balaam-Prophet and sorcerer who halfheartedly obeyed God; attempted to lead Israel into idol worship (22:1-24:25; 31:7, 8, 16).

DEUTERONOMY

Overview and Basic Outline
In this fifth book of the Pentateuch, we see again, the Hebrew reference to this book by the opening words. In this case, the reference is to "these are the words." The English title reflects the Greek word *Deuteronomion*, meaning "second law." The book contains a second version of the previously stated law, not a second law. It is an expansion of much of the law given on Mount Sinai.

Deuteronomy restates (although expressed differently) the covenant made between God and Israel at Sinai. The three-recorded speeches by Moses reminded the people of their position with God before he handed over the leadership to Joshua. In Moses' great speeches near the end of his life, he reminded the people of God's mighty acts, His covenant, and His many commands. It is a relevant book for all generations because of addressing faith under trial, marriage and family, worship, and stewardship.

We could accurately think of Deuteronomy as a covenant-renewal contract with a new generation of Hebrews. The first eleven chapters look back to what God already accomplished for His people. Chapter twelve begins the focus on the future. Whether past or present, the status of God's people is one of being a chosen, covenant people.

This book is one of the most frequently quoted Old Testament books by New Testament writers.

1. Remember God's Blessings, Cps 1-5
2. Respond to God's Goodness, Cps 6-11
3. Review God's Word, Cps 12-26
4. Renew God's Covenant, Cps 27-31
5. Recite to Israel, Cps 32-34

Thoughts About God in Deuteronomy:
God is revealed as One in Unity (Deut 6:4, 5). His names in Deuteronomy include:
- Yahweh, LORD
- El, Elohim, God
- El Kanna, Jealous God
- Esh Oklah, Consuming Fire (First appearance)
- El Chay, Living God (First appearance)
- Adonay, Lord, Master
- Ab, Father (First appearance)

- Elyon, Highest
- Ruach, Spirit

God is love; however, He will not allow idolatry or apostasy to overcome God's righteousness. His penalties will be judged against those who insult Him by turning away from Him.

Jesus Christ in Deuteronomy:
The Prophet is coming. He is the Messiah. Deuteronomy speaks of the coming of a new Prophet similar to Moses. Moses was spared death as a baby, and acted as priest, prophet, and leader.

Literary Form of Deuteronomy:
The primary genre is oration, as Moses delivers a series of formal speeches as he nears the end of his leadership of the nation of Israel. The content of his speeches is lawgiving (as hinted by the book's title, which conveys the idea of a repetition of the law given in the preceding three books of the Pentateuch). The motif of covenant renewal dominates; subordinate ideas are that obedience brings blessing while disobedience brings a curse. The last four chapters are a transfer-of-leadership story, as Joshua succeeds Moses when the latter dies.

The book is set apart from the other Pentateuch books by its sermonic style. At the end of the book, the extraordinary "Song of Moses" and "Moses' Blessings" show Moses to be a poet of considerable skill.

Highlights and Stories to Read in Deuteronomy:
- Cities of Refuge, chapter 19
- Joshua Appointed Israel's Leader, chapter 31
- Death of Moses, chapter 34

Author
Actually, we do not know absolutely. The early church accepted Moses, as did the Jewish historian Josephus. Scripture records Lev 1:1-2; Neh 13:1; Matt 8:4; Acts 26:22, all as accepting Moses as the author of the first five books of the Bible.

An alternative theory, the JEDP theory, suggests four basic sources of the Pentateuch: (J) Those generally using the name *Yahweh;* (E) Those generally using the name *Elohim;* (D) An author of Deuteronomy; (P) Portions of the Pentateuch authored by postexilic priesthood. See the author's book *Travel Through the Old Testament, Vol. 1* for detailed explanation of JEDP sources of authorship.

Deuteronomy

When the Book was Written
The accepted date is between 1491-1451 BCE.

The JEDP theory suggests the late seventh century BCE.

When the Events Took Place
1451 BCE.

Keys to the Book
    Key Theme: Remember what God has done and dedicate your life to Him.

    Key Word (s): *Covenant*
This word could be the primary theme of the entire Book. It could be an entire multi-week study. *Covenant.* The Hebrew means "a cutting." You have heard the words "to cut a covenant." When the explorer Livingston met a tribal chief, the two made an agreement. In order to continue on his journey, Livingston literally "cut" an agreement with the tribe's chief. They used blood to seal the covenant. From that time onward, Livingston never had a serious Problem in his travels. He had an agreement; he had "a covenant." All the chief's integrity, protection, and might now belonged to Livingston.

    The formal covenant occurs in Deuteronomy, cp 27 with Moses and all Israel agreeing, verse 9: *Be silent and listen, O Israel! This day you have become a people for the LORD your God.*

    The various covenants God made with His people in the Old Testament, With Noah, with Abraham, and with David, prefigure the supreme covenant made through Christ's sacrifice on the cross, which Jeremiah saw in Jer 31:31-4.

    Key Chapter: 27

    Key Verse (s):
10:12 "Now, Israel, what does the Lord your God require from you, but to fear the Lord your God, to walk in all His ways and love Him, and to serve the Lord your God with all your heart and with all your soul, 13 and to keep the Lord's commandments and His statutes which I am commanding you today for your good?

30:19 "I call heaven and earth to witness against you today, that I have set before you life and death, the blessing and the curse. So choose life in order that you may live, you and your descendants, 20 by loving the Lord your God, by obeying His voice, and by holding fast to Him; for this is your life and the length of your days, that you may live in the land which the Lord swore to your fathers, to Abraham, Isaac, and Jacob, to give them.

Key Characters
Moses-leader of Israel; instructed the people on the law of God but was not allowed to enter the Promised Land (1-5; 27; 29; 31-34).

JOSHUA

Overview and Basic Outline
This is the first of twelve books of the second division of the Old Testament, Books of History (Joshua-Esther). The title is based on the name of the central character, Joshua meaning, "The Lord is Salvation." The Greek equivalent is "Jesus."

The successor to Moses readies the new generation of God's nation to cross the Jordan and invade the land. Possessing the land was no easy task. This tribal nation was to subdue over thirty well-secured armies and city-states. However, God had promised to bring them into the Promised Land. He had made a covenant with Abraham that his descendants would take possession of Canaan (Gen 12:7). Joshua is the compelling history of the fulfillment of God's promises.

After the immediate victory in Jericho, the central, southern, and northern campaigns followed in which Joshua only achieved victories after following God's instructions. This is the story of the conquest and allocation of the land.

1. Preparation for Conquest, Cps 1-5
2. Conquest of Canaan, Cps 6-13
3. Settlement in Canaan, Cps 14-22
4. Two Speeches of Joshua, Cps 23-24

Thoughts About God in Joshua:
God is revealed as Faithful. His names in Joshua include:
- Yahweh, LORD
- El, Elohim, God
- El Chay, Living God
- Adonay, Lord, Master
- El Kanna, Jealous God

He always fulfills His promises. Any promise made, will be fulfilled. He promised to save Rahab in cp 2, with fulfillment in cp 6. His promise to save "whosoever" is truth, for He is faithful to complete every promise He made.

Jesus Christ in Joshua:
The Captain of your salvation. He is the only way to eternal life with God. Joshua represents a type of Christ, both in name and in deed. Joshua's

name means "Yahweh is Salvation" also translated as Jesus. Jesus appeared to Joshua (5:13, 14) and led Israel's army to victory.

Literary Form of Joshua:
The book follows a common biblical pattern known as mixed-genre format (which literary scholars also call encyclopedic form). The first twelve chapters are narrative, in the specific genres of military conquest story and epic (the story of a nation at a critical point of its history). Chapters 13-21 are documentary history, recording how the Promised Land was divided. The last three chapters return to the narrative mode with the final words and death of Joshua, who is the unifying hero of the book.

The book is positioned in the Hebrew Scriptures (see *The Hebrew Scripture Structure* at the beginning of this chapter) as the first of the four Former Prophets (Judges, Samuel, and Kings). Together, the four books describe the 800-year period from entry into Canaan through the destruction of the temple and Jerusalem.

Also note a most interesting feature, that of Joshua's military strategy.

Highlights and Stories to Read in Joshua:
- Joshua's Appointment, chapter 1
- Crossing the Jordan, chapter 3
- The Story of Rahab/Jericho, chapters 2, 6
- Joshua takes the Southern enemies, chapter 10
- Joshua takes the Northern enemies, chapter 11
- The Land Divided to the Twelve Tribes, chapter 14-19

Author
Joshua wrote a major part of the book. A later author added the narrative concerning his death.

When the Book was Written
Following the events in the book.

When the Events Took Place
1451-1424 BCE

Approximate Dates of Key Events	
1451 BCE	Joshua succeeds Moses; conquest begins
1445	Canaan apportioned
1424	Joshua dies

Joshua

Keys to the Book

Key Theme: Victory and conquest comes through faith in God and obedience to His word.

Key Word (s) *Rest*

The key word in Joshua is found in 1:13, 3:13, 10:20, and several other references. Joshua is a book of *rest*. It literally means, *"To be at peace."* Rest implies freedom from anxiety and conflict. God's Promise of a land to settle in was a Promise of *"rest,"* but would depend on God's command for His people to drive out the Canaanites. The New Testament speaks of Christians who are told that heaven will bring *"rest"* from death and all other earthly struggles (Hebrews 4:1).

Key Chapter: 24

Key Verse (s):

1:8 This book of the law shall not depart from your mouth, but you shall meditate on it day and night, so that you may be careful to do according to all that is written in it; for then you will make your way Prosperous, and then you will have success.

11:23 So Joshua took the whole land, according to all that the Lord had spoken to Moses, and Joshua gave it for an inheritance to Israel according to their divisions by their tribes. Thus the land had rest from war.

Key Characters

Joshua—taught by Moses, led Israel across the Jordan and into the Promised Land (1–24).

Rahab—a Prostitute living in Jericho; assisted the two spies; listed in the "seed" line, ancestor of David and Jesus (2; 6:17, 22, 23, 25).

Achan—after the victory in Jericho he kept some items for himself, thus disobeying God; this was the reason Israel failed in the battle against Ai; stoned to death (7; 22:20).

Eleazar—son of Aaron; became high priest; worked closely with Joshua (14:1; 17:4; 19:51; 21:1–3; 22:13–33; 24:33).

Phinehas—son of Eleazar, also a priest; helped to prevent civil war (22:13, 31–34; 24:33).

JUDGES

Overview and Basic Outline

This is the second of twelve books of the second division of the Old Testament, Books of History (Joshua-Esther). The title is based on the name of the central characters and its stories. The Hebrew title could be rendered "Leaders." The book traces the period between the death of Joshua and the rise of the Monarchy in Israel. It serves to sketch the dark period from the exciting days of Moses and Joshua to the promising time of Samuel and Saul.

The Promised Land was now to be made the permanent home of the Jews. As word of the success of the military campaigns spread, many difficult challenges arose.

The book of Judges records how the Jews adapted in the land that was dominated by the religious, cultural, and political ideologies of the Canaanites. No centralized government was established. Therefore, family and clan leadership responded to individual challenges. Judges is a compilation of selected independent stories, mostly centered on one individual.

Because of repeatedly turning from a worship of God to worship of Baal and other "gods" in the lands, God handed them over into the hands of invading nations. God then sent a military deliverer (twelve are mentioned in the book) or a "Judge" to fight the specific enemy. The particular territory would then remain at peace for the remainder of the Judge's life. Similar cycles followed, one after another, for over three hundred years.

     1. Review and Preview, Cps 1-2
     2. Times of Judges, Cps 3-16
     3. Time of Decay, Cps 17-21

Thoughts About God in Judges:

God is revealed as Mercy. His names in Judges include:
- Yahweh, LORD
- Yahweh Shalom, The LORD is Peace (First appearance)
- Elohim, God
- Ruach Yahweh, the LORD'S Spirit
- Shophet, Judge (First appearance)

God is shown as being serious against one who forsakes God after claiming His name. His mercy is available to one who cries out to Him after sinning. However, His patience is not endless. Do not "try" the LORD God.

The Spirit's power in enabling certain judges is noteworthy in the book.

Jesus Christ in Judges:
He is The Judge and Lawgiver. Failure happens! He is the savior of a fallen people. The judges are raised by God to bring forth deliverance for their time and place. Christ is represented as deliverer, who will indeed bring a final deliverance for His people. Judges pictures Christ in a confrontation with Satan and his forces, and His victory over them.

Literary Form of Judges:
A triumph of storytelling. More specifically, an anthology of hero stories (and we need always to remember that literary heroes are rarely completely good). Three "bigger than life" heroes stick out in our imagination—Eglon, Gideon, and Samson (the story of last meets all the criteria of literary tragedy). A cyclic narrative pattern governs the book: the people of Israel do evil in the sight of the Lord; God allows them to be conquered by an oppressive neighboring tribe or country; the people cry to God; God sends a deliverer.

Chapter 5 is a superb example of early Hebrew poetry, "Deborah's Song." The book is positioned as the second of the four Former Prophets (Joshua, Samuel, and Kings). The cyclical nature of the book is its most unusual literary feature. In addition, Judges is known for its long explanatory prologue.

Highlights and Stories to Read in Judges:
- Death of Joshua, chapter 2
- Deborah and Barak Defeat Their Enemies, chapter 4
- Gideon's Victory, chapter 6
- Samson and Delilah, chapters 12-16

Author
Most likely, Samuel.

When the Book was Written
Likely after the events in the book, during the days of Saul, David.

When the Events Took Place
1392-1050 BCE.

BOOK OF OLD TESTAMENT BIBLE LITERACY

Approximate Dates of Key Events	
1392-1050 BCE	Events in Judges
1175	Samuel is born
1392-1050	Events in Ruth during or following this period
1095	Saul becomes king

Keys to the Book

Key Theme: A repeated cycle of apostasy, oppression, repentance, and restoration.

Key Word: *Deliverance*
Found in 15:18, and few other places. It is more of a theme of the book. *Deliverance*. It is a different word from the key word in Exodus, which was *delivered*. This word in Judges means "victory" or even "safety. The Bible always associates this deliverance...with God. He is the one who brings victory or safety. Psalms 51:14 and 71:14 praise Him for it. Psalm 33:17 records deliverance is not found in horses but only in the Lord. Psalm 108:12 says it is not in the capabilities of people.

A Key Chapter: 2

Key Verse (s):
2:20 So the anger of the Lord burned against Israel, and He said, "Because this nation has transgressed My covenant which I commanded their fathers and has not listened to My voice, 21 I also will no longer drive out before them any of the nations which Joshua left when he died.

21:25 In those days there was no king in Israel; everyone did what was right in his own eyes.

Key Characters

Othniel—first Judge of Israel; defeated a powerful Mesopotamian king; brought forty years of peace to Israel (1:13–14; 3:7–11).

Ehud—second Judge of Israel; brought Israel eighty years of peace by helping to conquer the Moabites (3:15–31).

Deborah—Prophet and Israel's only female Judge; succeeded Shamar as fourth Judge of Israel (4:4–16; 5).

Judges

Gideon—Israel's fifth Judge; defeated the Midianite army (6–8).

Abimelech—Son of Gideon; made himself king of Israel; murdered his sixty-nine brothers (8:31–9:57).

Jephthah—Judge of Israel, also a warrior; defeated the Ammonites (11:1–12:7).

Samson—given to God from his birth; unusual strength; a Judge of Israel who was to defeat the Philistines (13:24–16:31).

Delilah—Samson's lover who betrayed him to the Philistines for money (16:4–21).

RUTH

Overview and Basic Outline
The name is from the Hebrew Bible. The Septuagint and Latin titles are also Ruth. The story is one of friendship, devotion, and redemption in the context of difficult days—a diamond in the midst of chaos. The events of Ruth occurred during the late days of Judges, a family story in a peaceful setting in contrast with the surrounding cycles of failure and defeat. These were difficult days of suffering for the Jews. Ruth was a non-Jew, a Moabite.

The book opens with the report of a famine, driving Naomi's family out of Bethlehem to the east side of the Dead Sea into Moab. Jesus could trace his ancestry back through Ruth (Matt 1:5). We get the background of marriage customs during ancient days and the duty of the next of Kin of a widow who had children.

We learn of Boaz, a relative of Naomi, and the obstacles, which were overcome for Boaz to marry Ruth. Boaz willingly fulfilled the responsibility of the "kinsman" or "family redeemer" for Ruth. As such, he illustrates God, who gladly redeems His people. Jesus descended from Ruth and Boaz.

The book is noteworthy because it includes the unusual expressions of (1) Gleaning, a kind of welfare provision; (2) Ruth's claim of protection by the covering of Boaz's cloak; (3) The real estate transaction made legal by exchanging sandals; (4) The law of farmland passed on to family lines.

1. The ten years of Naomi and Ruth, Cp 1
2. The two years of Boaz and Ruth, Cps 2-3-4

Thoughts About God in Ruth:
God is revealed as Sovereign in all circumstances. His names in Ruth include:
- Yahweh, LORD
- Elohim, God
- Shaddai, Almighty

A famine and deaths of three husbands are arranged circumstances, which lead to Ruth's salvation. Her journey parallels that of any person going from emptiness to fullness. Boaz exemplifies the position of redeemer, just as Christ has redeemed His people. The book illustrates how simple, obedient people can be saved by God's providence and become part of His larger plan.

Ruth

Jesus Christ in Ruth:
He is the redeemer shown in the life of Boaz. We see the coming of our Redeemer and King of all believers.

Literary Form of Ruth:
Ruth is the high point of storytelling in the Bible. The genre is idyll (a short narrative that describes a simple, pleasant aspect of rural and domestic life). The story is the most complete example in the Bible of a love story, and the genre of hero story likewise governs the book. Other unifying motifs are the quest story (quest for home) and a comic, U-shaped plot that begins in tragedy and then turns upward to a happy conclusion as obstacles are overcome.

The story of Ruth is told in four chapters, framed by a historical prologue (1:1-5) and a forward-looking epilogue (4:13-22). Between these are four scenes that trace the story.

Highlights and Stories to Read in Ruth:
- Naomi and Ruth Return to Judah, chapter 2
- Boaz marries Ruth, chapter 4

Author
Highly likely, Samuel.

When the Book was Written
*c.*1000 BCE. Written during the time of King David.

When the Events Took Place
Most likely during the final events in Judges, over a period of ten+ years.

Approximate Dates of Key Events	
1392-1050 BCE	Events in Ruth during or following the period of Judges
1095	Saul becomes king

Keys to the Book

Key Theme: Boaz, accepting the responsibility of a "redeemer," beautifully illustrates the redemption of sinners by Christ.

Key Word: *Redeemer*
Found in 2:1, 20; 3:9, 12, 13. The Hebrew word ga'al *Kinsman-Redeemer* is illustrated in the story of Ruth. It means to "play the part of a kinsman." It

refers to a close relative who becomes Protector. He was to guard the family rights; a redeemer. In Old Testament Law, a near relative had the right to act on behalf of a person in trouble or in danger. When persons or possessions were in the grip of a hostile power, the kinsman might act to redeem (to win release and freedom).

The marriage of Boaz to Ruth involved buying back Naomi's family land, and meant that their son would carry on Naomi's family line. Jesus, by taking on humanity, became our near Kinsman, with the right to redeem you and me.

Jesus is called our Redeemer in 1 Peter 1:18-19.

Key Chapter: 4

Key Verse (s):
1:16 But Ruth said, "Do not urge me to leave you or turn back from following you; for where you go, I will go, and where you lodge, I will lodge. Your people shall be my people, and your God, my God.

3:11 Now, my daughter, do not fear. I will do for you whatever you ask, for all my people in the city know that you are a woman of excellence.

Key Characters
Ruth—Naomi's daughter-in-law; marries Boaz; direct ancestor of Jesus (cps 1–4).

Naomi—the widow of Elimelech; mother-in-law of Orpah and Ruth; mentored/advised Ruth (cps 1–4).

Boaz—Prosperous farmer who married Ruth, the Moabite; direct ancestor of Jesus (cps 2-4).

1 SAMUEL

Overview and Basic Outline
We note that the books of 1 and 2 Samuel, along with 1 and 2 Kings, are a chronicle of the entire history of Judah's and Israel's kingship. Therefore, 1 Samuel is best understood after reviewing the historical period of Judges. Judges ended with the statement: *In those days there was no king in Israel; everyone did what was right in his own eyes.*

1 Samuel, named after Israel's last Judge and first Prophet, describes the transition of leadership from Judges to kings and from a nomadic, tribal form of government to a united kingdom under Saul and David. I Samuel spans Samuel's life from birth to death, chronicles Saul's entire reign as the first king of Israel, and the lengthy transition David underwent from shepherd boy to heir to the throne.

Originally, 1 and 2 Samuel were a single book in the Hebrew Bible, known as "Samuel." The books should be considered together. The single book of Samuel was divided into two in the Septuagint (they were then named 1 and 2 Kingdoms). The two books of Samuel and two books of Kings are one continuous story of the Israelite monarchies.

Samuel's call by God and his anointing Israel's first king are the focus of the book. We also read of Israel's defeat and capture of the ark by the Philistines. Saul's rivalry with David and his eventual suicide conclude the book.

1. Samuel: the last Judge, and first Prophet, Cps 1-7
2. Saul the first king, Cps 8-15
3. David and Saul, Cps 16-31

Thoughts About God in 1 Samuel:
God is revealed as Designer. His names in 1 Samuel include:
- Yahweh, LORD
- Elohim, God
- Yahweh Tsebaoth, the LORD of Hosts, the LORD Almighty
- Ruach Yahweh, the LORD'S Spirit
- Ruach Elohim, the Spirit of God
- El Chay, Living God
- Netsach Yisrael, Glory of Israel (First appearance)

God shaped His people's destiny. He allowed Israel to choose Saul. God chose David. The Spirit is seen as the divine enabler, empowering both Saul and David in God's designed plan.

Jesus Christ in 1 Samuel:
He is our *future king anointed by God*. Hanna's prayer anticipates this future king, an anointed one, also called the Messiah. He will fulfill God's promise to establish David's throne forever.

Literary Form of 1 Samuel:
A combination of historical chronicle and a collection of literary narratives in which history is told in sufficient detail that it comes alive in our imagination and embodies universal human experience (history tells what *happened*, while literature goes beyond that and tells what *happens* universally).

The three primary heroes are Samuel, Saul (a tragic hero), and David. The historical part records national history; the literary part is biography of individuals. Secondary characters in 1 Samuel include Hannah and Jonathan. The book was included in the Former Prophets.

```
1 Samuel
2 Samuel    = 1 Chronicles
```

Highlights and Stories to Read in 1 Samuel:
- Samuel dedicated, chapter 1
- Samuel hears God, chapter 2
- The Ark of the Covenant captured, chapter 4
- Saul anointed king, chapter 10
- David anointed king, chapter, chapter 16
- Goliath, chapter, chapter 17
- Saul consults a witch, chapter 28
- Death of Saul, chapter 31

Author
Generally accepted that the author is unknown, although Samuel perhaps wrote portions through I Sam 25. 1 Chron 29:29 suggests Nathan and Gad contributed.

When the Book was Written
930 BCE.

When the Events Took Place
1105-1055 BCE.

1 Samuel

Approximate Dates of Key Events	
Birth of Saul	c.1125 BCE
Ark moved to temple of Dagon	c.1100
Birth of Samuel	c.1105
Eli and his sons	c.1105
Ark moved again	1096
Samuel anoints Saul First King	1095
Civil war in Egypt	1090
David is born	1085
Samuel secretly anoints David king	1070
David and Goliath	1067
Jonathan visits/helps David	1064
David cuts off Saul's robe	1062
Death of Eli	1061
Death of Samuel	1060
Philistines took off Saul's head	1055
Death of Jonathan	1055

Keys to the Book:

Key Theme: In spite of disobedience causing interruption, God is committed to His plan and will work it out.

Key Word: *Hears*

Read 1 Samuel 1:13; 2:23; 7:9; 8:18. An important word used over 1,100 times in the Old Testament. It meant "total attention"; much more than listening; it also included obedience. God delights to use the one who hears and then acts. A "doer."

A Key Chapter: 15

Key Verse (s):

13:14 "But now your kingdom shall not endure. The Lord has sought out for Himself a man after His own heart, and the Lord has appointed him as ruler over His people, because you have not kept what the Lord commanded you."

15:22 Samuel said, "Has the Lord as much delight in burnt offerings and sacrifices as in obeying the voice of the Lord? Behold, to obey is better than sacrifice, and to heed than the fat of rams.

18:6 It happened as they were coming, when David returned from killing the Philistine, that the women came out of all the cities of Israel, singing and dancing, to meet King Saul, with tambourines, with joy and with musical instruments. 7 The women sang as they played, and said,

*"Saul has slain his thousands,
And David his ten thousands."*

Key Characters

Eli—Judged Israel for forty years; also a high priest; not a good father; trained Samuel (1:3–28; 2:11–4:18).

Hannah—Samuel's mother who dedicated him to the Lord when he was a baby (1:2–2:11, 21).

Samuel—ministered as priest, Prophet, and Judge of Israel; used by God to anoint Israel's first two kings (1:20; 2:11, 18–26; 3:1–21; 7:3–13:15; 15:1–16:13; 19:18–24; 25:1; 28:3–16).

Saul—chosen by God to be the first king of Israel; failed God; attempted to kill David; turned to a sorcerer and soon was killed (9:2–11:15; 13:1–19:24; 20:24–33; 21:10, 11; 22:6–24:22; 25:44–27:4; 28:3–31:12).

Jonathan—Saul's son and close friend of David; Protected David against his father, Saul (13:1–14:49; 18:1–23:18; 31:2).

David—greatest king of Israel; also a shepherd, musician, and poet; direct ancestor to Jesus Christ (16:11–30:27).

2 SAMUEL

Overview and Basic Outline
We note that the books of 1 and 2 Samuel, along with 1 and 2 Kings, are a chronicle of the entire history of Judah's and Israel's kingship.

2 Samuel continues the story of the early monarchy. David reigned for forty years (the first seven over only the tribe of Judah). The focus is on the second half of King David's life, whose name is mentioned over two hundred times. Faith and failure describe this king's life. It was one of both elation and adultery and the treason of his son Absalom. He is shown to be an excellent warrior and leader. God promised an unending dynasty, an "extension" of the covenant that was initiated with Abraham.

This second part of "Samuel," (1 and 2 Samuel were originally one book) centers on David's life both as a king and as a man. The writer "pulls no punches" telling the story. Transparency into David's life is shared, not skipped over and telling only the good. Despite David's flaws, it is clear that he valued his relationship with God and his heart was obedient to God.

We view David's rise and fall. The kingdom is expanded by conflicts with the Philistines, Moabites, Syrians, and Edomites. He established Jerusalem as his capital and brought the ark to the city.

David could be called the model of a king. In fact, later kings looked to him for inspiration.

1. David rules Judah, Cps 1-2
2. David rules all Israel, Cps 3-5
3. David's Glory years, Cps 6-8
4. David's Troubles, Cps 9-20
5. David's Final years, Cps 21-24

Thoughts About God in 2 Samuel:
God is revealed as Sovereign. His names in 2 Samuel include:
- Yahweh, LORD
- El, Elohim, God
- Yahweh Tsebaoth, the LORD of Hosts, the LORD Almighty
- Ab, Father
- Adonay, Lord, Master
- Metsuda, Fortress (First appearance)
- Elyon, Highest

- Ruach Yahweh, the Lord's Spirit

God always rules over His plans concerning His kingdom. He made covenant with David just as He did with Abraham. He is sovereign to carry out His designed plan.

God desires His people to approach Him in worship.

Jesus Christ in 2 Samuel:
God's promise in the *Davidic Covenant* outlined His plan to extend David's kingdom for eternity. Christ fulfilled this covenant.

Literary Form of 2 Samuel:
The prose epic of David, which can also be called court history (the history of what happened at court, as written by an official recorder). Elements of hero story and tragedy also enter.

The poetic sections were David's compositions: (1) The Song of the Bow (1:19-27); (2) "Song of Thanksgiving" (22:1-51); (3) David's last words (23:1-7).

2 Samuel was part of the Former Prophets.

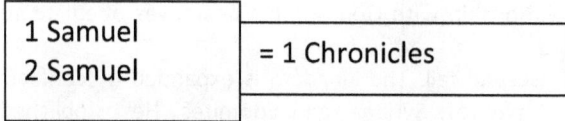

Highlights and Stories to Read in 2 Samuel:
- David anointed King of Judah, chapter 3
- David anointed King of all Israel, chapter 5
- Bathsheba, chapter 11
- "You are the man!" chapter 12
- David's last words, chapter 23

Author
It is generally accepted that the author is unknown, although Samuel perhaps wrote portions through I Sam 25. 1 Chron 29:29 suggests Nathan and Gad contributed.

When the Book was Written
930 BCE.

When the Events Took Place
1055-1015 BCE.

2 Samuel

Approximate Dates of Key Events	
David mourns Saul and David	1055 BCE
David, King over Tribe of Judah	1055-1048
David king over 12 tribes; David captures Jerusalem	1048
David brings Ark of Covenant to Jerusalem; David broke the Philistine hold	1047
Mephibosheth restored	1040
David and Bathsheba; Solomon is born	1037
Shalmaneser rules Assyria	1030-1018
Absalom revolts against David	1027
Absalom took possession of David's kingdom	1023
Saul's sons hung by Gibeonites	1022

Keys to the Book

Key Theme: God rewards a life lived before Him. However, the consequences of sin will always produce terrible consequences.

Key Word: *Ark*
In 2 Samuel we read the Key Word, *ark* in 6:2,4,20,12,17; 15:24. This was a wooden chest overlaid with gold and the "home" to the two tablets of Moses. It was always placed in the Holy of Holies, and represented His Covenant with them. The word itself just meant "a chest."

A Key Chapter: 11

Key Verse (s):
7:12 "When your days are complete and you lie down with your fathers, I will raise up your descendant after you, who will come forth from you, and I will establish his kingdom. 13 "He shall build a house for My name, and I will establish the throne of his kingdom forever.

22:21 "The Lord has rewarded me according to my righteousness; According to the cleanness of my hands He has recompensed me.

Key Characters
David—greatest king of Israel; also a shepherd, musician, and poet; direct ancestor to Jesus Christ (16:11–30:27).

Joab—David's military commander (2:13–3:39; 8:16; 10:7–12:27; 14:1–33; 18:2–24:9).

Bathsheba—committed adultery with David; mother of Solomon; direct ancestor of Jesus (11:1–26; 12:24).

Nathan—Prophet and advisor to David; used by God to reveal David's sin, urged him to repent (7:2–17; 12:1–25).

Absalom—David's son who attempted to overthrow the throne of Israel (3:3; 13:1–19:10).

1 KINGS

Overview and Basic Outline
In the Hebrew language, 1 and 2 Kings formed one book and was a sequel to the combined books of 1 and 2 Samuel. We note that the books of 1 and 2 Samuel, along with 1 and 2 Kings, are a chronicle of the entire history of Judah's and Israel's kingship.

The books of 1 and 2 Kings continue the history of God's people during four centuries. Kings immediately follows where Samuel left off, the final days of David's reign. The Hebrew title means "Kings," was divided into two books by Greek translators in the second century BCE. The books of 1 Kings and 2 Kings should be considered together.

We read of the death of David followed by the successor to the throne, his son Solomon and his great empire, and the division of Israel following Solomon's death. We read of the rivalry and political intrigue, which developed in the house of David to settle the question of who would be heir to the throne. 1 Kings will detail approximately 125 years following David. We travel from a united kingdom to the early kings of a divided kingdom.

The events concerning a large number of prophets are recorded in this book including Elijah.

1. God's Kingdom United: The Reign of Solomon, I Kings 1-11
2. God's Kingdom Divided: The Kings of Israel and Judah, 1 Kings 12-2 Kings 17
3. God's Kingdom Surviving: The Kings of Judah, 1 Kings 18-25

Thoughts About God in 1 Kings:
God is revealed as One True God. His names in 1 Kings include:
- Yahweh, LORD
- Elohim, God
- Adonay, Lord, Master
- Ruach Yahweh, the LORD's Spirit
- Yahweh Tsebaoth, the LORD of Hosts, the LORD Almighty

The only God is to be worshipped in His chosen place, the Temple in Jerusalem. He will not tolerate the worship from other sites such as the High Places or other places such as Bethel.

The Spirit of God is present to inspire His prophets.

Jesus Christ in 1 Kings:
Solomon's *great wisdom* symbolizes Christ. The New Testament refers to Christ "who became wisdom from God" (1 Cor 1:30).

Literary Form of 1 Kings:
Court history (a chronicle of what various kings did), but because of the strongly religious worldview it is also a religious history of a nation. When the prophet Elijah enters in the last six chapters, biography and hero story become part of the mix. If we take a wide-angle view, the book falls into three segments: history of Solomon's reign (1-11); succession narrative in which the kingdom splits into two kingdoms (12-16); conflict story between Ahab and Elijah (17-22).

The events in the life of Solomon are told with some detail. Later kings are mentioned with less emphasis on particulars. Then when Ahab arrives, the author again shares many details.

1 Kings was one of the Former Prophets.

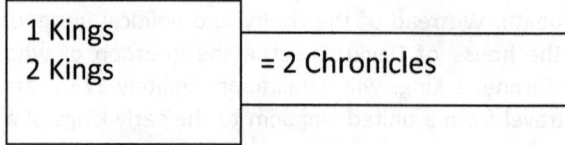

Highlights and Stories to Read in 1 Kings:
- David's final instructions to his son Solomon, chapter 2
- Solomon asks for wisdom, chapter 3
- Solomon builds the first Temple, chapter 6
- Solomon's wealth, chapter 10
- Kingdom divides, chapter 12
- Elijah appears suddenly, chapter 17
- Call of Elisha, chapter 19b

Author
Unknown; possibly Jeremiah. Several non-biblical books were used as sources in its final form (11:41, 14:19, 29).

When the Book was Written
*c.*580 BCE.

When the Events Took Place
*c.*1015-889 BCE.

1 Kings

Approximate Dates of Key Events	
Solomon anointed king; David Dies	1015 BCE
Solomon marries daughter of Pharaoh	1014
Temple built in Jerusalem	1012-1005
Temple dedicated	1004
Book of Ruth, Song of Solomon, Ecclesiastes written	1000-970
Rehoboam/Jeroboam	975
Elijah, Ahab, Jezebel	c.914-
Jehoshaphat rules Judah	914-889
Call of Elisha	c.889-

Keys to the Book
Key Theme
No matter how you live life, what your status is, the important focus is how you finish your race of life.

Key Word (s): *Baal*
Found in 1 Kings: 16:31; 18:19, 21, 26, 40; 22:53. *Baal* The word has the literal meaning of "master" or "owner." Baal was considered as the "son" of the god EL or "father bull" and the fertility goddess Asherah, who is mentioned in 2 Kings 21:7. Baal was the leader of all the Canaanites' gods and powerful forces. Terrible rituals were linked with this worship including Prostitution, self-mutilation, and infant sacrifice. Sadly, several times God's people were punished for their worship of Baal and Asherah (Judges 2:11–15; Jeremiah 19:4–6).

Key Chapter: 12

Key Verse (s):
4:29 Now God gave Solomon wisdom and very great discernment and breadth of mind, like the sand that is on the seashore.

9:4 As for you, if you will walk before Me as your father David walked, in integrity of heart and uprightness, doing according to all that I have commanded you and will keep My statutes and My ordinances, 5 then I will establish the throne of your kingdom over Israel forever, just as I Promised to your father David, saying, 'You shall not lack a man on the throne of Israel.'

11:11 So the Lord said to Solomon, "Because you have done this, and you have not kept My covenant and My statutes, which I have commanded you, I will surely tear the kingdom from you, and will give it to your servant.

Key Characters

David—king of Israel; chose his son Solomon to be the next king (1–2:10); also see info for Key People in 1 Samuel.

Solomon—third king of Israel; son of David and Bathsheba; builder of the first temple; God granted him his choice to become the wisest man ever born (1:10–11:43).

Rehoboam—son of Solomon; succeeded him as the fourth king of Israel; his evil actions led to the division of Israel into two kingdoms; later became king of the southern kingdom of Judah (11:43–12:24; 14:21–31).

Jeroboam—evil king of the northern ten tribes of Israel; erected idols and appointed non-Levitical priests (11:24–14:20).

2 KINGS

Overview and Basic Outline
In the Hebrew language, 1 and 2 Kings formed one book and was a sequel to the combined books of 1 and 2 Samuel. The Hebrew title means "Kings." It was divided into two books by Greek translators in the second century BCE. We note that the books of 1 and 2 Samuel, along with 1 and 2 Kings, are a chronicle of the entire history of Judah's and Israel's kingship.

2 Kings continues the drama begun in 1 Kings. Over half of the book details Elisha and his ministry. We read the tracing of the kings of Israel and Judah by first carrying forward the history of one nation, then retracing the same period for the other nation.

The author also emphasized two major sieges of Jerusalem. The first by Sennacherib of Assyria, the second by Nebuchadnezzar of Babylon. In fact, Kings was written to the people of the southern kingdom of Judah to explain that the fall of the northern kingdom of Israel was God's judgment of their idolatry.

2 Kings reflects the ongoing religious apostasy in both Israel and Judah, leading to the destruction of both nations. Nebuchadnezzar destroys the walls, temple, and buildings/houses of Jerusalem, 150 years following the fall of Israel.

Like 1 Kings, this book evaluates people by concluding if the people did what was right in the site of God, or not.

1. God's Kingdom United: The Reign of Solomon, 2 Kings 1-11
2. God's Kingdom Divided: The Kings of Israel and Judah, 2 Kings 12-2 Kings 17
3. God's Kingdom Surviving: The Kings of Judah, 2 Kings 18-25

Thoughts About God in 2 Kings:
God is revealed as Judge against unbelief. His names in 2 Kings include:
- Yahweh, LORD
- Elohim, God
- Ruach Yahweh, the LORD'S Spirit
- Yahweh Tsebaoth, the LORD of Hosts, the LORD Almighty
- El Chay, Living God
- Qedosh Yisrael, Holy One of Israel (First appearance)
- Adonay, Lord, Master

As in 1 Kings, God is the judge of those who rebel against Him. Above all else, God teaches His people that He values faithfulness to Him above all else.

The book ends with a hope; His promises are true.

Jesus Christ in 2 Kings:
A *Jewish remnant of God's people,* whom He spared, preserved the royal line through which Christ would enter the world. The line through which Jesus would redeem His people was saved by captivity.

Literary Form of 2 Kings:
Court history of the two kingdoms of Israel and Judah. Despite interspersed hero stories about virtuous kings, the overall pattern is that of the decline and fall of two nations. Subgenres include prophetic narrative, miracle story, political history, story of intrigue, and battle story. The storyteller is a master at recreating memorable moments that come alive in our imagination.

An interesting method, the author describes the period of the divided monarchy by alternating between the kings of Israel and the kings of Judah.

The single book of 1 Kings and 2 Kings was placed as the last of the four Former Prophets (Joshua, Judges, Samuel, and Kings). These four books describe the 800-year period from Israel's entry into Canaan through the destruction of the temple and Jerusalem and the exile to Babylon.

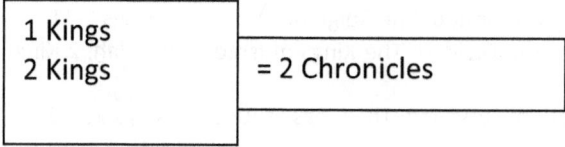

Highlights and Stories to Read in 2 Kings:
- Elijah taken to heaven, chapter 2
- Elisha heals Naaman, chapter 5
- The floating ax head, chapter 6
- Jerusalem falls to Babylonia, chapter 25

Author
Unknown; possibly Jeremiah.

When the Book was Written

2 Kings

c.580 BCE.

When the Events Took Place
889-587 BCE.

Approximate Dates of Key Events	
Elisha ministers	c.889- BCE
Jehu anointed king by Elisha	884
Jeroboam II begins his reign in Israel	826
Amos, Hosea Prophets to Israel	755-720
The Assyrian Empire strengthened under Tiglath-Pileser	745
Assyria (Shalmaneser, Sargon) - takes Israel	734-722
Josiah's reforms	c.640-
Babylonia takes Judah	605-586

Keys to the Book

Key Theme: Everyone's actions result in consequences. Israel and Judah learned the hard way.

Key Word (s): *High Places*
Found in 2 Kings: 12:3; 14:4; 15:4; 23:8, 15, 20. This refers to a sacred area located on high ground such as a hill or ridge. There was nothing wrong with this in the early days of worship before the temple was built (1 Kings. 3:2–4). At a later time, the Israelites started worshiping pagan gods at these sacred sites patterned after the Canaanite practice. Because of that, this term high places in the Old Testament became associated with Israel's religious rebellion and apostasy (1 Kings. 14:23; Psalms 78:58; Jeremiah 19:5).

Key Chapter: 25

Key Verse (s):
17:22 The sons of Israel walked in all the sins of Jeroboam which he did; they did not depart from them 23 until the Lord removed Israel from His sight, as He spoke through all His servants the Prophets. So Israel was carried away into exile from their own land to Assyria until this day.

23:27 The Lord said, "I will remove Judah also from My sight, as I have removed Israel. And I will cast off Jerusalem, this city which I have chosen, and the temple of which I said, 'My name shall be there.'"

Key Characters

Elijah—a Prophet of Israel; faced Ahab and Jezebel; raised a dead boy; called fire from heaven; never physically died; was carried directly to heaven in a chariot of fire (1:3–2:11; 10:10, 17).

Elisha—Prophet trained under Elijah; close companion, became Elijah's successor; many similarities in ministry; asked for twice the anointing; saw Elijah taken to heaven (2:1–9:3; 13:14–21).

The woman from Shunem—the woman visited by Elijah in her home; brought her son back to life (4:8–37; 8:1–6).

Naaman—a Syrian warrior who suffered from leprosy; healed by Elisha (5:1–27).

Jezebel—evil queen of Israel; Baal worship introduced; attempted to prevent Israel from worshiping God; eventually killed and eaten by dogs (9:7–37).

Jehu—anointed king of Israel; used by God to punish Ahab's family (9:1–10:36; 15:12).

Joash—king of Judah, saved from death as a child; followed evil advice of younger friends, ultimately assassinated by his own officials (11:1–12:21) *Hezekiah*—king of Judah who remained faithful to God (16:20–20:21).

1 CHRONICLES

Overview and Basic Outline
1 and 2 Chronicles originally formed one book and are located at the end of the Hebrew Bible. The original Hebrew book was first divided by the Greek translators in the second century BCE. The two books must be considered together. The Hebrew name of the books is "events of the days."

The book of 1 Chronicles covers the same time period and many of the same events as portions of 1 and 2 Samuel. 1 Chronicles focuses on Judah and David's reign including several selected events written in 2 Samuel and 1 Kings but also offering additional material not included in the earlier books. An extensive list (the most extensive in the Bible), beginning with Adam, of family genealogies of exiles in foreign lands is offered to verify them as rightful heirs of the Promised Land.

The books of Chronicles have been called a "priestly history" because it presents the history of Israel from a priestly perspective. The early chapters also include a brief mention of Saul's downfall and Solomon's accession.

Perhaps David's most important contribution, preparations to construct God's temple, are detailed in the later chapters.

1. Genealogies Cps 1-9
2. Saul Cp 10
3. David Cps 11-29

Thoughts About God in 1 Chronicles:
God is revealed as Sovereign. His names in 1 Chronicles include:
- Yahweh, LORD
- Elohim, God
- Yahweh Tsebaoth, the LORD of Hosts, the LORD Almighty
- Ruach, Spirit
- Ab, Father

God is shown as One who is sovereign and faithful to carry forth His plans. He desires the worship of His people in the ways he has revealed.

The Spirit revealed plans for construction of the Temple, and organizing the priests and Levites.

Jesus Christ in 1 Chronicles:

God made a covenant with David. He promised to establish David's throne forever. It would be through David's sons' sons and beyond, that the eternal kingdom of Christ would be established.

Literary Form of 1 Chronicles:
An expanded hero story that narrates the exploits of King David, as recorded by a court historian. Because David is the king of a nation, the genre of national history is also at work (with the repeated designation "all Israel" lending a corporate identity to the nation). The documentary impulse to record data and lists dominates (in contrast to earlier historical books, where people and events dominate).

The genealogical material is the most extensive found in Scripture. In addition, the lists of names in 1 Chronicles is quite interesting: David's Warriors (cp 11); divisions of the Levites (cp 23); divisions of the Priests (cp 24); the Levitical musicians (cp 25); the Levitical gatekeepers (cp 26); David's officials (cp 27).

David is portrayed as almost perfect in 1 Chronicles, whereas in 2 Samuel his adultery with Bathsheba and the treason of Absalom is considered.

A poetic section (16:29) adds David's prayers.

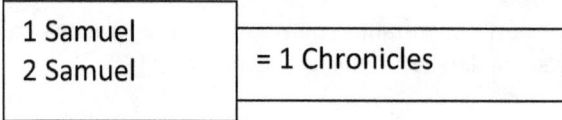

Highlights and Stories to Read in 1 Chronicles:
- Death of King Saul, chapter 10
- David becomes King of all Israel, chapter 11
- David and moving the Ark, chapters 13, 15, 16
- David instructs his son, Solomon, chapter 28
- Solomon becomes King, chapter 29

Author
It is speculated to have been Ezra. More likely, it was compiled by a Levite compiler referred to as "the Chronicler."

When the Book was Written
c.430-420 BCE.

When the Events Took Place

1 Chronicles

c.1055-1015 BCE.

Approximate Dates of Key Events	
David mourns Saul and David	1055 BCE
David, King over Tribe of Judah	1055-1048
David king over 12 tribes; David captures Jerusalem	1048
David brings Ark of Covenant to Jerusalem; David broke the Philistine hold	1047
Mephibosheth restored	1040
David and Bathsheba; Solomon is born	1037
Shalmaneser rules Assyria	1030-1018
Absalom revolts against David	1027
Absalom took possession of David's kingdom	1023
Saul's sons hung by Gibeonites	1022

Keys to the Book

Key Theme: Even though there are difficult and disappointing times in life, God's Promises are still available and dependable.

Key Word: *Sons*
Found in 1 Chronicles 1:43; 3:12; 4:25; 5:14; 9:4; 11:22; 26:28. This word has the literal meaning of "to build." The Hebrews considered their children to be "builders" of the future generations. The word may refer to a direct son or to a future descendant. (1 Kings 2:1; 1 Chronicles 7:14). Benjamin in the Old Testament means "Son of my Right Hand." In the plural, *ben* can be translated as "children" regardless of gender (see Exodus 12:37—"children of Israel"). Even God used this term to describe His relationship with Israel: *"Israel is My son, My firstborn"* (Exodus 4:22).

Key Chapter: 17

Key Verse (s):
17:11 "When your days are fulfilled that you must go to be with your fathers, that I will set up one of your descendants after you, who will be of your sons; and I will establish his kingdom. 12 "He shall build for Me a house, and I will establish his throne forever. 13 "I will be his father and he shall be My son; and I will not take My lovingkindness away from him, as I took it from him who was before you. 14 "But I will settle him in My house and in My kingdom forever, and his throne shall be established forever."'"

29: 11 Yours, O Lord, is the greatness and the power and the glory and the victory and the majesty, indeed everything that is in the heavens and the earth; Yours is the dominion, O Lord, and You exalt Yourself as head over

Key Characters

David—king of Israel and ancestor of Jesus Christ; described by God as "a man after My own heart" (2:8–29:30; see Acts 13:22) See Key People information from 1 Samuel and 1 Kings.

The mighty men—a special group of soldiers who were dedicated to fight for King David (11:10–28:1).

Nathan—a Prophet and advisor to David; told Solomon of God's will for him to build the great first temple (17:1–15).

Solomon—David's son who became the third king of Israel (3:5–29:28).

2 CHRONICLES

Overview and Basic Outline
1 and 2 Chronicles originally formed one book and are located at the end of the Hebrew Bible. The Hebrew name of the books is "events of the days." The book was divided in to two books in the second century BCE.

2 Chronicles covers over four centuries of history. Beginning with Solomon's plans to build the Jerusalem temple and ending with its destruction. The book concludes with the Persian King Cyrus' edict ordering the rebuilding of the temple.

The book focuses on the building and dedication of the temple, along with the strong emphasis of honoring and serving God. In addition, emphasis is place on the kings of Judah who led the nation in religious reform and renewal. 2 Chronicles coves the same period as 1 and 2 Kings, but with a focus on the kings of Judah.

1. Solomon, 1-9
2. Judah's Monarchy in the Divided Kingdom, 10-36:21
3. Judah's Release From Their Seventy-year Captivity, 36:22, 23

Thoughts About God in 2 Chronicles:
God is revealed as the One who blesses His people. His names in 2 Chronicles include:
- Yahweh, LORD
- Elohim, God
- Ruach Elohim, the Spirit of God
- Ruach Yahweh, the LORD's Spirit

God stated His program to help His people to become more knowledgeable in His ways. Above all else, He values faithfulness to Him. The book ends the history of the Israelites with the hope of return to the Promised Land. The Spirit of God inspires the priests and prophets.

Jesus Christ in 2 Chronicles:
The *line of David* remained protected throughout 2 Chronicles. Jesus is pictured in *the temple* built by Solomon; however, this temple (Jesus) will be eternal.

BOOK OF OLD TESTAMENT BIBLE LITERACY

Literary Form of 2 Chronicles:
Another historical chronicle, with a focus on personalities. A strongly religious viewpoint is imposed on the reigns of successive kings of Judah, as God rewards obedience to his covenant and punishes disobedience.

King Hezekiah of Judah reigned at the time of Israel's fall. Therefore, he was the Davidic king in Jerusalem and ruled all Israel (31:1; 35:3).

Chronicles was placed in the Writings section of Hebrew Bible, and was the last book in their writings.

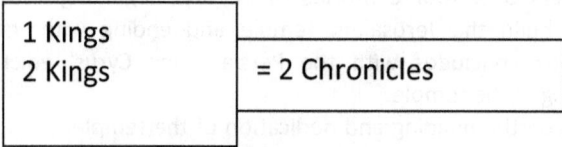

Highlights and Stories to Read in 2 Chronicles:
- Solomon asks for wisdom, chapter 1
- Solomon and the first Temple, chapters, 2-5
- Solomon dies in Jerusalem
- The kingdom divides, chapter 10
- Joash repairs the Temple, chapter 24
- Assyria attacks Jerusalem, chapters 28b, 32
- Jerusalem falls to Babylonia, chapter 36b
- Cyrus' heart stirred by God, chapter 36c

Author
Speculated to have been Ezra. More likely, it was compiled by a Levite compiler referred to as "the Chronicler."

When the Book was Written
c.430-420 BCE.

When the Events Took Place
c.1025-537 BCE.

Approximate Dates of Key Events	
Solomon anointed king; David Dies	1015 BCE
Solomon marries daughter of Pharaoh	1014
Temple built in Jerusalem	1012-1005
Temple dedicated	1004
Book of Ruth, Song of Solomon, Ecclesiastes written	1000-970
Rehoboam/Jeroboam	975

	2 Chronicles
Elijah, Ahab, Jezebel	c.914-
Jehoshaphat rules Judah	914-889
Call of Elisha	c.899-

Keys to the Book

Key Theme: Hope is always alive. Even though you may look at difficult circumstances in life, God is with you and will restore you. God always blesses faithfulness to Him.

Key Word (s): *Passover*
Found in 2 Chronicles 30:1, 15; 35:1, 9, 11, 13, 18, 19. This word has a literal meaning of "to pass" or "to leap over." An important word to consider, the Passover celebration commemorated the day God spared the firstborn children of the Israelites from the death plague brought on Egypt. The Lord "passed over" those who sprinkled the blood from the Passover lamb on their doorposts (Exodus 12). It was the first of the three annual Hebrew festivals at which all the men must appear at the sanctuary (Exodus 13:3-10). Passover, as specified in the Law of Moses, reminds the Israelites of God's great mercy on them (Leviticus 23:5–8; Numbers 28:16–25; Deuteronomy 16:1–8). The Passover meal is a type of Christ, our "Passover Lamb," whose blood rescues us from death. King Hezekiah's great Passover in 2 Chronicles 30:14 signaled spiritual renewal in Judah.

Key Chapter: 34

Key Verse (s):
7:14 and My people who are called by My name humble themselves and pray and seek My face and turn from their wicked ways, then I will hear from heaven, will forgive their sin and will heal their land.

16:9 "For the eyes of the Lord move to and fro throughout the earth that He may strongly support those whose heart is completely His. You have acted foolishly in this. Indeed, from now on you will surely have wars."

Key Characters
Solomon—a king of Israel and builder of the first temple; asked for/received great wisdom to rule God's people (1:1–9:31).

Queen of Sheba—heard of Solomon's great reputation; visited him seeking information about his success (9:1–12; see Matt. 12:42).

Rehoboam—evil son of Solomon who became a king of Israel; soon divided the kingdom and later led the southern kingdom of Judah (9:31–13:7).

Asa—king of Judah; used very corrupt methods to accomplish God's purposes (14:1–16:14).

Jehoshaphat—son of Asa, followed him as king of Judah; attempted to follow God but made poor decisions (17:1–22:9).

Jehoram—wicked son of Jehoshaphat who succeeded him as king of Judah; Promoted idol worship and killed his six brothers (21:1–20).

Uzziah—(also called Azariah) succeeded his father, Amaziah, as king of Judah; mostly followed God, but prideful (26:1–23).

Hezekiah—succeeded his father, Ahaz, as king of Judah; restored the temple; followed God and started religious reform (28:27–32:33).

Manasseh—succeeded his father, Hezekiah, as king of Judah; did evil in the sight of the Lord but repented later in his reign (32:33–33:20).

Josiah—succeeded his father, Amon, as king of Judah; followed the Lord; found the Book of the Law while restoring the temple; took the Book to the people. Brought revival/reforms (33:25–35:27).

EZRA

Overview and Basic Outline
Originally, Ezra and Nehemiah was one book and should be considered together. Ezra is a book of hope and restoration. The book is named for the leading character. The Latin translator Jerome named the two separate books.

Two groups of Israelites returned from Babylonian captivity thirty years apart. Each group numbered approximately 40,000. Zerubbabel led the first group, Ezra the second.

Ezra continues the history of Israel at the point where 2 Chronicles ended. Notice the last two words of 2 Chronicles and the first two of Ezra, indicating that the two books belonged together.

God worked through the pagan King Cyrus to bring about the return to the Promised Land of those who would help His people. The rebuilding of the temple and a stable, organized people were vital for the future of the nation.

We notice in Ezra that the returning Jews were now free of any idolatry, which was the reason for so much failure of their ancestors. The returning Israelites' first act was to build an altar on which to offer the required sacrifices.

1. The First Return Under Zerubbabel, Cps 1-6
2. The Second Return Under Ezra, Cps 7-10

Thoughts About God in Ezra:
God is revealed as Judge for the righteous. His names in Ezra include:
- Yahweh, LORD
- Elohim Elah, (in the Aramaic portions of Ezra, 4:8-24; 5:1-17; 6:1-18; 7:12-26)

God acts for His people, because of His righteousness. He will work through pagan kings and godly teachers if needed to accomplish His plan. He may ask one to sever family ties in order follow Him.

Jesus Christ in Ezra and Nehemiah:
He's your rebuilder and restorer of the broken down walls of human life. Israel's return to a Promised Land represents the forgiveness of Christ available to all people.

Literary Form of Ezra:

A return story that narrates the return of two waves of Jewish exiles to Jerusalem after captivity in Babylon. The main archetype is the rebirth of a nation in its homeland. The three dominating motifs are returning, rebuilding, and reforming.

The author had access to many official Persian documents, lists, and memoirs. The use of lists indicates the author of Ezra and Chronicles was the same person. The official records include: (1) the Decree of Cyrus (1:2-4); (2) Letter of Rehum to Artaxerxes (4:8-16); (3) Artaxerxes' Reply to Rehum (4:17-22); (4) Letter of Tattenai to Darius (5:6-17), and several other official Persian documents.

Aramaic portions of Ezra include 4:8-6:18 and 7:12-26. Aramaic was the international trade language of the ancient Near East under the Persians.

Highlights and Stories to Read in Ezra:
- The return to Jerusalem, chapter 1
- Opposition to rebuilding the Temple, chapter 4
- Resume building the Temple, chapter 5
- Ezra comes to Jerusalem, chapter 7

Author
Ezra, according to Jewish tradition. Notice the narration switches from third person to first person after Ezra appears in the story (chapter 7).

When the Book was Written
c.430-420 BCE.

When the Events Took Place
537-467 BCE.

Chronology of Ezra		
539 BCE	Capture of Babylon	Daniel 5:30
536	Cyrus's first year as sole ruler of kingdom	Ezra 1:1-4
536	Return under Sheshbazzar (Zerubbabel) -	Ezra 1:11
536	Building of altar	Ezra 3:1
535	Work on temple begun	Ezra 3:8
535-529	Opposition during Cyrus' reign	Ezra 4:1-5
529-520	Work of temple ceased	Ezra 4:24
520	Work on temple renewed under Darius	Ezra 2:2
516	Temple completed	Ezra 6:15
467	Ezra departs from Babylon, 2nd return	Ezra 7:6-9
467	Ezra arrives in Jerusalem	Ezra 7:8-9
467	People assemble	Ezra 10:9
467	Committee begins investigation	Ezra 10:16
456	Committee ends investigation	Ezra 10:17

Ezra

Keys to the Book

Key Theme: Set the priorities of your life in God; worship Him first, then work for Him in all you do.

Key Word (s): *Jews*
Found in 4:12, 23; 5:1, 5; 6:7, 8, and 14.
The word means "to praise." Jacob used the word in Genesis 49:8 in a blessing of his son.
We mentioned, a Jew was one from the tribe of Judah or an Israelite living in Judah. During this period of restoration, "Jew" referred to the Israelites as a group.
Jesus was called King of the Jews, then Paul clarified it for all of us in Romans 2:28 *For ⟨?⟩ ⟨?⟩he is not a Jew who is one outwardly, nor is circumcision that which is outward in the flesh. 29 But ⟨?⟩he is a Jew who is one inwardly; and ⟨?⟩ circumcision is that which is of the heart, by the ⟨?⟩ Spirit, not by the letter; ⟨?⟩ and his praise is not from men, but from God.*

Key Chapter: 6

Key Verse (s):
1:3 'Whoever there is among you of all His people, may his God be with him! Let him go up to Jerusalem which is in Judah and rebuild the house of the Lord, the God of Israel; He is the God who is in Jerusalem."

6:16 And the sons of Israel, the priests, the Levites and the rest of the exiles, celebrated the dedication of this house of God with joy

7:10 For Ezra had set his heart to study the law of the Lord and to practice it, and to teach His statutes and ordinances in Israel.

Key Characters
Ezra—scribe and teacher of God's Word who began religious reform among the people; led the second group of exiles from Babylon to Jerusalem (Ezra 7:1–10:16).

Cyrus—Persian king who conquered Babylon; assisted the return of the Israelite exiles to their homeland (Ezra 1:1–6:14).

Zerubbabel—led the first group of Israelite exiles from Babylon to Jerusalem; completed the rebuilding of the temple (Ezra 2:2–5:2).

Haggai—post-Exilic (after the Exile) Prophet who encouraged Zerubbabel and the Israelite people to continue rebuilding the temple (Ezra 5:1–2; 6:14).

Zechariah—post-Exilic Prophet who encouraged Zerubbabel and the Israelite people to continue rebuilding the temple (Ezra 5:1–2; 6:14).

Darius I—Persian king who supported the rebuilding of the temple by the Israelites (Ezra 4:5–6:14).

Artaxerxes—Persian king (Xerxes I) who allowed Ezra to return to Jerusalem (Ezra 7:1) and reinstitute temple worship and the teaching of the Law.

NEHEMIAH

Overview and Basic Outline
This book centers on the rebuilding of the city walls around Jerusalem. It is named for the major character, the cupbearer to the King of Persia, Artaxerxes. It follows the book of Ezra, actually the second part of the original book (Ezra and Nehemiah).

Nehemiah was greatly disturbed in hearing the wall of Jerusalem was still in ruins. In the ancient world, a city without walls was helpless before its enemies. The temple was in construction, but the wall was ignored. For Jerusalem to have its walls complete was evidence of divine favor.

Therefore, Nehemiah sought and received permission to travel to Jerusalem to oversee the building of the wall. Thirteen years after Ezra had arrived to begin the temple construction, and with many obstacles to overcome, he led the project to construct the wall in two months.

Nehemiah became governor of Jerusalem and served for the following twelve years.

1. Nehemiah's First Term as Governor of Jerusalem, Cps 1-12
2. Nehemiah's Second Term as Governor of Jerusalem, Cp 13

Thoughts About God in Nehemiah:
God is revealed as a worker on behalf of His people. His names in Nehemiah include:
- Yahweh, LORD
- El, Elohim, God
- Adonay, Lord, Master
- Ruach, Spirit

God will do whatever is needed to enable them to accomplish His purposes. His teachers are sent to encourage and lead. He will even use a king in order to work His plan for the time. He never changes. The plan He offered to Moses remains true for the people who returned to Jerusalem.

Jesus Christ in Ezra and Nehemiah:
He's your rebuilder and restorer of the broken down walls of human life. Nehemiah is the example of rebuilding of the city of God, which will be completed at the coming of Christ with His saints.

Literary Form of Nehemiah:

A kaleidoscopic book that combines hero story, return story, civil record, governor's report, and management handbook. Rebuilding the wall of Jerusalem occupies half of the book and takes on a symbolic meaning in addition to being a literal event. The popularity of this book for retreats and seminars shows that "principles for living" is a good summary statement.

The book has an extensive first-person narrative, using words such as "I," "my," and "me." The preaching of Ezra, and the use of the "Memoirs of Nehemiah" further indicate the authorship of a single book.

Highlights and Stories to Read in Nehemiah:

- Nehemiah's concern, chapter 1
- Nehemiah goes to Jerusalem, chapter 2
- The wall is rebuilt, chapters 3, 4, 12b
- Ezra reads the Law, chapter 8

Author

Ezra, however 1:1 identifies the speaker as Nehemiah. Some scholars believed Nehemiah was the author, other attribute the writer or compiler of Chronicles and Ezra-Nehemiah to an unknown "Chronicler."

When the Book was Written

c.430-420 BCE.

When the Events Took Place

454-430 BCE.

	Chronology of Nehemiah	
454 BCE	20th year of Artaxerxes I	Nehemiah 1:1
454	Nehemiah approaches king	Nehemiah 2:1
454	Nehemiah arrives in Jerusalem, 3rd return	Nehemiah 2:11
454	Completion of wall	Nehemiah 6:15
454	Public assembly	Nehemiah 7:3-8:1
454	Feast of Tabernacles	Nehemiah 8:4
442	32nd year of Artaxerxes	Nehemiah 5:14; 13:6
442	Nehemiah's recall and return from Persia	

Keys to the Book

Key Theme: Arise and build the walls of your life with respect and urgency in spite of all opposition.

Key Word: *Awesome*

Nehemiah

Found in 1:5, 11; 6:14, 19. It means, "to fear," and carries the meaning of virtue. A reverence and respect for God's character. In some Bible passages, "fearing" and godly living are so closely related that they are almost synonymous; Lev 19:14; 2 Kings 17:324. Psalms 128:1 reads *How blessed is everyone who fears the Lord, Who walks in His ways.*

Key Chapter: 9

Key Verse (s):
6:15 So the wall was completed on the twenty-fifth of the month Elul, in fifty-two days. 16 When all our enemies heard of it, and all the nations surrounding us saw it, they lost their confidence; for they recognized that this work had been accomplished with the help of our God.

8 :8 They read from the book, from the law of God, translating to give the sense so that they understood the reading.

Key Characters
Nehemiah—influential cupbearer of the Persian king Artaxerxes; led the third group of exiles to Jerusalem to rebuild the city walls (1:1–13:31).

Ezra—led the second group of exiles to Jerusalem; worked with Nehemiah as Israel's priest and scribe (8:1–12:36).

Sanballat—governor of Samaria who attempted to discourage the people and thwart the rebuilding of Jerusalem's wall (2:10–13:28).

Tobiah—Ammonite official who mocked the rebuilding of the wall and discouraged the people (2:10–13:7).

ESTHER

Overview and Basic Outline
Esther's name was derived from the Persian word for "star." Esther and Ruth are the only books in the Bible named for women. The book is named in the Hebrew Bible, from the heroine of the story.

The book tells the story of God's protection on behalf of His people, though His name does not appear one time. The evil Haman plots to destroy all Jews, but Mordecai and Esther counter with a wise plan of their own. Their quick thinking saved the Jewish people from disaster.

Esther is selected as Queen and Haman's attempt to manipulate King Xerxes is foiled. In a dramatic twist, Haman is hanged on the very gallows he built for the execution of Mordecai. Mordecai is promoted to prime minister (the position Harman held).

The annual Jewish feast of Purim was established by Mordecai. The book of Esther preserves the historical origins of the celebration.

1. Esther replaces Vashti, 1:1-2:18
2. Mordecai overcomes Haman, 2:19-4:17
3. Israel survives, 5:1-10:3

Thoughts About God in Esther:
God is revealed as never changing. His name is not mentioned in Esther. However, He is seen throughout the events. God's covenant people will never be forgotten. In spite of the opposition of kings, leaders, or even nations, God will work out His plans.

Jesus Christ in Esther:
He is YOUR deliverer and preserver. Jesus is the sovereign protector over His people. Christ is shown in Esther who was willing to lay down her life to save her people.

Literary Form of Esther:
A hero story par excellence, and equally a triumph of storytelling. In fact, this book possesses virtually all of the ingredients that the human race likes best in a story. The overall pattern is a U-shaped descent into potential tragedy followed by a rise to a successful conclusion; literary scholars call this plot pattern comedy. In this story, the comic plot is also a rescue story.

Esther

It is a carefully crafted short story centered on true events. It is positioned as the last of the historical books of the Old Testament. The Greek translators were troubled by its lack of reference to God. They therefore inserted more than a hundred verses that refer to God. However, these were never accepted as canon.

Interesting is the use of paired elements. Two banquets of both Ahasuerus and Esther, two festivals of Purim, two lists of servants, and two letters establishing Purim.

Highlights and Stories to Read in Esther:
- Esther becomes Queen, chapter 2
- Haman plots to destroy all Jews, chapter 3
- Mordecai and Esther stopped the genocide, chapters 4, 5
- Harman executed, chapter 7
- Festival of Purim initiated, chapter 9b

Author
The author remains unknown; some name Mordecai.

When the Book was Written
460-400 BCE.

When the Events Took Place

Approximate Dates of Key Events	
Ahasuerus (Xerxes) - divorces Vashti	487BCE
Esther marries Ahasuerus	487
Haman's plot against the Jews	482
Haman hanged	481
Mordecai made Prime Minister	481
Jews delivered	480
Ezra arrived in Jerusalem	458
Nehemiah's work begins	445

Keys to the Book

Key Theme: God will always preserve His people. That includes you. In the midst of Satan's opposition, nothing happens beyond God's ability to work things for His glory.

Key Word: *Fasting*
Found in 4:3, 14. Pretty clear meaning, "to abstain from food." At various times it meant to abstain from drinking, bathing, anointing with oil, or sexual relations.

A fast, which was very common in ancient days, varied in length. 1 Samuel 14:24 "one day"; 1 Samuel 31:13 "seven days." It could last up to forty days.

We have passages in connection with mourning for the dead, intercessory prayer, repentance, and times of distress. Isaiah told the people to always include acts of righteousness with their fasting (Isaiah 58:3-9).

Key Chapter: 8

Key Verse (s):
4:14 *"For if you remain silent at this time, relief and deliverance will arise for the Jews from another place and you and your father's house will perish. And who knows whether you have not attained royalty for such a time as this?"*

8:17 *In each and every Province and in each and every city, wherever the king's commandment and his decree arrived, there was gladness and joy for the Jews, a feast and a holiday. And many among the peoples of the land became Jews, for the dread of the Jews had fallen on them.*

Key Characters
Esther—replaced Vashti as queen of Persia; saved the Jews against Haman's evil plot (2:7–9:32).

Mordecai—adopted and raised Esther; advisor to Esther as queen; later replaced Haman as second in command under King Xerxes (2:5–10:3).

King Xerxes I—king of Persia; married Esther and made her queen (1:1–10:3).

Haman—second in command under King Xerxes; plotted to kill the Jews (3:1–9:25).

JOB

Overview and Basic Outline
One of three books (Proverbs, Ecclesiastes) from Israel's wisdom teachers.

Job is perhaps the earliest book of the Bible, the first to be written. The name of the book comes from the Hebrew Bible, named after the main character and chief speaker in the dialogues. The Hebrew title means "Persecuted One." Job is the major biblical treatment on the issue of why people suffer. The book is written in the form of a dramatic poem.

The first two chapters set the stage for the remainder of the book. Satan makes an accusation before God, to test the integrity of Job.

The man Job lost family, health, and possessions. Job and four acquaintances debate the age-old question of "Why do the righteous suffer?" The "comforters" conclude that misfortune is always sent by God as punishment for sin. Job counters with the belief that he is an upright man and has done nothing to deserve this treatment by God.

God does not have to explain of justify His actions. He is all-powerful and all-knowing. Even though Job's patience was not peaceful and done in silence, Job learns to trust where he cannot understand. Restoration for Job concludes the book.

1. Job's Dilemma, Cps 1-2
2. Job's Debate, Cps 3-37
3. Job's Deliverance, Cps 38-42

Thoughts About God in Job:
God is revealed as sitting in His high court. His names in Job include:
- El, Elohim, Eloah, God
- Yahweh, LORD
- Shaddai, Almighty
- Adonay, Lord, Master
- Ruach EL, God's Spirit
- Ab, Father
- Go'el, Redeemer (First appearance)

We are shown that God allows Satan to challenge His righteousness. He has no concern for failure. He is almighty. Christ is portrayed as the coming redeemer (19:25) and the Spirit of God is shown as creator in 33:4.

Jesus Christ in Job:
Our *everlating Redeemer*. Our hope is in One who identifies with our suffering. Job eventually cries out to Christ, His mediator.

Literary Form of Job:
Many literary scholars claim that Job is the supreme literary achievement of the Old Testament. The main genre is poetic drama. Additionally, a drama like this that was never intended for performance on a stage is called a closet drama. Thematically, this book is the only book in the Bible that is a full-fledged theodicy—a reconciliation of God's goodness and omnipotence with the fact of evil and suffering in the world (the problem of evil, as philosophers call it). This highly poetic book needs to be read slowly and reflectively while relishing its poetry.

The narrative prologue of the first two chapters, and the epilogue in cp 42, are the framework for the extended body of the book. The poetic dialogues and monologues of the "in between" chapters, were composed entirely in the form of Hebrew parallelism found in Psalms and the other wisdom books.

Highlights and Stories to Read in Job:
- Satan before God, chapter 1a
- Satan's Action to Job, chapters 1b, 2a
- Eliphaz and Job, chapters 4-7, 5, 15-16, 22-23
- Bildad and Job, chapters 8-10, 18-19, 25-26
- Zophar and Job, chapters, 11-12, 20-21
- Job's request to argue his case, chapter 13-14
- Why are the wicked not punished? Chapter 24
- Final words of Job, chapters 27-31
- Elihu presents his argument, chapters 32-36
- God and Job, chapter 38

Author
The book is anonymous.

When the Book was Written
Could have been written anytime between Moses and the end of the Old Testament.

When the Events Took Place
c.2000-1500 BCE; most probable, Job took place sometime during the period of Abraham, Isaac, and Jacob.

Job

Keys to the Book

Key Theme: Human reasoning alone can never conclude in knowing the thoughts of God.

Key Word (s): *Affliction*

A Key Word in Job is found in 10:15; 30:16, 27; 36:8. *Affliction* comes from a root word which means "misery." It pictures someone bowed down under the weight of a heavy burden. We can relate sometimes to this.

The Bible says our Father sees the afflictions of His kids, He urges us to cast every burden upon HIM. He knows everyone of them. Since He controls all events, we can be assured that He is accomplishing good out of the difficulties we face. This is the setting of Job.

Key Chapter: 42

Key Verse (s):

11:21 *"Naked I came from my mother's womb,*
And naked I shall return there.
The Lord gave and the Lord has taken away.
Blessed be the name of the Lord."

13:15 *Though He slay me, I will hope in Him. Nevertheless I will argue my ways before Him.*

37:23 *"The Almighty — we cannot find Him; He is exalted in power And He will not do violence to justice and abundant righteousness. 24 "Therefore men fear Him; He does not regard any who are wise of heart."*

Key Characters

Job—suffered much loss; faith was tested by God; Job never blamed God; restoration (1:1–42:16).

Eliphaz the Temanite—a friend of Job; believed Job was suffering because of his sin (2:11; 4:1–5:27; 15:1–35; 22:1–30; 42:7–9).

Bildad the Shuhite—a second friend of Job; believed Job had not repented of his sin and therefore suffered (2:11; 8:1–22; 18:1–21; 25:1–6; 42:9).

Zophar the Naamathite—a third friend of Job; believed Job deserved to suffer more for his sins (2:11; 11:1–20; 20:1–29; 42:9).

Elihu the Buzite—a younger "advisor," stood up against Job's three friends; believed God was using suffering to mold Job's character (32:1–37:24).

PSALMS

Overview and Basic Outline

The Hebrew title of this book is a wonderful word, the Hebrew word "Tehillim" meaning *Praises*. The Greek and Latin versions name it "Book of Psalms." The book explores both our depth of need and height of our praise. In addition, it explores a wide range of topics such as peace, war, worship, and messianic Prophecy. The Psalms were generally meant to be put to music, and this book preserves the inspired words of Israelite songwriters. They are songs of exultation and high worship, songs of respect for God's Word, and other expressions of true religion.

The Book of Psalms is the largest and most referred to book in the Bible.

An attempt has been made to classify the Psalms by their form: hymns, laments (cries to God for help), and songs of thanksgiving. A few others were classified as royal psalms, kingship psalms, Zion (Jerusalem) psalms, or songs of trust. Israel's psalms were generally used in community worship, to express both praise and needs to God.

1. Book I (Genesis) MAN 1-41
2. Book II (Exodus) ISRAEL 42-72
3. Book III (Leviticus) THE SANCTUARY 73-89
4. Book IV (Numbers) THE EARTH 90-106
5. Book V (Deuteronomy) THE WORD OF GOD 107-150

Thoughts About God in Psalms:

God is revealed as Creator, Redeemer, and Covenant-maker. His names in Psalms include:
- Yah, Yahweh, LORD
- Melek, King (First appearance)
- El, Elohim, Eloah, God
- Shopet, Judge
- Elyon, Highest
- Adonay, Lord, Master
- Machseh, Refuge (First appearance)
- Metsuda, Fortress
- Roeh, Shepherd (First appearance)
- Go'el, Redeemer
- Yahweh Roi, the LORD is My Shepherd
- Yahweh Tsebaoth, the LORD of Hosts, the LORD Almighty

- El Chay, Living God
- Ruach, Ruach Qodesh, Spirit (First appearance)
- Migdal-Oz, Strong Tower (First appearance)
- Ab, Father
- Shaddai, Almighty
- Maon, Dwelling Place (First appearance)
- Qedosh Yisrael, Holy One of Israel
- Mashiach, Christ, Messiah
- Yahweh Tsur, the LORD My Rock (First appearance)

God is everywhere in the Psalms. His attributes are praised. The Spirit is active in accomplishing His purposes.

Jesus Christ in Psalms:
Christ is shown in many of the Psalms. He is identified as the direct descendant of David several places. (See the author's *Travel Through the Old Testament, Vol. 2* for a list of Psalms of Christ). *He is your Shepherd.*

Literary Form of Psalms:
A poetry anthology. All of the poems are lyric poems—poems that express the thoughts or feelings of a speaker. As with all poetry anthologies, the individual poems are self-contained and do not form part of a larger story. The verse form in which all the Psalms are written is parallelism, and this can be relished as reflective of the poet's skill with language. Although all of the psalms are lyric poems (either reflective/meditative or emotional/affective), they usually fall into a further genre, the most numerous being lament psalms, praise psalms, nature poems, and worship psalms.

Psalms was the first book in the Writings division of Hebrew Scripture.

Author
David wrote seventy-three of the Psalms, Moses (Psalm 90), Solomon (Psalms72 and 127), Asaph wrote twelve Psalms, the sons of Korah wrote eleven, Heman (Psalm 88), Ehan (Psalm 89), and forty-nine Psalms include no mention of its author.

When the Book was Written
Collected over an extensive period, *c.*1450-400.

When the Events Took Place
*c.*1500-538 BCE.

Keys to the Book

Psalms

Key Theme: I will praise Him with my whole heart.

Key Word: *Praise*

Praise is God's method to bind together His family. Everything else falls into insignificance in the midst of praise.

1. In 2 Chronicles 20:19 we see the Hebrew word HALAL. It means "to make a clear boast, to rave, to be shiny, to celebrate, or to be clamorously foolish."
2. In Psalm 50:23 we find TOWDAH. TOWDAH has some HALAL inside—celebration. It means, "To extend the hand in thanksgiving."
3. Found in Psalm 63:3, SHABACH, "to address in a loud tone, to shout
4. We find another praise in Ps 72:15, BARAK (baw-rak'). It means "to bow down in worship as an act of adoration." *Let them bless him all day long.*
5. Psalms 57:7, ZAMAR, meaning, "To rejoice in music before the Lord." It is used "to touch the strings."

Key Chapter: 100

Key Verse (s):

19:14 *Let the words of my mouth and the meditation of my heart Be acceptable in Your sight, O Lord, my rock and my Redeemer.*

145:21 *My mouth will speak the praise of the Lord, And all flesh will bless His holy name forever and ever.*

Key Characters

David—King of Israel; called a man after God's own heart by God Himself (Psalms 2–41; 51–70; 72:20; 78:70, 71; 86; 89; 96; 101; 103; 105; 108–110; 122; 124; 131–133; 138–145).

PROVERBS

Overview and Basic Outline

The Hebrew title was "Proverbs of Solomon." Solomon was named because he was the major contributor. It is one of three books (Job, Ecclesiastes) from Israel's wisdom teachers. Proverbs suggests how to succeed in the practical affairs of daily life. The book gives positive and negative principles for successful living, no matter the situation. It could be summarized by Pro 1:7.

It is a book of wisdom. It is skill of living, a practical knowledge. Wise people know what to say and when to say it. They choose wise words in their response. In addition, wisdom begins with God and one's reverence towards Him. It is an awe that a person should feel when in the presence of the sovereign Creator of the universe.

1. The Proverbs of Solomon, son of David 1-9
2. The Proverbs of Solomon 10-22a
3. The Words of the Wise 22b-24
4. The Proverbs of Solomon, transcribed by King Hezekiah 25-29
5. The Words of Agur 30
6. The Words of King Lemuel 31:1-9
7. The Christian Woman 31:10-31

Thoughts About God in Proverbs:

God is revealed as the One who has set the principles of the world. His names in Proverbs include:
- Yah, Yahweh, LORD
- El, Elohim, Eloah, God
- Migdal-oz, Strong Tower

The awesome reverence for the Lord is the highest virtue. He set up the principles of the world so that the one, who lives by them, will find blessings, joy, and success.

Jesus Christ in Proverbs:

He is your Wisdom. Trust His Word for every step of your life's journey. The wisdom of Proverbs "became for us wisdom from God" according to 1 Cor 1:30. We also know that all the wisdom of God became flesh in Christ (Col 2:3). What a comfort to realize that Christ in us is the wisdom of God.

Proverbs

Literary Form of Proverbs:
If we do not naturally think of the book of Proverbs as poetry, it is because our standard for poetry is lyric (as in the book of Psalms). But a glance at the format of the book of Proverbs shows that it is written in the verse form of parallelism. The primary literary unit of the book of Proverbs is the proverb—a concise, memorable statement of a general truth. A proverb is an observation about life, and the wisdom that it imparts is skill for living.

Both the Mesopotamians and the Egyptians developed wisdom traditions. However, Israelite wisdom surpassed that of other nations. It was placed in the Wisdom section of Hebrew Scriptures. Hebrew poetry had two or three lines in parallel thought. Both "synonymous" parallelism (both lines having the same meaning) and "antithetic" parallelism (the second line the opposite of the first) were in use.

Author
Solomon spoke many Proverbs (1 Kings 4:32). However, see references below.

When the Book was Written
Many compiled during the time of Hezekiah (Pro 25:1) 726-697 BCE. It is suggested that the final form took place after the return from the Babylonian exile.

When the Events Took Place
Collections over a period of years. See 22:17-24:22; 24:23-34; 30: 31:1-9; 31:10-3.

Keys to the Book
    Key Theme: The wise are those who heed God's commands while the foolish ignore them. This is God's plan for everyday life.

    Key Word: *Wisdom*
Of course, the KEY WORD in Proverbs is *Wisdom*. The Hebrew word carries a meaning of "skill." It may be wisdom in a trade (Ezekiel 28:4, 5), ability (Exodus 31:6), or even war (Isaiah 10:13). However, the most common wisdom would be in daily living—what we do when it is aligned with His Word is wisdom. It is an ability to Judge correctly and follow the best course of action, based on knowledge and understanding of His Word.

The greatest reward that comes from wisdom is the fear and knowledge of God (Proverbs 2:5). Wisdom then is vitally connected with knowing God and having a Proper relationship with Him. The biblical concept of wisdom is quite different from the classical view of wisdom, which is sought through philosophy and man's rational thought to determine the mysteries of existence and the universe.

The first principle of biblical wisdom is that man should humble himself before God in reverence and worship, obedient to His commands. The source of real wisdom is God who by it, numbered the clouds (Job 38:37), founded the earth (Proverbs 3:19), and made the world (Jeremiah 10:12).

Key Chapter: 31

Key Verse (s):
1:5 A wise man will hear and increase in learning, And a man of understanding will acquire wise counsel, 6 To understand a Proverb and a figure, The words of the wise and their riddles. 7 The fear of the Lord is the beginning of knowledge; Fools despise wisdom and instruction.

3:5 Trust in the Lord with all your heart And do not lean on your own understanding. 6 In all your ways acknowledge Him, And He will make your paths straight.

Key Characters
Solomon-king of Israel asked for, received, great wisdom from God (1 Kings 4:20-34).

Agur-son of Jakeh (30:1).

Lemuel-king whose mother's teachings are included in chapter 31. Some identify this as Solomon; otherwise unknown.

ECCLESIASTES

Overview and Basic Outline
One of three books (Job, Proverbs) from Israel's wisdom teachers. The Greek translators used this name when they titled it in the second century BCE. It was the rendering of the Hebrew title, "Preacher" or "Teacher."

The message comes from someone looking back on a life of experiences with little to show from it. It presents a view of life from a very human perspective. Materialists find life's object in the abundance of possessions or achievements. Sensualists discover meaning in physical pleasure. Scholars seek purpose through intellectual inquiry. All these answers are futile. Life can only be revealed by God. The writer of Ecclesiastes concludes the matter: Honor God and keep His Word and only then will life have meaning.

Meaning of life is of concern to each of us. We learn from Solomon to go through life and all its experiences while keeping the ultimate focus on God.

1. Solomon's Investigation, 1:12-6:9
2. Solomon's Conclusions, 6:10-12:8
3. Solomon's Advice, 12:9-14

Thoughts About God in Ecclesiastes:
God is revealed Creator or Elohim. His names in Ecclesiastes include:
- Elohim, God

God is displayed in relationship to all humanity. All humankind and their relationship to God; their accountability to Him. A distinction is made between God's relationship with Israel and with all human beings.

Jesus Christ in Ecclesiastes:
While not found directly in Ecclesiastes, He is the source of all wisdom and has placed the knowledge of eternity in the heart of all believers.

Literary Form of Ecclesiastes:
Although English translations print most of this book as prose, it possesses all the qualities of poetry. The primary unit is the proverb. Unlike the book of Proverbs though, this collection of proverbs is tightly structured. Though the book is not organized as a story, the individual units tell the story of the author's quest to find satisfaction in life. Further, the whole collection is structured as a prolonged contrast between "under the sun"

passages in which we are made to feel the emptiness of life lived by purely human and earthly values, and God-centered "above the sun" passages that offer an alternative. The book resembles a personal journal, consisting of passages of reflection, recollection of experiences, and mood pieces.

Highlights and Stories to Read in Ecclesiastes:
- Everything is meaningless, chapter 1
- There is a time for everything, chapter 3
- Wisdom to live by, chapters 7-8
- Remember your Creator, chapter 12

Author
Probably Solomon in his later years.

When the Book was Written
c.930; alternative date c.450.

When the Events Took Place
Time of Solomon, 970-931 BCE.

Keys to the Book

Key Theme: All accumulations in life mean little unless the life is lived in fellowship with, and obedience to, God.

Key Word: *Vanity*

Vanity, used 37 times, means "vapor" or "breath." One's warm breath vanishing in a cool day. And with this word, the writer of Ecclesiastes describes

>Wealth
>Honor
>Fame, etc

Jeremiah used the same word to denounce idolatry (18:15).
Job used it for the length of life (7:16).
Solomon uses it much more than any other Old Testament writer.

A Key Chapter: 12

A Key Verse (s):
2:24 There is nothing better for a man than to eat and drink and tell himself that his labor is good. This also I have seen that it is from the hand of God.

12:13 The conclusion, when all has been heard, is: fear God and keep His commandments, because this applies to every person. 14 For God will bring every act to Judgment, everything which is hidden, whether it is good or evil.

Key Characters
Solomon-king of Israel asked for and received great wisdom from God. Became the wisest person ever born (1:1-14).

SONG OF SOLOMON

Overview and Basic Outline
The Hebrew title is "Song of Songs" meaning "The best song." English Bibles include Solomon in the title because of verse 1:1.

The book is the passionate love story of a man and his bride. We read of the celebration of God's gift of love by describing the intimacy of a husband and wife. It is the Bible's romance manual for marriage, both the period leading to, and the period following.

Too often, people abuse or distort sexual love. Song of Solomon explores this "big issue" of life. It is a wondrous and normal part of marriage to be savored as a gift from God.

The progression into and after marriage reminds us in a general way of the love of Christ for His bride.

1. Falling in Love 1:1-3:5
2. United in Love 3:6-5:1
3. Struggling in Love 5:2-7:10
4. Growing in Love 7:14-8:14

Thoughts About God in Song of Solomon:
His names in Song of Solomon include:
- Yah, LORD

God is not directly names in this book. He is referred indirectly as the Creator who gave romantic love between husband and wife. Also, and indirect reference is made to Adam and Eve coming together as one flesh (Gen 2:18-25).

Jesus Christ in Song of Solomon:
He is our Lover and Bridegroom. This book represents the spiritual relationship between God and the individual believer.

Literary Form of Song of Solomon:
An anthology of love poems. Since these poems are built around a single courtship and marriage, they have the quality of an epithalamion (marriage poem). As a love poem, the Song of Solomon resembles love poetry, as it has always existed. The poems variously express the emotions of romantic love in heightened language, praise the beloved, compare the beloved to the best things in nature, invite the beloved to a life of mutual love, and portray typical moments in a courtship and

marriage. There is nothing about this anthology of pastoral (rural) love lyrics that is out of the norm for love poetry, and we should resist a common practice of arbitrarily allegorizing the details. A love poem is a love poem, and we should abandon ourselves to the poems in this "best of the best" collection (which is the implication of the title—"the song of songs").

The poetic imagery is exquisite, lavish, and delicate, even if the vivid metaphors from the ancient Near East are not fully appreciated. We may also understand the book as a deeper, truer meaning of its declaration of God's love for Israel.

Highlights and Stories to Read in Song of Solomon:
- A bride considers her beloved, chapter 1
- A groom speaks to his bride, chapters 3, 4, 5a
- A bride describes her husband, chapter 6
- A groom speaks in intimate terms, chapter 7
- A groom and his bride together, chapter 8

Author
Solomon, probably in his early days. Others attribute the writing to one who dedicated it TO King Solomon.

When the Book was Written
c.980-970 BCE.

When the Events Took Place
Time of Solomon, 970-931 BCE.

Keys to the Book
   Key Theme: Love, honor, and cherish your life-long spouse.

   Key Word: *Beloved*
Found in—1:14; 2:8; 4:16; 5:1, 6:10; 6:1; 8:14—it is a Hebrew word in Hebrew poetry used for a male loved one, (also Isaiah 5:1). The writer of the Song of Solomon uses this word thirty-two times.

   Key Chapter: Since the whole book is a unity, there is no Key Chapter; rather, all eight beautifully depict the love of a married couple.

   A Key Verse (s):
7:10 "I am my beloved's, And his desire is for me.

8:7 Many waters cannot quench love, Nor will rivers overflow it; If a man were to give all the riches of his house for love, It would be utterly despised."

Key Characters

King Solomon-identified as king in several verses; called "beloved"; type of the bridegroom.

Shulamite woman-the (Probably first) bride of King Solomon (1:1-8:13).

Daughters of Jerusalem-young women who encouraged their friend to go to King Solomon. (1:4; 2:14; 3:5, 11; 5:1, 8; 6:1; 8:4).

ISAIAH

Overview and Basic Outline
One of the five books in the Major Prophets section (Jeremiah, Lamentations, Ezekiel, and Daniel), Isaiah's name means "The Lord saves" or "the Lord is salvation." The Book of Isaiah is considered the greatest prophetic book in the Old Testament.

Not much is known about the prophet other than what he reveals in his book. Little is known about his personal life. It is thought his death was described in Hebrews 11:37.

Isaiah warned the people that because of their continue idolatry, God would send them into captivity. However, He would then restore them through the offering of a perfect lamb (Jesus Christ). He would usher in His kingdom, which will be unending. His prophecies were given during the reign of four Judean kings (Uzziah, Jotham, Ahaz, and Hezekiah).

Isaiah made many prophecies during his forty years of ministry, effecting both Israel and Judah. His prophecy on the suffering Servant (52:13-53:12) is the most detailed Prophecy about Jesus' death in the Bible. It is the fifth longest book in the Bible.

Isaiah's special name for God was "the Holy One of Israel" used twenty-six times.

1. Judah and Jerusalem Under the Monarchy, Cps 1-39
2. Exile In Babylon (an interim period), Cps 40-55
3. Prophecies of Israel's Glorious Future, (back in Jerusalem), Cps 56-66

Thoughts About God in Isaiah:
God is revealed as both comfort and judge. His names in Isaiah include:
- Yahweh, Yah, LORD
- Qedosh Yisrael, Holy One of Israel
- El, Elohim, God
- Yahweh Tsebaoth, the LORD of Hosts, the LORD Almighty
- Adonay, Lord, Master
- Melek, King
- Sar Shalom, Prince of Peace (First appearance)
- Ruach, Spirit
- Shaddai, Almighty
- Elyon, Highest
- Shopet, Judge
- Elohim Chay, Living God

- El Olam, the Everlasting God
- Go'el, Redeemer
- Ish Makoboth, Man of Sorrows (First appearance)
- Ab, Father

God desires for every one of His people to fulfill His requirements. God hates sin and will judge it.

He is also God of hope. The book is well known for its detailed prophecies about Messiah. His birth (7:14; 9:6, 7) and His death (52:13-53:12) reveal details of both events, found nowhere else in Scripture.

The Spirit of God will empower both the Messiah and the servants of Messiah.

Jesus Christ in Isaiah:
He's the Prince of Peace. Isaiah depicts the future Christ as the *Suffering Servant* who would bear the iniquities of mankind. See the author's book *Travel Through the Old Testament, Vol. 2* for a detailed list of Christ in Isaiah.

Literary Form of Isaiah:
Falls into the category known as encyclopedic form (a substantial anthology comprised of diverse genres and forms). The book is so massive that it has been called by such labels as "a Bible within the Bible" and "a miniature Bible." Because of these qualities, we should focus on individual passages as self-contained, not looking for an ongoing narrative line. We need to be prepared for abrupt shifts in genre, mood, and time frame. Regarding the time frame, biblical prophecy sometimes predicts the immediate future, sometimes an intermediate future (especially the coming of Christ), and sometimes an "end times" future.

The book includes a mastery of Hebrew vocabulary and style. It also has a larger vocabulary than any other Old Testament book. The author writes of events that cover centuries, and it can be difficult in places to tell if he speaks of the present, the near future, or the long-range future.

Highlights and Stories to Read in Isaiah:
- Unfaithful Jerusalem, chapter 1
- Judgment against Judah, chapter 3
- Isaiah's call, chapter 6
- The coming Assyrian invasion, chapter 9
- The Branch from David's line, chapter 11
- Message to Babylon, chapters 13, 14, 21
- Message about Egypt, chapter 19
- Assyria invades Judah, chapter 36

- The coming of Christ, chapter 40a
- The Savior of Israel, chapter 43
- The Lord chooses Cyrus, chapter 45
- Babylon will fall, chapter 47
- Christ will die as a sacrifice, chapter 52
- Future glory of Jerusalem, chapters 54, 60

Author
Isaiah is accepted as the author of the entire book. However, it has been suggested that Isa 40-66 may have been written by other authors because the focus is on a later period, the Babylonian captivity.

When the Book was Written
c.680 BCE.

When the Events Took Place
742-680 BCE.

Keys to the Book
    Key Theme: God is Judge, Redeemer, and Savior.

    Key Word: *Salvation*
Found in Isa 12:2 "Behold, God is my salvation, I will trust and not be afraid; For the Lord God is my strength and song, And He has become my salvation."
Isaiah 25:9 *And it will be said in that day, "Behold, this is our God for whom we have waited that He might save us. This is the Lord for whom we have waited; Let us rejoice and be glad in His salvation."*
Isaiah 49:6 *He says, "It is too small a thing that You should be My Servant To raise up the tribes of Jacob and to restore the preserved ones of Israel. I will also make You a light of the nations. So that My salvation may reach to the end of the earth."* There are many other references in Isaiah of this same word, salvation.

    This great word describes deliverance from distress because of victory. It's God's work on your behalf, carrying a meaning of the deliverance of a single Individual...YOU...ME.

    Then, always realize, this word is much, much more than a new birth. This word includes—deliverance from the power of sin, including forgiveness as well as wholeness for the whole personality.

    In the Old Testament, the word salvation sometimes refers to deliverance from danger (Jeremiah 15:20), deliverance of the weak from an oppressor (Psalm 35:9-10), the healing of sickness (Isaiah 38:20), and deliverance from guilt and its consequences.

All this is in salvation.

Key Chapter: 53

Key Verse (s):
9:6 For a child will be born to us, a son will be given to us; And the government will rest on His shoulders; And His name will be called Wonderful Counselor, Mighty God, Eternal Father, Prince of Peace. 7 There will be no end to the increase of His government or of peace, on the throne of David and over his kingdom, to establish it and to uphold it with justice and righteousness from then on and forevermore. The zeal of the Lord of hosts will accomplish this.

53:6 All of us like sheep have gone astray, each of us has turned to his own way; but the Lord has caused the iniquity of us all to fall on Him.

Key Characters

Isaiah—Prophet who ministered throughout the reigns of four kings of Judah; gave both a message of Judgment and hope (1–66).

Shear-Jashub—Isaiah's son; name means "a remnant shall return," denoting God's Promised faithfulness to His people (7:3; 8:18; 10:21).

Maher-Shalal-Hash-Baz—Isaiah's son; name means "hasting to the spoil, hurrying to the prey," denoting God's coming punishment (8:1, 3, 18).

JEREMIAH

Overview and Basic Outline
One of the five books in the Major Prophets section (Isaiah, Lamentations, Ezekiel, and Daniel). The name Jeremiah in Hebrew means, "Exalted by the Lord" or "The Lord Throws Down." It is the longest book in the Bible.

The book is highly autobiographical, and more can be learned about the prophet from his work than from any other historical source. He probably died in Egypt after the exile of 586 BCE.

Jeremiah was called to a ministry at the time of the descent of the Assyrian Empire and the emergence of the Babylonian Empire. Jeremiah encountered God in three opening chapter dialogues. He faced great rejection of his message, but witnessed what he warned about, the Babylonian captivity.

His prophecy took place during the Judah's last five kings: Josiah, Jehoahaz, Jehoiakim, Jehoiachin, and Zedekiah. Judah was in a state of decline following King Josiah's death in 609 BCE. Jeremiah witnessed the destruction of Jerusalem by the Babylonian military.

The book is not in chronological order; however, his historical portions follow that of 2 Kings.

1. The Call of Jeremiah, Cp 1
2. The Prophecies to Judah and Jerusalem, Cps 2-45
3. The Prophecies to the Nations, Cps 46-51
4. The Fall of Jerusalem, Cp 52

Thoughts About God in Jeremiah:
God is revealed as omnipresent and omnipotent. His names in Jeremiah include:
- Yahweh, LORD
- Adonay, Lord, Master
- Yahweh Tsebaoth, the LORD of Hosts, the LORD Almighty
- El, Elohim, God
- Ab, Father
- Melek, King
- Elohim Chay, Living God
- Miqweh Yisrael, the Hope of Israel (First appearance)
- Yahweh Tsidqenu, the LORD Our Righteousness (First appearance)
- Tsemach, Branch (First appearance)
- Qedosh Yisrael, Holy One of Israel

- Go'el, Redeemer

God's well known attributes of "all knowing" and "all powerful" are on display in Jeremiah. No one can hide from God (23:24). Neither Christ nor the Spirit is directly mentioned in the book (however, see below).

Jesus Christ in Jeremiah:
He is *the Righteous Branch*. He is the *fountain of living waters*. It is quite evident from Jeremiah that Christ is the One to come who will be the prophesied *shepherd*. He also is the *balm in Gilead*. Reading Jeremiah and looking for Christ is indeed a joyful experience.

Literary Form of Jeremiah:
An elegiac ("sad, funeral") book that partly recounts the persecuted life of Jeremiah, the central personality, and partly reports the decline of the nation of Judah. The overall story is the difficult life of a godly man who is forced to endure hard times. Oracles of judgment dominate the book, and the takeaway message for us is the need to avoid the mistakes that the people of Judah made in ignoring God's call to reform their lives. Major archetypes include the wicked city, crime, and punishment.

The majority of the book is poetic. However, several sections are prose. It was the second of the four Latter Prophets in the Hebrew canon. The material on Jerusalem's last days is agonizing.

Highlights and Stories to Read in Jeremiah:
- The call of Jeremiah, chapter 1
- Judgment coming against Judah, chapter 4a, 16a
- Jeremiah weeps, chapter 4b, 8b
- Final warning to Jerusalem, chapter 6
- The Potter and the clay, chapter 18
- The righteous descendant of King David, chapter 23
- Jeremiah escapes death, chapter 26
- Jeremiah's letter to the exiles, chapter 29
- Jeremiah's message and their destruction, chapter 36a
- Jeremiah rewrites his messages, chapter 36b
- Jerusalem falls, chapter 39
- Babylon will fall, chapter 50, 51
- Fall of Jerusalem, chapter 52

Author
Jeremiah

Jeremiah

When the Book was Written
c.585 BCE.

When the Events Took Place
628-586 BCE.

Keys to the Book

Key Theme: Sin and rebellion will always be punished. However a call to repentance is always heard.

Key Word: *Heal*
Found in 3:22, 6:14, 8:11, 15:18. It literally means the work of a physician. Generally the idea of restoring to normal. God is praised for His healing:
Disease (Psalms 103:3);
Brokenhearted (Psalms 147:3);
The soul (Psalms 30:2; 107:20);

Key Chapter: 31

Key Verse (s):
7:23 *"But this is what I commanded them, saying, 'Obey My voice, and I will be your God, and you will be My people; and you will walk in all the way which I command you, that it may be well with you.' " 24 Yet they did not obey or incline their ear, but walked in their own counsels and in the stubbornness of their evil heart, and went backward and not forward.*

8:11 *"They heal the brokenness of the daughter of My people superficially ,saying, 'Peace, peace,' but there is no peace. 12 Were they ashamed because of the abomination they had done? They certainly were not ashamed, and they did not know how to blush; therefore they shall fall among those who fall; at the time of their punishment they shall be brought down," says the Lord.*

Key Characters

Jeremiah—priest and Prophet in the Southern Kingdom of Judah.

King Josiah—sixteenth king of the Southern Kingdom of Judah; attempted to follow God (1:1–3; 22:11, 18).

King Jehoahaz—evil son of Josiah and seventeenth king of the Southern Kingdom of Judah (22:9–11).

BOOK OF OLD TESTAMENT BIBLE LITERACY

King Jehoiakim—evil son of Josiah and eighteenth king of the Southern Kingdom of Judah (22:18–23; 25:1–38; 26:1–24; 27:1–11; 35:1–19; 36:1–32).

King Jehoiachin—evil son of Jehoiakim and nineteenth king of the Southern Kingdom of Judah (13:18–27; 22:24–30).

King Zedekiah—evil uncle of Jehoiachin and twentieth king of the Southern Kingdom of Judah (21:1–14; 24:8–10; 27:12–22; 32:1–5; 34:1–22; 37:1–21; 38:1–28; 51:59–64).

Baruch—served as Jeremiah's scribe (32:12–16; 36:4–32; 43:3–45:4).

Ebed-Melech—Ethiopian palace official who feared God and helped Jeremiah (38:7–39:16).

King Nebuchadnezzar—greatest king of Babylon; led the people of Judah into captivity (21–52).

The Rechabites—obedient descendants of Jonadab; contrasted to the disobedient people of Israel (35:1–19).

LAMENTATIONS

Overview and Basic Outline
One of the five books in the Major Prophets section (Isaiah, Jeremiah, Ezekiel, and Daniel). Lamentations is a book that cries out and expresses emotional distress. Its setting follows Jeremiah's preceding book.

The original Hebrew title is simply the first word of the book, "How!" The English name comes from the translators in the second century BCE.

Five poems using a variety of metaphors provide us with the outline. The book comes to grips with the destruction of Jerusalem. Grief and sorrow from a people breaking God's covenant permeates the book. We learn from the book that it is okay to speak openly about one's agony. It is the author's view of the horror remaining after Babylon invaded Judah.

1. Jerusalem's Devastation, Cp 1
2. The Lord's Anger, Cp 2
3. Jeremiah's Grief, Cp 3
4. God's Grief, Cp 4
5. The Remnants' Prayers, Cp 5

Thoughts About God in Lamentations:
God is revealed as mercy and faithfulness. His names in Lamentations include:
- Yahweh, LORD
- Adonay, Lord, Master
- Elyon, Highest
- El, God

He is mentioned with a faithful love in 3:22, 23. As in Jeremiah, there is no mention of Christ or the Spirit (however, see below).

Jesus Christ in Lamentations:
He is our Unfailing Compassion. The weeping over Jerusalem pictures Jesus deep love for the people of the city. He wept over Jerusalem crying "O Jerusalem, Jerusalem..." Jesus is the only One who weeps with us in time of need.

Literary Form of Lamentations:
An elegy (funeral poem) that laments the metaphoric death of Jerusalem. The outpouring of grief (in its intensity rarely matched in all the annals of literature) is not inartistic, however. In addition to being highly poetic, four of the five chapters are arranged in the form of an acrostic (a poem

in which successive units begin consecutively with the letters of the Hebrew alphabet). We can call the book a formalized expression of grief in a highly literary form.

It was quite normal for people of the ancient Near East to compose laments in the face of tragedy. David's "Song of the Bow" (2 Sam 1:19:27" is an example. The entire book of Lamentations is Hebrew poetry, more than any other book.

Highlights and Stories to Read in Lamentations:
- Sorrow in Jerusalem, chapter 1
- Restore us Lord! Chapter 5b

Author
Jeremiah. However, no author is named in this specific book, and there is no place in the rest of the Bible where this writing is attributed to Jeremiah.

When the Book was Written
c.545-586 BCE.

When the Events Took Place
586 BCE.

Keys to the Book
  Key Theme: Grief may be for a moment, but God is always present and never fails.

  Key Word: Weeps
It expresses emotions—from grief to happiness. It certainly is in this area of "Laments." Of course, in this book, it is associated with a wailing over the destruction of Jerusalem and their sins. However, in Genesis 29:11 it is weeping with joy. Ruth 1:9 weeps over the departure. Ezra 3:12 a weeping with joy over the rebuilt temple.

  Key Chapter: 3

  Key Verse (s):
2:5 *The Lord has become like an enemy. He has swallowed up Israel; He has swallowed up all its palaces, He has destroyed its strongholds and multiplied in the daughter of Judah mourning and moaning. 6 And He has violently treated His tabernacle like a garden booth; He has destroyed His appointed meeting place. The Lord has caused to be forgotten the*

appointed feast and sabbath in Zion, and He has despised king and priest in the indignation of His anger.

3:22 The Lord's lovingkindnesses indeed never cease, for His compassions never fail. 23 They are new every morning; Great is Your faithfulness.

Key Characters

Jeremiah—Prophet of Judah; mourned the destruction of Jerusalem (1:1–5:22).

People of Jerusalem—people Judged by God because of their great sins (1:1–5:22).

EZEKIEL

Overview and Basic Outline
One of the five books in the Major Prophets section (Isaiah, Jeremiah, Lamentations, and Daniel). The name Ezekiel means, "God strengthens." He was called while in Babylon captivity, in the second of three deportations, and prophesied the impending destruction of Jerusalem. He lived among the Jewish exiles in Babylon along the river just east of the Euphrates. God's people needed a prophet in Babylon because they carried all the spiritual baggage from years of idolatry and apostasy. At the time, Judah was in its darkest days. A few years later, he spoke of the restoration of the city.

   1. Ezekiel's Early Sermons Before Judah's Fall, Cps 1-24
   2. Ezekiel's Messages Against the Nations, Cps 25-32
   3. Ezekiel's Latter Sermons After the Fall, Cps 33-48

Thoughts About God in Ezekiel:
God is revealed as Sovereign. His names in Ezekiel include:
- Elohim, God
- Yahweh, LORD
- Yahweh Shammah, The LORD is there
- Shaddai, Almighty
- Ruach, Spirit
- Adonay, Lord, Master

All of God's actions on behalf of His people are for His glory. He is sovereign in all the affairs of all people and nations. Christ, as a fulfillment of the Davidic line, is mentioned in various places in Ezekiel (17:22-24; 37:24-28). The Spirit will enable His people to obey Him from their hearts.

Jesus Christ in Ezekiel:
He's the Messiah who reigns. He's pictured as *a branch* in both 17:22-24 and 34: 23, 24. The Branch will grow and become a majestic cedar, hiding Israel in His shadow. He is also the *shepherd* over His sheep.

Literary Form of Ezekiel:
Like Isaiah, an encyclopedic book comprised of many different genres, so we have no good alternative but to assimilate the successive units individually. Symbolism and fantasy (visionary writing) abound. We need to be clear, however, that with symbolism and fantasy the prophet uses

imaginary details to portray realities that actually exist. A common paradigm at work in Ezekiel is one that this book shares with many other Old Testament prophecies: oracles of judgment against the prophet's nation, oracles of judgment against neighboring nations, and oracles of future blessing on God's people.

Ezekiel's three visions are a special kind of prophecy. More than any other prophet, he performed actions with symbolic meaning, which he then interpreted. Both poetry and prose are used to tell his story.

Highlights and Stories to Read in Ezekiel:
- A vision of living beings, chapter 1
- Ezekiel's call, chapter 2
- A clay model of Jerusalem's fall, chapter 4
- The glory departs from the Jerusalem temple, chapter 10
- Ezekiel to be exiled, chapter 12
- Jerusalem is useless, chapter 15
- The soul who sins will die, chapter 18
- Babylon used for judgment, chapter 21
- Jerusalem compared to a cooking pot, chapter 24
- Dry bones, chapter 37
- Gog, chapters 38, 39
- Future restoration of God's glory, chapters 40-48

Author
Ezekiel. He was a priest, but not able to serve in the usual traditional capacity. His call came at age thirty.

When the Book was Written
c.592-570 BCE.

When the Events Took Place
594-571 BCE.

Keys to the Book
　　Key Theme: A faithful God when His own people are unfaithful.

　　Key Word: *Son of Man*
A Key Word in Ezekiel was easy to pick. It is found in 2:1; 3:17; 12:18. Ezekiel uses this phrase *"son of man,"* over 90 times in referring to himself. He was chosen by God to be a spokesperson for God.

It simply means "human one." Only found two other times in the Old Testament. Daniel saw a heavenly being *"like the Son of Man"* (Daniel

7:13). Of course, Jesus later adopted the title "Son of Man," as He too was a living sign to all.

So Ezekiel was to be a living example, a representative of God to the captives.

Key Chapter: 37

Key Verse (s):
36:24 "For I will take you from the nations, gather you from all the lands and bring you into your own land. 25 "Then I will sprinkle clean water on you, and you will be clean; I will cleanse you from all your filthiness and from all your idols. 26 "Moreover, I will give you a new heart and put a new spirit within you; and I will remove the heart of stone from your flesh and give you a heart of flesh."

36:33 Thus says the Lord God, "On the day that I cleanse you from all your iniquities, I will cause the cities to be inhabited, and the waste places will be rebuilt. 34 "The desolate land will be cultivated instead of being a desolation in the sight of everyone who passes by. 35 "They will say, 'This desolate land has become like the garden of Eden; and the waste, desolate and ruined cities are fortified and inhabited."

Key Characters

Ezekiel—Prophet to the people of Israel in Babylonian captivity (1:1–48:35).

Israel's leaders—led the people of Israel into idolatry (7:26–8:12; 9:5, 6; 11; 14:1–3; 20:1–3; 22:23–29).

Ezekiel's wife—unnamed woman whose death symbolized the future destruction of Israel's beloved temple (24:15–27).

DANIEL

Overview and Basic Outline
One of the five books in the Major Prophets section (Isaiah, Jeremiah, Lamentations, and Ezekiel). Daniel is a unique Old Testament book, classified as apocalyptic or "unveiling." Daniel's name means, "God is my judge." He was a contemporary of Jeremiah and Ezekiel, and was taken captive to Babylon. Daniel demonstrated remarkable trust in God and revealed God's plans for the future. The book records events at the beginning of Nebuchadnezzar's first invasion of Jerusalem to the third year of Cyrus.

Daniel, a descendant of King Hezekiah, was in a high-level position in Babylon because of his gift of interpreting dreams. A section of his book, 2:4-7:28 was written in Aramaic to give authenticity to the stories. His vision of four kingdoms is the focus of much of the book.

1. Daniel's Background, Cp 1
2. Visions of Worldly Powers, Cps 2-7
3. Visions of Israel's Future, Cps 8-12

Thoughts About God in Daniel:
God is revealed as omniscient and sovereign. His names in Daniel include:
- Adonay, Lord, Master
- Elohim, God
- Yahweh, LORD
- Elan Illa-ah, God Most High (Aramaic)
- El Elyon, God Most High
- Elyonin, Illa-ah, Highest (Aramaic)
- Elyon, Highest
- Bar-Enash, Son of Man (Aramaic)
- Mashiach, Christ, Messiah

God reveals secrets and is over the universe. Ultimately, His desire is to present all things to His Son.

Jesus Christ in Daniel
He's the 4th *Man in your fiery furnace of life*. Also Daniel pictures Christ as a *great mountain,* covering all and standing forever. Christ is called the *coming Messiah* and *One like the Son of man*. Little doubt as to the eternal existence of Jesus Christ, our Creator and Savior.

Literary Form of Daniel:

Two books in one—six chapters of narrative (in the specific form of hero stories) and six chapters of prophetic visions. The hero stories focus on individuals, while the prophetic visions of the future present a history of nations. The commanding figure of Daniel is a unifying factor in the book, and so is the sovereign presence of God.

God exhibits his sovereignty in the book. God took the most powerful man in the world at the time and sent him through a period of insanity. The prophecies of four world kingdoms are the most extensive view of history written.

Highlights and Stories to Read in Daniel:
- Daniel trained in Babylon, chapter 1
- Nebuchadnezzar's dream, chapter 2
- Nebuchadnezzar's image of gold, chapter 3
- Daniel in a den of lions, chapter 6
- Daniel's dream of four kingdoms, chapter 7
- The seventy sevens, chapter 9b
- The time of the end, chapter 12

Author
Daniel. He came from a royal family and always gave God complete credit.

When the Book was Written
c.537-530 BCE.

When the Events Took Place
606-536 BCE.

Keys to the Book
   Key Theme: Maintain a reputable life and walk with integrity under all circumstances.

   Key Word (s): *Vision*
Found in 8:1, 13; 15:26. It means, "to see" (Isaiah 1:1 uses the same word). It is associated with a revelation from God, in Daniel's case revelation accompanied by symbols that required an interpretation by an angel. His ministry was entirely in Babylon, at least 70 years from 604-536 BCE.

Several other Prophets lived at this same time including Ezekiel, Habakkuk, Jeremiah, and Zephaniah.

   A Key Chapter: 9

Daniel

A Key Verse (s):

2:20 Daniel said, "Let the name of God be blessed forever and ever, for wisdom and power belong to Him. 21 "It is He who changes the times and the epochs; He removes kings and establishes kings; He gives wisdom to wise men and knowledge to men of understanding. 22 "It is He who reveals the Profound and hidden things; He knows what is in the darkness, and the light dwells with Him."

2:44 "In the days of those kings the God of heaven will set up a kingdom which will never be destroyed, and that kingdom will not be left for another people; it will crush and put an end to all these kingdoms, but it will itself endure forever."

Key Characters

Daniel—also called Belteshazzar; later became a royal advisor (1:1–12:13).

Nebuchadnezzar—the greatest king of Babylon; went temporarily insane for not acknowledging God's sovereign position (1:1–4:37).

Shadrach—also called Hananiah; exiled Jew placed in leadership in Babylon; saved by God from the "fiery furnace" (1:7; 2:49; 3:8–30).

Meshach—also called Mishael; exiled Jew placed in leadership in Babylon; saved by God from the "fiery furnace" (1:7; 2:49; 3:8–30).

Abed-Nego—also called Azariah; exiled Jew placed in leadership in Babylon; saved by God from the "fiery furnace" (1:7; 2:49; 3:8–30).

Belshazzar—successor of Nebuchadnezzar as king of Babylon; also used Daniel as an interpreter (5:1–30).

Darius—Persian successor of Belshazzar as ruler of Babylon; his advisors tricked him into sending Daniel to the lions' den (5:31–6:28).

HOSEA

Overview and Basic Outline
Hosea's name means "salvation." He was a native of the northern kingdom of Israel and prophesied to them. The opening three chapters convey a message of Israel's unfaithfulness to God, even sending a message through the names of Hosea's children. This was demonstrated by Hosea's marriage to an adulterous wife. The book illustrates the love story between God and humanity.

Israel was beginning to deteriorate following the death of Jeroboam II. The call for people to return to God went unheeded, even though they claimed to know Him. However, God continued to offer His favor and love, but Hosea's words warned of death and destruction would come to those unfaithful.

Hosea prophesied at the same time as Isaiah, about ten years before Jonah.

1. An Unfaithful Wife, And A Faithful Husband, Cps 1-3
2. An Unfaithful Israel, And A Faithful God, Cps 4-14

Thoughts About God in Hosea:
God is revealed as the judge of unfaithfulness. His names in Hosea include:
- Yahweh, LORD
- El, Elohim, God
- Ehyeh, I Am
- El chay, Living God
- Ish, Husband (First appearance)
- Adonay, Lord, Master

God is shown as an analogy of a husband-wife relationship. The Lord loves His people and will not tolerate them lusting after other gods. He will judge unfaithfulness. The Spirit is not directly mentioned in the book.

Jesus Christ in Hosea:
He is your Redeemer! Your redemption is a completed act. Accept it! Thank Him for it. He is called the *only savior*.

Literary Form of Hosea:
The distinctive feature by which we remember the prophecy of Hosea is a symbol or metaphor rooted in a real-life event in Hosea's life: a husband's

marrying a wife who would be an adulteress, and returning to her after she had deserted him. The wayward wife is a metaphor for Israel's disobedience to God's covenant.

The majority of the book is poetry, with some prose in chapters 1 and 3.

Hosea is the first of twelve Minor Prophets, shorter than Isaiah, Jeremiah, or Ezekiel. In the Hebrew Bible, "The Twelve" were a single book and the last of the Latter Prophets.

Highlights and Stories to Read in Hosea:
- Hosea's wife and children, chapter 1
- Buy back your wife, chapter 3
- Israel's love is like a morning mist, chapters 6, 7
- Israel is punished, chapter 9
- God loves Israel, chapter 11
- Repentance will bring blessing, chapter 14

Author
Hosea. Little is known about his life other than being the son of Beeri (1:1). It is thought Hosea's prophecy may have existed in spoken form, and then later gathered together in written form by scribes.

When the Book was Written
722 BCE.

When the Events Took Place
755-722 BCE.

Keys to the Book
    Key Theme: God's mercy and love call out to every human being.

    Key Word: *Stumble*
Found in 4:5; 5:5. It literally means, "to totter, to trip and fall." It was generally used to describe the Hebrews spiritual life. Isaiah used it (40:30) to warn those who rely on their own strength would fall. Then again in Isaiah 63:13 he says those who are led by the Lord will NOT stumble. Also see 1 Samuel 2:4. Hosea wrote the book during this same period of Jonah and Amos; actually, his career spanned the last six kings of Israel—longer than the others. He probably knew a lot more than what we glean from his book.

    Key Chapter: 4

Key Verse (s):
4:1 Listen to the word of the Lord, O sons of Israel, For the Lord has a case against the inhabitants of the land, because there is no faithfulness or kindness or knowledge of God in the land.

6:6 For I delight in loyalty rather than sacrifice,
And in the knowledge of God rather than burnt offerings.

11:7 So My people are bent on turning from Me. Though they call them to the One on high, None at all exalts Him. 8 How can I give you up, O Ephraim? How can I surrender you, O Israel? How can I make you like Admah? How can I treat you like Zeboiim? My heart is turned over within Me, All My compassions are kindled. 9 I will not execute My fierce anger; I will not destroy Ephraim again. For I am God and not man, the Holy One in your midst, And I will not come in wrath.

Key Characters

*Hosea-*Prophet to the ten tribes of the northern kingdom of Israel. His marriage was a picture of God's relationship to the kingdom (1:1-14:9).

*Gomer-*a Prostitute or "strange woman" who became Hosea's wife. (1:3-9).

*Jezreel, Lo-Ruhamah, and Lo-Ammi-*the children of Hosea and Gomer whose names depicted God's relationship with Israel (1:3-2:1).

JOEL

Overview and Basic Outline
Joel's name means, "The Lord is God." He was a prophet to Judah and Jerusalem. He described a swarm of locusts, which devoured the land of Judah, to be followed by an invasion from the north (perhaps a warning of the Assyrian invasion). Joel saw in the locust invasion, a foretaste of the Day of Judgment. The repentance of the people served as the basis for Joel's remarks concerning the future day of God's spirit outpouring and His final judgment of the wicked.

1. Devastation of Judah (historical), Cp 1
2. Destroyers From The North (transitional), Cp 2:1-17
3. Restoration By God, Cp 2:18-3:21

Thoughts About God in Joel:
God is revealed as Righteous Judge. His names in Joel include:
- Yahweh, LORD
- Elohim, God
- Shaddai, Almighty
- Ruach, Spirit
- Machseh, Refuge

There is coming a "Day of the Lord" when God will bring a devastation to all who have opposed Him. In it all, He will spare His children (2:18).

Jesus Christ in Joel:
He is the baptism with the Holy Ghost and Fire. We have His Spirit in our life as a believer. The final fulfillment will come in the millennial kingdom when God's Spirit is poured out on all creation.

Literary Form of Joel:
Whereas the central metaphor of Hosea is the faithless wife, the controlling image in Joel is the killer locust, symbolizing God's judgment against an apostate nation. The book thus has affinities with the genre of the horror story. Surprisingly (and unlike the usual prophetic practice of being weighted on the side of judgment), the Joel's prophecy is divided between a "bad news" half (two oracles of judgment) and a "good news" half (two oracles of redemption).

Joel is one of the shortest prophetic books, consisting of only seventy-three verses. His poetry is vivid and visual. It is the second of the twelve Minor Prophets. The twelve Minor Prophets belonged to the single book called "The Twelve." He is the first prophet to use the phrase "the day of the Lord."

Highlights and Stories to Read in Joel:
- Invasion of locusts, chapter 1
- Invasion of Assyrian army, chapter 2
- The Day of the Lord, chapter 2b
- Blessings of His people, chapter 3b

Author
Joel

When the Book was Written
835 BCE.

When the Events Took Place
c.750 BCE.

Keys to the Book

Key Theme: God's blessing follows one's obedience to Him.

Key Word: *Spirit*
Breath, "to breathe" or "to blow." Actually, the word could be associated with an evil spirit or the Spirit of God, (1 Samuel 16:14-16; Psalm 51:11).

A Key Chapter: 2

A Key Verse (s):
2:11 The Lord utters His voice before His army; Surely His camp is very great, for strong is he who carries out His word. The day of the Lord is indeed great and very awesome, and who can endure it?

2:28 It will come about after this That I will pour out My Spirit on all mankind; and your sons and daughters will Prophesy, your old men will dream dreams, your young men will see visions. 29 "Even on the male and female servants I will pour out My Spirit in those days."

Key Characters
Joel—Prophet to the people of Judah during the reign of Joash (1:1–3:21).

The people of Judah—the southern kingdom punished for their sins by a locust plague (1:2; 2:1; 3:1–2, 19–21).

AMOS

Overview and Basic Outline
His name means "burden bearer." He was a shepherd without the status of a prophet but with a prophet's message to Israel. His explanation for his words is the *Lord God showed me*. He and Hosea were the only writing prophets to the northern kingdom of Israel.

He was a contemporary of Isaiah and Micah in Judah, his words declared judgment upon Judah, Israel, and the northern neighbors of Syria, Philistia, Phoenicia and others. His visions in chapters 7-9 displayed the seriousness of God's approaching judgment. Amos prophesied during a time of material prosperity and peace not known since the reign of Solomon. A united Israel is enjoying domestic affluence, international power, and military expansion.

The people of Israel corrupted the worship of God and treated the less fortunate with injustice. However, the book ends with hope for the future rebuilding and prosperity for the surviving remnant. Archeologists have discovered the occurrence of the earthquake referred to in the opening verses.

1. Messages of Judgment Against Nations, Cps 1-2
2. Messages Against Israel, Cps 3-6
3. Visions, Cps 7-9

Thoughts About God in Amos:
God is revealed as sovereign. His names in Amos include:
- Yahweh, LORD
- Adonay, Lord, Master
- Yahweh Tsebaoth, the LORD of Hosts, the LORD Almighty

He places and removes nations because He has absolute authority. He shows Himself to His prophets (3:7) and is judge of all people, good and evil. He has a wonderful future for His people (9:11-15).

Jesus Christ in Amos:
He is your Burden Bearer. Cast your burden on Him.

Literary Form of Amos:
In terms of literary technique, one of the most packed books in the whole Bible. The plainspoken prophet Amos is a master of metaphor and parody (imitating an established genre with inverted effect). He is a passionate defender of the oppressed classes, and his prophecy is almost entirely a

literary satire (which is commonly yet incorrectly assumed to involve humor).

From his beginning, we notice his startling word pictures, *The Lord roars from Zion* and *"the summit of Carmel dries up."* Amos is the It is the third of the twelve Minor Prophets. The twelve Minor Prophets belonged to the single book called "The Twelve."

Highlights and Stories to Read in Amos:
- Judgment on Israel and her neighbors, chapters 1, 2
- Assyria will attack, chapter 3b
- Call to repentance, chapter 5
- The Day of the Lord, chapter 5b
- Three visions of Amos, chapter 7
- Vision of Ripe Fruit, chapter 8
- Vision of judgment, chapter 9

Author
Amos. See 1:1. Amos was from a town in Judah, but directed his prophecy to the northern kingdom.

When the Book was Written
750 BCE

When the Events Took Place
760-750 BCE

Keys to the Book
   Key Theme: Everyone, rich or poor, are accountable to God.

   Key Word: Seek
Found in 5:4. It means just about what you would think, "to inquire" or "to ask." It carries the thought of going to someone and seeking an answer. You can see this same word in Ezra 6:21, Psalms 119:10 and Isaiah 34:16.

   Key Chapter: 9

   Key Verse (s)
3:1 Hear this word which the Lord has spoken against you, sons of Israel, against the entire family which He brought up from the land of Egypt: 2 "You only have I chosen among all the families of the earth; Therefore I will punish you for all your iniquities."

8:11 "Behold, days are coming," declares the Lord God, "When I will send a famine on the land, Not a famine for bread or a thirst for water, but rather for hearing the words of the Lord. 12 People will stagger from sea to sea And from the north even to the east; They will go to and fro to seek the word of the Lord, but they will not find it.

Key Characters
Amos-Prophet from Judah warned Israel of God's Judgment (1:1-9:15)

Amaziah-king of Judah, the southern kingdom; son of King Joash (7:10-17)

Jeroboam II-king of Israel following his father, King Jehoash (7:7-13)

OBADIAH

Overview and Basic Outline
Obadiah means "the servant of the Lord." It is the shortest book in the Bible and offers no background on the author (there are thirteen people in the Bible with this name). The prophecy is to Judah concerning judgment against Edom. We can only speculate as to the author, period of writing, and date of writing. The rebellion of Edom could refer to several events.

The prophet spoke about the pride and arrogance of the Edomites who maintained a consisted hatred toward Israel. They were the descendants of Esau and lived south of the Dead Sea. Obadiah prophesied God's plan to make Edom unimportant or forgotten because of its false confidence.

Obadiah contains similarities with Jeremiah.

1. Announcement of Doom, vv 1-9
2. Judgment of Doom, vv 15-16
3. Deliverance of Israel Promised, vv 17-21

Thoughts About God in Obadiah:
God is revealed as justice. His names in Obadiah include:
- Yahweh, LORD
- Adonay, Lord, Master

His justice in dealing with human sin is shown in Obadiah. His destruction of Eden is dealt with in the book (v. 15).

Jesus Christ in Obadiah:
He is the Mighty One. Obadiah pictures Christ as both *Judge* and *Savior*.

Literary Form of Obadiah:
One of five one-chapter books in the Bible, and accordingly noted for its compactness. This prophetic book denounces neither Israel nor Judah but rather the pagan nation of Edom. The usual prophetic paradigm of judgment followed by a golden age prophecy of future glory is present.

Obadiah is one of three prophetic books written for an initial audience other than God's people (Jonah and Nahum). The book is written in Hebrew poetry. It is the fourth of the twelve Minor Prophets. The twelve Minor Prophets belonged to the single book called "The Twelve."

Obadiah

Highlights and Stories to Read in Obadiah:

- Concerning Edom, chapter 1a
- Edom will not recover, chapter 1b
- The coming Day of the Lord, 1c

Author
Obadiah. Personal facts are scarce concerning Obadiah. No family references or known locations are offered in determining the author or time period.

When the Book was Written
c.600 BCE; alternative date 840 BCE

When the Events Took Place
c.840

Keys to the Book
> **Key Theme:** Sin will not go unpunished.

> **Key Word: Pride**

Found in v. 3. The same word in Jeremiah 49:16 and Proverbs 11:2. It means, "To boil up."

This was the key characteristic of the nation of Edom. Jeremiah used the word as a synonym for Babylon. It insights rebellion toward God and brings shame and destruction.

> **Key Chapter:** 1

> **Key Verse (s)**

10 Because of violence to your brother Jacob, You will be covered with shame, and you will be cut off forever.

21 The deliverers will ascend Mount Zion to Judge the mountain of Esau, and the kingdom will be the Lord's.

> **Key Characters**

The Edomites—the nation originating from Esau, despised and Judged by God v. 1-16

JONAH

Overview and Basic Outline
Jonah's name means, "dove." The account of a real man's disobedience to God's command to go and preach to Nineveh. It is the only recording in the Bible of a prophet who is running away from God. His experience of spending three days and three nights in the belly of a fish has been debated for many years. Jesus mentioned Jonah in comparison to His own three days before resurrection. Jonah eventually follows the command of God to preach to the people in Nineveh. The people respond to him, his message reaching the very seat of government. As a result, Nineveh was saved from destruction. Jonah was the Missionary Prophet and contemporary of Amos.

1. Running From God, Cp 1
2. Submitting to God, Cp 2
3. Following God, Cp 3
4. Angry with God, Cp 4

Thoughts About God in Jonah:
God is revealed as Creator. His names in Jonah include:
- Yahweh, LORD
- El, Elohim, God

God has authority over storms, fish, plants, and worms. He is also shown as loving and compassionate to people and nations.

Jesus Christ in Jonah:
He is your deliverer. Jesus identified Himself with Jonah in Matt 12. Both would be in three days and three nights in a captive place.

Literary Form of Jonah:
A satire in narrative form, as the prophet himself is held up to satiric rebuke from start to finish. The object of the satiric attack is ethnocentrism—wanting to claim God for one's own nation and being angry when God's grace extends to all nations and groups. Jonah is portrayed as a great nationalist, and God as a great internationalist. Of course the image by which we remember the story is the "great fish" that swallows Jonah and then spits him out.

Jonah is one of three prophetic books written for an initial audience other than God's people (Obadiah and Nahum). The book is written in

Hebrew prose except for Jonah's prayer. Jesus affirmed both that Jonah was swallowed by a fish and Nineveh repented of, so there can be no doubt that the events reported in this book happened in history. A belief in God's sovereignty over nature and history settles the event. It is the fifth of the twelve Minor Prophets. The twelve Minor Prophets belonged to the single book called "The Twelve."

Highlights and Stories to Read in Jonah:
- Jonah flees from God, chapter 1
- Jonah prays to God, chapter 2
- Jonah repents, goes to Nineveh, chapter 3
- Jonah is angry, chapter 4

Author
Unknown

When the Book was Written
760 BCE

When the Events Took Place
*c.*600 BCE

Keys to the Book
    Key Theme: Obey God and follow His guidance. Wasted time and experience will be avoided.

    Key Word: Prepared
Found in 1:17; 6-8. The word means "to count" or "to assign." Psalms 147:4 praises God for knowing the number of stars and counting each one. In Jonah, it carries the meaning of "appointing" or "ordaining" and shows God's intervention in natural events to bring about His will. God "appoints" a fish. He "assigns" a small worm to teach Jonah about His mercy.

    Key Chapter: 3

    Key Verse (s)
2:8 "Those who regard vain idols forsake their faithfulness, 9 But I will sacrifice to You with the voice of thanksgiving. That which I have vowed I will pay. Salvation is from the Lord."

4:2 He prayed to the Lord and said, "Please Lord, was not this what I said while I was still in my own country? Therefore, in order to forestall this I fled to Tarshish, for I knew that You are a gracious and compassionate God, slow to anger and abundant in loving-kindness, and one who relents concerning calamity.

Key Characters

Jonah-an evangelist/missionary to Nineveh; swallowed by a large fish in order to bring his repentance. Reluctantly obeyed God (1:1-9)

The crew of the ship avoided killing him, opted for throwing him overboard in order to stop the storm (1:5-16)

MICAH

Overview and Basic Outline
Micah, meaning, "Who is like Yahweh?" speaks of justice and righteousness in the body of faith through a series of several speeches. He is a contemporary of Isaiah and speaks a similar message. He prophesied during several kings of Judah including Hezekiah (causing him to repent). His main message was against Judah, but also prophesied against Israel. His ministry was during the corrupt period of oppression and abuse of evil power in Judah.

The prophecy references the destruction of Samaria and the invasion of Sennacherib in 701 BCE.

Opposition from false prophets caused confusion regarding God's requirements. It was a period when Egypt and Assyria were battling for supremacy. Micah reminds us of hope and confidence in God, regardless of the sinfulness of society. Micah saw a "ruler" from Bethlehem, referred to by Matthew as the birth of Jesus.

      1. Judgment of the Leaders and the People, Cps 1-3
      2. Restoration (Prophecies of Christ), Cps 4-5
      3. Repentance (What Does the Lord Demand of Us?), Cps 6-7

Thoughts About God in Micah:
God is revealed with wrath against idolatry and human sin. His names in Micah include:
- Yahweh, LORD
- Adonay, Lord, Master
- Ruach, Spirit
- Elohim, El, God
- Yahweh Tsebaoth, the Lord of Hosts, the Lord Almighty

The two captivities, Assyrian and Babylonian, were the result of God's justice with His people.

Christ's birth in Bethlehem is prophesied (5:2). The Spirit of God empowered the prophet (3:8).

Jesus Christ in Micah:
He is the Majesty and Glory of God! Micah prophesied of Christ's birthplace and eternality. Jesus used Micah 7:6 to explain the nature of His coming.

Literary Form of Micah:
The book is structured as three alternating cycles of oracles of judgment followed by oracles of redemption. The prophet self-identifies as coming from an agricultural region, and his book is filled with images from nature and farming. Like Amos, Micah focuses on social sins of oppression of the poor and legal injustice.

Micah, using poetic style, sometimes uses "I" to voice God's own words (chapter six), while other times the "I" is his own voice (chapter seven). He is also known for quoting false prophets (2:6, 7). It is the sixth of the twelve Minor Prophets. The twelve Minor Prophets belonged to the single book called "The Twelve."

Highlights and Stories to Read in Micah:
- Judgment against Samaria (capital of Israel) and Jerusalem (capital of Judah), chapter 1
- God's plan of disaster, chapter 2
- God's future rule over the world, chapter 4
- A Ruler from Jerusalem, chapter 5
- What does the Lord require? Chapter 6

Author
Micah (1:1) was probably the compiler of the book; perhaps being authored by other persons, especially chapters 4-7. He is mentioned in Jer 26:17-19.

When the Book was Written
c.740-710

When the Events Took Place
c.750-697 BCE

Keys to the Book
    Key Theme: A daily walk with God is more important than the following of religious "rites" and traditions.

    Key Word: Compassion
We read in 7:19 *He will again have compassion on us; He will tread our iniquities under foot. Yes, You will ▯cast all ▯their sins Into the depths of the sea.* The Hebrew word means, "to love from the womb." Several times, it's also translated *mercy*. Isaiah 14:1 uses the same word, and the AMP and NKJV both translate it *mercy*.

Micah

We know this word expresses the deepest of emotion; "from the womb." God loves His people with a deep compassion that is beyond expression. The Lord expressed this same love to Moses when it's recorded Exodus 34:6 *Then the Lord passed by in front of him and Proclaimed, "The Lord, the Lord God, compassionate and gracious, slow to anger, and abounding in loving-kindness and truth; 7 Who keeps loving-kindness for thousands, who forgives iniquity..."*

Key Chapters: 6-7

Key Verse (s)
6:8 He has told you, O man, what is good; and what does the Lord require of you but to do justice, to love kindness, and to walk humbly with your God?

7:18 Who is a God like You, who pardons iniquity and passes over the rebellious act of the remnant of His possession? He does not retain His anger forever, because He delights in unchanging love

Key Characters
The people of Israel—the northern kingdom, which was about to fall into Assyrian captivity (1:2–7:20)

NAHUM

Overview and Basic Outline
Nahum's book reveals God's response to cruelty and violence in the world. His name means "comfort." God provided comfort to Judah upon the destruction, which was coming, and upon their response to the message. God warned His people about God's judgment against the Assyrian capital of Nineveh. Noah turned Nineveh towards a compassionate God and extended their existence for another two hundred years. Nahum reveals God's judgment because of Nineveh's violence and evil. His people received cruel treatment at the hands of the Assyrians, and he will judge and destroy His enemies.

Nahum is one of three prophetic books written for an initial audience other than God's people (Obadiah and Jonah). The entire book is written in Hebrew poetry. His style is vivid, with use of metaphors and word pictures. It is the fifth of the twelve Minor Prophets. The twelve Minor Prophets belonged to the single book called "The Twelve."

1. Destruction Declared, Cp 1
2. Destruction Detailed, Cp 2
3. Destruction Deserved, Cp 3

Thoughts About God in Nahum:
God is revealed as holiness. His names in Nahum include:
- Yahweh, LORD
- El Kanna, Consuming Fire, Jealous God
- Yahweh Tsebaoth, the LORD of Hosts, the LORD Almighty

Even though God is patient, His wrath against ungodliness is a certainty. He promised wrath on Nineveh because of wickedness and violence (1:2).

Jesus Christ in Nahum:
He is the All Powerful One. He is your stronghold in any time of trouble. Call upon the All Powerful One to help you. He will deliver you and place your feet on the solid Rock. He also is the coming Christ who will judge every human being.

Literary Form of Nahum:
From the fields of Micah we are transported to a world of military combat. The prophecy is directed not to the covenant nations of Israel

and Judah but to the Assyrian capital Nineveh. Oracles of redemption are totally absent in this prophecy of judgment.

Nahum is one of three prophetic books written for an initial audience other than God's people (Obadiah and Jonah). The entire book is written in Hebrew poetry. His style is vivid, with use of metaphors and word pictures. It is the seventh of the twelve Minor Prophets. The twelve Minor Prophets belonged to the single book called "The Twelve."

Highlights and Stories to Read in Nahum:
- The Lord's anger against Assyria, chapter 1
- Assyria will fall, chapter 2
- I am against you, Assyria, chapter 3

Author
Nahum

When the Book was Written
c.650 BCE

When the Events Took Place
665-612 BCE

Keys to the Book
    Key Theme: Any unrepentant nation is vulnerable to God's judgment.

    Key Word: Jealous
Found in 1:1. It is a word meaning "to be eager" or even "to be furious." It's even one of God's names in Exodus 34:14. Usually, the word is associated with idol worship. God is Jealous when it comes to His people. He is creator and redeemer, furious and eager, for His people. He will tolerate no rival.

    Key Chapter: 1

    Key Verse (s)
1:7 The Lord is good, a stronghold in the day of trouble, and He knows those who take refuge in Him. 8 But with an overflowing flood He will make a complete end of its site, and will pursue His enemies into darkness.

3:5 "Behold, I am against you," declares the Lord of hosts";And I will lift up your skirts over your face, and show to the nations your nakedness and to the kingdoms your disgrace. 6 "I will throw filth on you and make you vile, and set you up as a spectacle. 7 "And it will come about that all who see you will shrink from you and say, 'Nineveh is devastated!' Who will grieve for her?' Where will I seek comforters for you?"

Key Characters
The people of Nineveh—Assyrians who returned to evil and were destined for destruction (2:1–3:19)

HABAKKUK

Overview and Basic Outline
Habakkuk was a contemporary of Jeremiah. His name means "one who embraces." Very little is known about the author's background. He offers us a challenge to continue trusting God in the midst of adversities and trials in life.

Nebuchadnezzar invaded Judah as he was returning from Egypt, taking Daniel and his friends to Babylon. Nebuchadnezzar invaded Jerusalem two more times, finally destroying the city and temple in 586 BCE. The events take place during the period of the Neo-Babylonian Empire and view the invasion as God's judgment against Judah. Habakkuk refers a great deal to the Chaldeans, which is a representation of the Babylonians.

1. Habakkuk's Questions, Cps 1-2
2. Habakkuk's Song, Cp 3

Thoughts About God in Habakkuk:
God is revealed as Revealer of truth. His names in Habakkuk include:
- Yahweh, LORD
- Elohim, Eloah, God
- Yahweh Tsebaoth the LORD of Hosts, the LORD Almighty

God reveals Himself as the authority over human history. Habakkuk tells of making known the name of God among all people

Jesus Christ in Habakkuk:
He is the God of Glory and Greatness. Habakkuk calls Christ the *Anointed One* and *God of my salvation.*

Literary Form of Habakkuk:
After the farmer prophet (Micah) and the warrior prophet (Nahum), we come to the prophet who questioned God. Even more famous is the last chapter, containing the prophet's "though the fig tree should not blossom" assertion of trust in God. In this book, the question-and-answer dialogue between the prophet and God takes the place of the customary oracles of judgment and redemption.

The entire book is written in Hebrew poetry. The author was determined to express honor for God's name (1:12; 3:3). It is the eighth of the twelve Minor Prophets. The twelve Minor Prophets belonged to the single book called "The Twelve."

BOOK OF OLD TESTAMENT BIBLE LITERACY

Highlights and Stories to Read in Habakkuk:
- Habakkuk complains, chapter 1
- The Lord answers, chapter 2
- Habakkuk prays, chapter 3

Author
Habakkuk

When the Book was Written
c.607

When the Events Took Place
612-598 BCE

Keys to the Book
  Key Theme: A righteous person lives by faith.

  Key Word: Image
Found in 2:18. It is a word meaning "to hew out stone" or "to cut or carve wood." You can see the word in Exodus 34:4. God Prohibited this at Mt Sinai in Exodus 20:4. The Bible calls them worthless and anyone who worships them, shameful. Isaiah mentions the images several times.

  Key Chapter: 3

  Key Verse (s)
2:4 "Behold, as for the Proud one, his soul is not right within him; but the righteous will live by his faith."

3:17 Though the fig tree should not blossom and there be no fruit on the vines, though the yield of the olive should fail and the fields Produce no food, though the flock should be cut off from the fold and there be no cattle in the stalls, 18 Yet I will exult in the Lord, I will rejoice in the God of my salvation. 19 The Lord God is my strength, and He has made my feet like hinds' feet, and makes me walk on my high places. for the choir director, on my stringed instruments.

  Key Characters
Habakkuk—the last Prophet sent to Judah before its fall into Babylonian captivity (1:1–3:19)

The Chaldeans—Babylonians raised up by God to punish Judah (1:6–11; 2:2–20)

ZEPHANIAH

Overview and Basic Outline
The genealogy traces Zephaniah's ancestry to King Hezekiah, his great-great grandfather. Zephaniah's name means "the Lord hides." He was a prophet and resided in Jerusalem during the time of King Josiah, Judah's last Godly leader. He announced judgments against Philistia, Moab, Ammon, Cush, and Assyria because of their hostility towards God and the people of Judah.

     1. Judgments Promised, Cps 1-2
     2. Salvation Promised, Cp 3

Thoughts About God in Zephaniah:
God is revealed as righteous and jealous. His names in Zephaniah include:
- Yahweh, LORD
- Adonay, Lord, Master
- Elohim, God
- Yahweh Tsebaoth, the LORD of Hosts, the LORD Almighty

God will bring about justice to all persons. Those who claim to be His, but in actuality perform evil will experience His justice. Christ is the King of Israel (3:15).

Jesus Christ in Zephaniah:
He is Savior. Portrayed as the *Mighty One* who will bring salvation to any person on earth. Christ referred to Zephaniah in Matt 13:41 and 24:29.

Literary Form of Zephaniah:
Three oracles of judgment and one of redemption. Dispensing with the usual features of describing and condemning evil, Zephaniah mainly predicts judgment against it. There are nearly twenty references to the coming "day of the Lord." The two bookends are "I will utterly sweep away everything" (1:2) and "I [will] restore your fortunes" (3:20).

    The entire book, consisting of only fifty-three verses, is written in Hebrew poetry. The author's style is largely dark telling of the coming "Day of the Lord" as bitter with severe penalties. Yet a remnant will be restored in righteousness. It is the ninth of the twelve Minor Prophets. The twelve Minor Prophets belonged to the single book called "The Twelve."

Zephaniah

Highlights and Stories to Read in Zephaniah:
- Judgment against Judah, chapter 1
- Judgments against Philistia, Moab, Ammon, Cush, and Assyria chapter 2
- The future of Jerusalem, chapter 3

Author
Zephaniah

When the Book was Written
c.622 BCE

When the Events Took Place
640-622 BCE

Keys to the Book
   Key Theme: Unrepentant sin inevitably brings God's judgment.

   Key Word: Humble
Found in 2:3 and 3:12. The Hebrew word may be translated "meek." It means "to be bowed down" or "to be afflicted." Sometimes it refers to the oppressed but also signifies the strength of character in enduring suffering without resentment. This is a character, which is rooted in God.

   Key Chapter: 3

   Key Verse (s)
1:14 Near is the great day of the Lord, near and coming very quickly; listen, the day of the Lord! In it the warrior cries out bitterly. 15 A day of wrath is that day, a day of trouble and distress, a day of destruction and desolation, a day of darkness and gloom, a day of clouds and thick darkness.

2:3 Seek the Lord, all you humble of the earth who have carried out His ordinances; seek righteousness, seek humility. Perhaps you will be hidden in the day of the Lord's anger.

   Key Characters
Zephaniah—Prophet who warned Judah of coming Judgment and future hope (1:1–3:20)

BOOK OF OLD TESTAMENT BIBLE LITERACY

The People of Judah—led by King Josiah to repent but eventually fell into Babylonian captivity (1:6–11; 2:2–20)

The Edomites—the nation originating from Esau, despised and Judged by God (vv 1–16)

HAGGAI

Overview and Basic Outline
The name Haggai means "my feast" or "festive." He lived in exile in Babylon and was an old man when he delivered his words. He was one of three post-exilic prophets (Zechariah, Malachi). His recorded ministry lasted less than four months during the reign of Darius the Great, king of Persia. The book consists of four addresses.

Haggai uplifted the people concerning the work of God. The foundation of the Temple lay untouched for eighteen years. He gave God's promise that the glory of the second temple would exceed that of the first temple. Haggai directed his words to Zerubbabel the governor and Joshua the high priest.

1. Temple of God, 1:1-2:9
2. Blessings of God, 2:10-23

Thoughts About God in Haggai:
God is revealed as the honored One. His names in Haggai include:
- Yahweh, LORD
- Yahweh Tsebaoth, the LORD of Hosts, the Almighty One
- Elohim, God

Honor is due God. He establishes that which pleases Him. In Haggai, God desires proper worship in the Temple. The rebuilt Temple will one day receive the wealth of the nations (2:7). A promise of the coming Messiah is revealed in 2:23.

Jesus Christ in Haggai:
He is your Restorer. What has been taken away from you? Christ is the One who repays, and gives you more than that which is lost.

Literary Form of Haggai:
Haggai does not predict coming exile to a covenant nation but denounces exiles who had returned to Jerusalem after the Babylonian captivity. The sin that is denounced is the failure to rebuild the temple, symbolic of Israel's devotion to God. After the temple is rebuilt, the prophet paints a picture of national prosperity. Instead of the usual poetry, this prophecy comes to us as prose.

He precisely dated the four occasions on which he received the Word of the Lord. Haggai saw the completion of the second temple. It is the tenth of the twelve Minor Prophets. The twelve Minor Prophets belonged to the single book called "The Twelve."

Highlights and Stories to Read in Haggai:
- The call to build the house of the Lord, chapter 1
- Promised Glory of the temple, chapter 2a
- Zerubbabel as the Lord's signet ring, chapter 2b

Author
Haggai

When the Book was Written
c.510-505 BCE

When the Events Took Place
520-505 BCE

Keys to the Book
   Key Theme: Never give up! In the midst of trials, recommit your life to God.

   Key Word: Signet Ring
Found in 2:23, really two words in our English Bibles. We could think of this as affixing a seal or even "to seal up." When it was pressed into wax, the ring left the personal identification of the owner, the sender. Much more meaning than our ID badges. Haggai compared Zerubbabel to a signet ring. Zerubbabel restored or sealed the royal authority to the line of David.

   Key Chapter: 2

   Key Verse (s)
1:7 Thus says the Lord of hosts, "Consider your ways! 8 "Go up to the mountains, bring wood and rebuild the temple, that I may be pleased with it and be glorified," says the Lord.

2:7 'I will shake all the nations; and they will come with the wealth of all nations, and I will fill this house with glory,' says the Lord of hosts. 8 'The silver is Mine and the gold is Mine,' declares the Lord of hosts. 9 'The latter glory of this house will be greater than the former,' says the Lord of hosts, 'and in this place I will give peace,' declares the Lord of hosts."

Haggai

Key Characters

Haggai—Prophet of Judah after the return from the Babylonian exile; urged the people to rebuild the temple (1:3–2:23)

Zerubbabel—led the Jews out of Babylonian exile; stood as the symbolic representative of the line of David; called "the signet ring" (1:1–2:23)

ZECHARIAH

Overview and Basic Outline
Zechariah means, "The Lord remembers." He was a contemporary of Haggai, continuing the message of rebuilding the Temple. The books of Haggai, Zechariah, and Malachi were composed in the postexilic period of Israel's history. The messages in the first eight chapters came while the Temple was under construction in Jerusalem.

Zechariah served as both prophet and priest, provided encouragement to complete the work. The later chapters take place after the Temple's completion, and have been understood as the hope for a future Messianic Age. In addition, we gain understanding of the final week of Jesus' life.

1. Eight Visions of Zechariah, Cps 1-6
2. Four Messages of Zechariah, Cps 7-8
3. Two Burdens of later writers, Cps 9-14

Thoughts About God in Zechariah:
God is revealed as mercy. His names in Zechariah include:
- Yahweh, LORD
- Yahweh Tsebaoth, the LORD of Hosts, the LORD Almighty
- Elohim, God
- Ruach, Spirit
- Adonai, Lord, Master
- Melek, King

One day His people will dwell in security and blessing in Jerusalem for eternity. God's Spirit enables His people. The coming Jesus is shown in 9:9, 11:12, and 3:8, 6:12.

Jesus Christ in Zechariah:
He is the Reigning King. Zechariah portrays Christ as the *Branch*, a *priest on His throne*, and as *(Him) whom they pierced*. Even as we know Him as King, he came *lowly and riding on a donkey*.

Literary Form of Zechariah:
The longest and most complex of the twelve Minor Prophets. An apocalyptic book that is commonly called the Revelation of the Old Testament. Features that those two books share are the technique of symbolic reality (a preponderance of symbols, so that the reality that we encounter as we read is primarily a world of symbols) and an apocalyptic

Zechariah

(end times) orientation. In addition to being futuristic, the book belongs to the genre of visionary writing (as we are given visions of a future reality or a reality that transcends our earthly reality).

Like Ezekiel and Daniel, Zechariah received symbolic visions as a part of his ministry, written mainly in Hebrew prose. Chapters 9 and 10 are the only poetry section. His prophecies sometimes ad so condensed that one cannot conclude whether it is near or far. It is the eleventh of the twelve Minor Prophets. The twelve Minor Prophets belonged to the single book called "The Twelve."

Highlights and Stories to Read in Zechariah:
- The call to the people, chapter 1a
- Zechariah's visions in a single night begin, chapter 1a
    - Red Horse, chapter 1b
    - Four horns and four craftsmen, chapter 1c
    - The measuring line, chapter 2
    - Clean garments, chapter 3
    - Lampstand and olive trees, chapter 4
    - Flying scroll, chapter 5a
    - Woman in a basket, chapter 5b
    - Four chariots, chapter 6
- Promises to bless Jerusalem, chapter 8
- Armageddon, chapter 14

Author
Zechariah

When the Book was Written
c.520-518 BCE

When the Events Took Place
522-470 BCE

Keys to the Book
   Key Theme: Hope is revived following a renewal of trust in God.

   Key Word: *Angel*
Found several times, 1:9; 2:3; 3:1, 5. *Angel, which* we looked at earlier in this Section.

The word could refer to angelic beings or human messengers. Both Prophets and priests are mentioned as messengers from God, using this word. In Zechariah, angels bring revelations from God and interpret dreams and visions (1:14; 6:4, 5).

Key Chapter: 14

Key Verse (s)

8:3 "Thus says the Lord, 'I will return to Zion and will dwell in the midst of Jerusalem. Then Jerusalem will be called the City of Truth, and the mountain of the Lord of hosts will be called the Holy Mountain.'"

9:9 Rejoice greatly, O daughter of Zion! Shout in triumph, O daughter of Jerusalem! Behold, your king is coming to you; He is just and endowed with salvation, Humble, and mounted on a donkey, Even on a colt, the foal of a donkey.

Key Characters

Zechariah—Prophet of Judah after the Exile; encouraged Judah to finish building the temple (1:1–14:20)

Zerubbabel—leader of the Judean exiles; carried out the work on the temple (4:6–10)

Joshua—Israel's high priest after the remnant returned to Israel (3:1–10; 6:11–13)

The Jews rebuilding the temple—who returned to Jerusalem after the Exile in obedience of God (1:16; 4:9; 6:15; 8:13)

MALACHI

Overview and Basic Outline
Little is known about the author whose name means "my messenger." He was a contemporary of Nehemiah. The books of Haggai, Zechariah, and Malachi were composed in the postexilic period of Israel's history. His ministry took place during the period of Ezra and Nehemiah. Some scholars believe that it is likely Malachi preached before the reforms of Ezra and Nehemiah, preparing the way for them. Malachi directed his thoughts to the lack of worship, marriage and divorce, injustice and tithing. He charged the people with violations of the covenant and gave specific examples. However, he also looked ahead to a time of wonderful blessing. The temple and city had been rebuilt. The interesting pattern of the book follows a stated issue followed by a response by the people, and then God's message of challenge.

1. Past Privilege of Israel, 1:1-5
2. Present Promise to Israel, 1:6-3:15
3. Future Promise to Israel, 3:16-4:6

Thoughts About God in Malachi:
God is revealed as immutable. His names in Malachi include:
- Yahweh, LORD
- Yahweh Tsebaoth, the LORD of Hosts, the LORD Almighty
- Adonay, Lord, Master
- Melek, King
- Elohim, God

God never changes. His promises last forever and are always the same. He is consistently the judge of all people. Christ is shown in 3:1-5.

Jesus Christ in Malachi:
He's the Son of Righteousness with healing in His Wings. Malachi speaks of the *messenger of the covenant.* He ends the Old Testament writings with "behold He is coming."

Literary Form of Malachi:
We rightly think of this book as the ending point of the Old Testament. A predominantly "bad news" book consisting of a litany of spiritual and moral failings of the priests and ordinary Jews who had returned to the

homeland after the Babylonian captivity. The accusations are packaged as an imagined dialogue between God and his wayward people.

The entire book is written in Hebrew prose. The author used a number of vivid metaphors. It is the last of the twelve Minor Prophets. The twelve Minor Prophets belonged to the single book called "The Twelve."

Highlights and Stories to Read in Malachi:
- The Lord assured the people He loved them, chapter 1a
- Your sacrifices were defiled, chapter 1b
- The priests were an abomination, chapter 2a
- Robbing God, chapter 3
- Revere the name of the Lord, chapter 4

Author
Unknown for certain. However, there is no reason to believe that Malachi is written by anyone other than Malachi himself.

When the Book was Written
c.430-410

When the Events Took Place
c.536-510

Keys to the Book
 Key Theme: Spiritual apathy should never be named among God's people. Repentance and renewal must be a Christian's commitment.

 Key Word: *Try*
A Hebrew word meaning "to put to the test." When God uses the word in connection with His people, it means a Proving in such a way that they become stronger, more established. Malachi challenged the Israelites to "try" God to test His faithfulness. It's also found in Genesis 42:15, 16; and Psalms 26:2

 Key Chapter: 3

 Key Verse (s)
3:1 "Behold, I am going to send My messenger, and he will clear the way before Me. And the Lord, whom you seek, will suddenly come to His temple; and the messenger of the covenant, in whom you delight, behold, He is coming," says the Lord of hosts.

Malachi

4:5 "Behold, I am going to send you Elijah the Prophet before the coming of the great and terrible day of the Lord. 6 "He will restore the hearts of the fathers to their children and the hearts of the children to their fathers, so that I will not come and smite the land with a curse."

Key Characters

Malachi—Prophet to Judah; last of the Old Testament Prophets.

The priests—revealed their unfaithfulness by marrying foreign wives and giving false interpretation of the Law (1:7, 8; 2:1–9)

The people of Judah—married foreign wives and fell into idolatry (2:11–17)

TWO

COLLECTION/DICTIONARY of People, Titles, Positions, and Nations Concerning The Old Testament Scriptures

People, Titles, Positions, Nations

Additional expanded details on many of these words are located in Chapter Six.

With many of the following persons, there are several identical names. This author does not include every name. Several are connected to ancient/Biblical history but not listed in the Scriptures.

Aaron (AIR uhn) - The older brother of Moses. He plays a key role in the events of Exodus and Numbers. He served as Moses' spokesman. He failed God after Moses went and met with God. He gave in to the people's demand and made a golden calf for them to worship. He also became the high priest of Israel; subsequent priests were descendants of Aaron. Refer to Ex 4:14-16.

Abdon (AB done) – Hillel's son who judged Israel for eight years; very wealthy man. Refer to Jud 12:13-15.

Abednego (uh BED nih go) – the name given to Azariah, one of the three friends and captives of Daniel at Babylon. Refer to Dan 1:7.

Abel (AY bel) – The second son of Adam and Eve. H was a shepherd and brought a good sacrifice to God. The brother of Cain, a farmer who brought some of his crops to God as a bloodless sacrifice. Cain became angry with Abel and God and murdered Abel. God marked him and caused him to wander. Refer to Gen 4:2-8.

Abiathar (uh BIGH uh thar) - A high priest during David's time. Ahimelech was his father. Refer to 1 Sam 22:20-22; 1 Kings 1:24, 25.

Abiel (A bih ell) – Father of Kish and Ner and grandfather of King Saul. Refer to 1 Sam 9:1, 14:51.

Abiezer (uh BIGH uh zur) – Member of Benjamin's tribe and warrior among David's mighty men. Refer to 2 Sam 23:27; 1 Chron 11:28.

Abigail (AB ih gayl) – The beautiful, wise, and poised wife of David. Refer to 1 Sam 25.

Abihail (AB ih hail) – Esther's father, and uncle of Mordecai. Refer to Est 2:15; 9:29.

Abihu (a BIGH hoo) – The second son of Aaron and a priest. He accompanied Moses and Aaron toward Mount Sinai to worship God. Refer to Ex 24:1, 9.

Abijah (a BIGH juh) – (1) Samuel's second son, a corrupt judge in Beersheba (1 Sam 8:2); (2) Son of Jeroboam I of Israel (1 Kings 14:1, 2).

Abijam (a BUY han) – The son and successor of King Rehoboam of Judah for three years, 958-955 BCE. He made war against King Jeroboam. Refer to 14:31.

Abimelech (uh BIM uh leck) – A Philistine King who tried to add Abraham's wife to his harem. However, God made it clear that he was not to do so. Refer to Gen 20:2.

Abinadab (uh BIN a dab) – The second son of Jesse and brother of David. Refer to 1 Sam 17:13.

Abishai (uh BISH i) – David's nephew, in command of one of David's three armies. Refer to 1 Chron 2:16; 2 Sam 18:1-15.

Abner (AB nur) - He served Saul as commander and bodyguard. Refer to 1 Sam 14:50.

Abraham (A bruh ham) - He left his homeland and took everything he possessed to follow the direction of God. He is regarded as the spiritual father of Judaism, Christianity, and Islam. Refer to Gen 17:5.

Abram - Original name, later called Abraham.

Absalom (AB suh luhm) – He murdered his half brother and led a coup against his father, King David. The third son of David. Refer to 2 Sam 3:3.

Achan (AY kuhn) - The first Hebrew in the Promised Land executed for disobeying God. He kept the spoils of the Jericho battle. Refer to Josh 7:1.

Achish (A kish) – The son of Maoch and King of Gath. He befriended David during the persecution by Saul. Refer to 1 Sam 21:10-15.

Acsah (ack SAH) – Caleb's daughter. Refer to 1 Chron 2:49.

Adaiah (a DYE yuh) - A descendant of Aaron who returned to Jerusalem following the captivity. Refer to 1 Chron 9:10-12.

Adam (ADD um) - The world's first human, directed to reign over the earth, sky, and waters. Refer to Gen 2:19. His, along with Eve's, disobedience, damaged all Creation. He was expelled from Eden and brought sin upon all humans. Refer to Gen 1:27.

Adna (AD nuh) – Priest under the high priest Joiakim who returned to Jerusalem with Zerubbabel. Refer to Neh 12:15.

Adnah (ADD nuh) – Captain from Manasseh's tribe who left Saul to join David's army. Refer to 1 Chron 12:20.

Adonai (ADD o nigh) - A word for God. The Israelites spoke this word where the word *Jehovah* occurred.

Adoni-zezek (a DAWN ih ZEH deck) – One of five kings of the Amorites who fought against Joshua at Gibeon. Refer to Josh 10:1-27.

Adonijah (ad oh NIGH juh) – The fourth son of David who tried without success to take over his father's throne. The Hebrew meaning is "Yahweh is Lord." Refer to 2 Sam 3:4; 1 Kings 1:5-2:25.

Adonikam (ad oh NYE kum) – A Jewish leader who returned from Babylon with Zerubbabel and Ezra. Refer to Ezra 2:1, 13.

Adoniram (ad oh NYE rum) –

People, Titles, Positions, Nations

Important official during the reigns of David and Solomon. Refer to 1 Kings 4:6; 5:14.

Adversary - An opponent or an enemy; a word used for Satan. Refer to Deut 32:43; 1 Pet 5:8.

Agag (A gag) – A king of the Amalekites, a race of Canaanites descended from Esau. He was captured by Saul, and later executed by Samuel.

Ahab (A hab) – A king of Israel (Northern Kingdom) for twenty-one years, He married Jezebel and was at constant war with Judah, 918-897 BCE. Refer to 1 Kings 16:29.

Ahasuerus (uh haz you EE russ) A king of Persia (Xerxes I) who married Esther, mentioned in Ezra 4:6, Dan 9:1, and Est 1:1.

Ahaz (A has) – A king of Judah for sixteen years. His rule was full of idolatry; a wicked king, 742-726 BCE.

Ahaziah (ay huh ZIGH uh) – A son of Ahab and Jezebel. King of Israel (Northern Kingdom), two years, installed calf worship, war with Judah, fell out of window, died, 898-897. Refer to 1 Kings 22:51-53; 2 Kings 8:24.

Ahiezer (ah hih EE zur) – A leader of Dan's tribe following the Israelites escape from Egypt. Refer to Num 1:12, 2:25.

Ahijah (ay HIGH juh) – (1) One of King Solomon's secretaries (1 Kings 4:3); (2) Warrior among David's mighty men (2 Sam 34:34).

Ahimaaz (a HIM a az) – Father of Ahinoam, King Saul's wife. Refer to 1 Sam 14:50.

Ahimelech (a HIM eh leck) - The high priest of Nob in the days of Saul. Refer to 1 Sam 21:1.

Ahinoam (a HIN oh am) – Daughter of Ahimaaz and wife of King Saul. Refer to 1 Sam 14:50.

Ahithophel (a HIGH throw fell) – King David's trusted counselor who turned traitor. Refer to 2 Sam 16:23; 16:20-22.

Ahitub (ah HIGH tub) – Member of the priestly line of Aaron's son. A descendant of Eli. Refer to 1 Sam 14:3; 22:9-12.

Akkub (ACK cub) – (1) Ancestor of a group of Temple assistants who returned to Jerusalem with Zerubbabel (Ezra 2:45); (2) Ezra's assistant who explained to the people passages from the law (Neh 8:7).

Alexander the Great (al eg ZAN dur) – He led Greece to a world power, 356-323. Mentored by Aristotle, he thought he would rule the world. Made the people of the lands he conquered to adopt the Greek culture.

Alien - A stranger or foreigner from another country. Refer to Ex 18:3; Ps 69:8.

Amalek (AM uh lek) – A grandson of Esau. His descendants were enemies of Israel. Refer to Gen 36:12; 1 Chron 1:36.

Amalekites (AM uh leck ites) - Descendants of Amalek. Tried to keep the Israelites from entering the Promised Land. Refer to Gen 36:12; Ex 17:8-1.

Amariah (am ah RYE uh) - (1) A son Azariah who was high priest during Solomon's reign (1 Chron6:11); (2) Helped seal the covenant along with Nehemiah (Neh 10:3).

Amasa (ah MOS ah) – David's nephew; son of David's sister. Refer to 2 Sam 17:25; 1 Chron2:17.

Amasai (a MASS a eye) – Leader of thirty warriors who joined David. Refer to 1 Chron 1:24.

Amaziah (am ah ZIE uh) – A king of Judah for twenty-nine years 839-811 BCE. He invaded Israel.

Ambassador - A person who represented one government at the seat of another. Refer to Num 20:14; Josh 9:4.

Ammiel (AM ih ell) – (1) A son of Gemalli sent by Moses to spy out the land of Canaan (Num 13:12); (2) Father of David's wife, Bathsheba (1 Chron3:5).

Ammon (AM muhn) – He descended from Ben-ammi, the son of Lot by his younger daughter. Refer to Gen 19:30-38.

Ammonites (AM muhn ites) - Descendants of Ammon who became enemies with Israel. Refer to Gen 19:38.

Amnon (AM nahn) - David's oldest son, first in line to become Israel's next king. His sin cut his life short. Absalom directed his death, becoming the next in line to the throne.

Amon (A mun) – A king of Judah for two years, evil reign, 642-640 BCE.

Amos (A muhs) - A Prophet from the southern nation of Judah. A layman who owned herds and an orchard. A masterful writer, with great knowledge of history. His Prophecy concerning Assyria came true in 722 BCE. Refer to Amos 1:1-7.

Amram (Am ram) - A Levite, father of Moses, Aaron, and Miriam. Refer to Ex 6:18-20.

Amraphel (AM rah fell) - A king of Shinar who invaded Canaan during Abraham's time. Refer to Gen 14:1, 9.

Anak (A knack) – A race of giants. Goliath was probably one of them. Refer to Josh 15:13.

Antiochus (an TIE oh kus) - Several members of the Seleucid dynasty of Syria who governed Palestine during the intertestament period.

Aram (A ram) – (1) A descendant of Shem (Gen 10:22-23); (2) A Son of Shemer of the tribe of Asher (1 Chron7:34).

Arameans (AIR ah mee unz) - Ancient desert people who lived with the Israelites. David subdued sections of them, but no all. Refer to 1 Kings 11:23,24; Judg3:8-10.

Aranunah (air a NOON ah) – Jebusite whose threshing floor was the scene of some significant events in biblical history. refer to 2 Sam 24:15, 16; 1 Chron 21:27-30.

Araunah (a ROW nah) – His threshing floor was the scene of significant events in biblical history. (1) the Lord stopped an angel from inflicting Israel (2 Sam 24:15-16); (2) David chose the threshing floor as the site for the Temple, and Solomon built it there on Mt. Moriah (2 Chron 3:1). The Dome of the Rock is located on the site of Araunah's threshing floor.

Arioch (AIR ih ock) - Captain of Nebuchadnezzar's bodyguard. Refer to Dan 2:14-15.

Arphaxad (ar FAX uhd) – Shem's son and Noah's grandson born after the flood. Refer to Gen 10:22-24; 1 Chron 1:17, 18.

Artaxerxes (art uh ZERK sees) – Stopped the rebuilding of the Temple, later allowed its rebuilding, 522 BCE. Refer to Ezra 4:7.

Artaxerxes II Mnemon – A ruler of Persia, 404-358 BCE.

Artaxerxes III Ochus – He brought peace to the empire by diplomacy, but was assassinated. Not mentioned in the OT.

Asa (A suh) – A king of Judah, forty-one years, 955-914. He emptied the temple treasury to pay Syria's king to attack Baasha. Refer to 1 Kings 15:8.

Asahel (ah SAIL) – Warrior among David's mighty men. Refer to 2 Sam 23:24.

Asaph (A saf) – David's appointed music minister in Jerusalem. Asaph led the Jews in praise when the ark arrived in Jerusalem. Refer to 1 Chron 6:39.

Asher, Tribe of (ASH ur) - One of the twelve tribes descended from Jacob. Refer to Josh 17:7).

Asher (ASH er) – Jacob's son born to Leah's maid Zilpah. Refer to Gen 30:12, 13.

Ashurbanipal (ASH ur van ah paul) – Assyrian ruler who reigned in the years during which kings Manasseh, Amon, and Josiah governed Judah.

Asshur (ASH er) – Shem's son. Refer to Gen 10:22; 1 Chron 1:17.

Assyria, Assyrians (as SIHR ih ah) - A kingdom that dominated the ancient world. It defeated the northern kingdom of Israel, carried away thousands of Israelites, and resettled them in parts of the Empire. Refer to Gen 10:22; 2 Kings 15:19; Ezek 16:28.

Astrologers - Magicians who claimed to be able to foretell the future by studying the stars. Refer to Deut 4:19; Jer 10:2.

Athaliah (ath uh LIE uh) – the only Queen of Judah. Reigned for six years, daughter of Jezebel, slayer of all Judah leaders except Joash, 884-878 BCE. Refer to 2 Kings 8:26.

Attai (AT tie) – Warrior from Gad's tribe who joined David against King Saul. Refer to 1 Chron 12:11.

Azarel (AS a rell) – (1) Warrior from Benjamin's tribe who joined David against King Saul (1 Chron12:2, 6; (2) Assisted in the music of the sanctuary (1 Chron25:18).

Azariah (as uh RIGH uh) – A friend of Daniel, who was renamed Abednego. Refer to Dan 1:5, 6. At least twenty-five persons in the OT have the same name. Refer to 1 Chron 2:38; 2 Chron 23:1; Ezra 2:2;Neh 10:2.

Azmaveth (AS mah veth) – Warrior among David's mighty men. Refer to 1 Sam 23:31.

Azzur (A sir) – Political leader who signed Ezra's covenant of faithfulness to God with Nehemiah after the Exile. Refer to Neh 10:17.

B

Baal (BAY uhl) - Canaanite God of fertility; sometimes worshiped with sex rituals. Refer to Judg2:11; Isa 46:1.

Baanah (BAY UH nah) – (1) A Benjamite who helped murder Ish-bosheth. Executed By David. Refer to 2 Sam 4:2-12. (2) A Babylonian captive who returned with Zerubbabel. Refer to Ezra 2:2; Neh 7:7.

Baasha (BAY uh sha) - King of Israel (Northern Empire) - , twenty-four years, 953-930 BCE. Became king after murdering the son of the nation's founding king, Jeroboam.

Balaam (BAY lum) - A seer, asked to put a curse on Israel. Hebrew soldiers killed him during a battle with Midian.

Balak (BAY lack) - King of the Moabites when the Israelites invaded the plains of Moad. Refer to Nu 22-24.

Bani (BAY nee) - One of David's mighty men. A man of the tribe of Gad. Refer to 2 Sam 23:36

Barak (BAY rack) - Encouraged by Deborah, enlisted 10,000 men, and routed an enemy.

Baruch (BAY ruke) - Confirmed by archeologists on a seal. The scribe who wrote Jeremiah's dictated Prophecies. Refer to Jer 36:4-32.

Barzillai (bar ZILL ah) – One of three men who offered hospitality to David during Absalom's rebellion. Refer to 2 Sam 17:27.

Basemath (BASE math) – Ishmael's daughter, who married Esau. Refer to 36:3.

Bathsheba (bath SHE buh) - David saw her bathing, had her brought to him, sent her husband into battle. Married her, their child lived only seven days. Refer to 2 Sam 6.

Bealiah (BEE a LIE uh) – Warrior from Benjamin's tribe who joined David against King Saul. Refer to 1 Chron12:5.

Bedan (BEE dan) – One of Israel's deliverers, along with Gideon, Jephthah, and Samuel. Refer to 1 Sam 12:11

People, Titles, Positions, Nations

Bela (BEE luh) – Benjamin's oldest son. Refer to Gen 46:21.

Belteshazzar (bel teh SHAZ ur) - Name given to Daniel in Babylon. Refer to Dan 1:7; 5:12.

Belshazzar (bell SHAZ ur) - The Babylonian leader who died following Daniel's interpretation of the mysterious words on the wall. The Persians and Medes stormed the capital and conquered Babylon. Refer to Dan 5:1.

Benaiah (BENA iah) - Captain in David's bodyguard. Refer to 2 Sam 8:18.

Ben-hadad (ben HAY dad) - Three Kings of Syria with this name, helped build the Assyrian Empire in conquest of the known world. Refer to 2 Kings 8:7.

Ben-Hur (ben HER) – one of twelve officers appointed to requisition food for King Solomon's household. Refer to 1 Kings 4:8.

Benjamin (BEN juh muhn) - The last of Jacob's twelve sons. Refer to Gen 35:16-18.

Benjamin, tribe of - One of the tiniest strips of lnad went to Benjamin. The cities of Jericho and Gibeon were in its borders. Refer to Josh 18:11.

Ben-Oni (BEN o nigh) – Name of Rachel's last son when she died. Refer to Gen 35:18.

Berechiah (behr ah KIE uh) – Son of Zerubbabel. Refer to 1 Chron3:20

Berekiah (bear ah KIAH) – (1) Son of Zerubbabel and descendant of David (1 Chron3:20); (2) Asa's son who returned to Judah after the Babylonian exile (1 Chron9:16).

Beriah (bear RI ugh) – (1) Asher's son who migrated to Egypt with Jacob (Gen 46:17); (2) Ephraim's youngest son, born after his brothers were killed (1 Chron7:20-23).

Bethuel (beh THEW al) – Youngest son of Abraham's brother Nahor. Refer to Gen 22:23.

Bildad (BIL dad) - One of Job's friends, called "the Shuhite." Refer to Job 2:11, 8:1).

Bilhah (BILL hah) - Maidservant of Rachel, Jacob's wife. Mother of Dan and Naphtali. Refer to Gen 30:1-8; 1 Chron7:13.

Bilshan (BILL shan) - One of twelve princes of the Jews who returned from "Babylon under Zerubbabel. Refer to Ezra 2:2; Neh 7:7.

Birsha (burr SHAY) – Ruler of Gomorrah in the days of Abraham and Lot. Refer to Gen 14:2.

Biztha (BIZZ thuh) – One of the seven eunuchs commanded to bring Queen Vashti to his party. Est 1:10.

Boaz (BOE az) - Resided in Bethlehem, a man of wealth, kinsman to Elimelech, married Ruth. Refer to Ruth 2-4.

Branch, Jesus as the - A title of Jesus that emphasizes His succession through the lineage of David. Refer to Isa 11:1; Zech 6:12.

Bukki (buh KI) – Assisted Joshua in dividing the land of Canaan. Refer to Num 34:22.

Buz (buhz) – Nephew of Abraham. Refer to Gen 22:21.

Buzi (BYOO zie) – Father of the prophet Ezekiel. Refer to Ezek 1:1-3.

C

Cain (KAYN) - First son of Adam and Eve, murdered his brother Abel. Refer to Gen 4.

Cainan (KAYN uhn) – Adam's great-grandson also called Kenan. Refer to Gen 5:9-14; Luke 3:37).

Caleb (KAY luhb) - Appointed one of twelve spies sent to scout the land of Canaan. Refer to Num 13:14; 1 Chron4:15.

Cambyses (kam BEE zees) - Ruler of Persian Empire, conquered Egypt, died 522 BCE.

Canaan (KAY none) - Son of Ham and grandson of Noah. Father of the Canaanite people. Refer to Gen 10:6; 1 Chron1:8.

Canaanites (KANE ites) - A highly developed ancient tribe long before the Hebrews arrived. They had a well-developed system of walled cities. Refer to Josh 6-12.

Captain- Title for a leader of a group of soldiers. Refer to Deut 1:15; Josh 10:24.

Chaldean (Kal DEE uhn) - Chaldeans were settled on the shores of the Persian Gulf. They conquered Babylonia, but later defeated by Assyria.

Chilion (KIL ih ahn) - The younger of the two sons of Elimelech and Naomi. Husband of Orpah, brother-in-law of Ruth.

Chosen People - Family of Abraham, Israel. Called Hebrews or Jews. Refer to Gen 17:7; Ps 89:3; 1 Pet 2:9.

Concubine (CON cue bine) - A wife of lower rank, usually from slaves or captives. Not wedded in the usual manner, and did not have the same status as a wife. Refer to Gen 16:2-3, 21:10.

Cupbearer - A high ranking officer who was expected to sample the king's food to make sure it did not contain poison. Refer to Neh 1:11; 2:1.

Cush (KOOSH) – eldest of Ham's four sons. Refer to Gen 10:6.

Cyrus, King of Persia (CY russ) - Founder of the Persian Empire. Named by Isaiah as the divine instrument for the release of the Jews from the Babylonian exile. Refer to Isa 44:28, 45:1-14.

D

Dagon (DAY gone) – The chief god of the Philistines. Refer to Judg16:23.

People, Titles, Positions, Nations

Dan (DAN) – The fifth son of Jacob. Mother was Bilhah, Rachel's maid. Refer to Gen 30:5-6.

Dan, Tribe of - (1) The second largest of the twelve tribes. Samson was a Danite. Refer to Josh 19:40-43, 21:5, 23. (2) A city in the northern part of Palestine. Refer to Judg20:1.

Daniel (DAN yull) - Carried captive to Babylon, named Belteshazzar and made a governor under Darius. Refer to Dan 1-2; 6:2.

Darius, King of Persia (duh RIGH uhs) – A common name for three rulers of the Medes and Persians. Refer to Dan 5:31; Ezra 4:5; Neh 12:22.

Darius I the Great – Reigned for thirty-seven years. One of the most able Persian kings. An effective organizer and administrator, who developed trade, built a network of roads and established a postal system. He continued the policy of Cyrus allowing Jews to restore worship in Jerusalem. Refer to Haag 1:1; Zech 1:1.

Darius the Mede - Ruled Babylon briefly following Belshazzar. He made Daniel a governor. Refer to Dan 5:31; 6:1-2.

David (DAY vid) - The eighth son of Jesse. He was anointed king by Samuel, to succeed Saul. He united the twelve tribes into one kingdom and established a capital in Jerusalem. Refer to 1 Sam 16:13; 17:12.

Debir (duh BEER) – One of the kings of Eglon, executed by Joshua. Refer to Josh 10:22-27.

Deborah (DEB uh rah) - Prophetess and Judge. Refer to Judg4:5-14.

Dedan (DEE dun) – (1) Grandson of Cush (Gen 10:7; (2) Grandson of Abraham (Gen 25:3).

Delilah (duh LIE lah) - A woman of Sorek who discovered the secret of Samson's strength Samson fell in love with Delilah who betrayed him to the Philistines for money. Refer to Judg16:4-20).

Diblaim (DIB laum) – Father of Gomer, Hosea's wife. Refer to Hos 1:3.

Dinah (DIE nah) – A daughter of Jacob and Leah who was attacked by Shechem. Refer to Gen 30:21, 34:1-29.

Dodo (DOE doh) - Father of Eleazar, one of David's mighty men. Refer to 2 Sam 23:9.

Doeg (DOE egg) – Official of Saul who was commanded to kill innocent priests at Nob. Refer to 1 Sam 21-22.

Dumah (DEW ma) – Ishmael's son who founded an Arab tribe. Refer to Gen 25:14.

Eber (EE bur) - A descendant of Shem and ancestor of Abraham and Christ. Perhaps the word "Hebrew." Refer to Gen 10:21, 24-25.

Eglon (EGG lon) – An overweight Moabite king who was stabbed and killed by the Jewish hero, the left-handed Ehud. Refer to Judg3:12).

Ehud (EE hud) - The second of Israel's twelve Judges. Freed his people from King Eglon of Moab. Refer to Judg3:15.

Elah (EE la) – (1) A king of Israel (Northern Kingdom) for two years, 930-929 BCE. (2) A son of Caleb (1 Chron4:15).

Elam (EE luhm) – (1) A Son of Shem (Gen 10:22). (2) A head of a family, which returned from Babylon (Ezek 2:1,2, 7). (3) A priest during the rebuilding of the temple.

Eldad (EL dad) - One of the seventy appointed by Moses to aid him in governing the people. Refer to Num 11:17.

Eleazar (EL ee A zur) – (1) The third son of Aaron, father of Phinehas. Refer to Ex 6:23, 25. (2) A son of Abinadab in whose house the ark was kept after its return to the Israelites. Refer to 1 Sam 7:1-2.

Elhanan (el HAY nun) - One of David's thirty heroes. Refer to 2 Sam 23:24.

Eli (EE lie) – The high priest at the temple of Shilo. He helped train Samuel, but was unable to control his own sons. Refer to 1 Sam 1:9, 24-28, 2:23-25.

Eliab (e LIE ab) – The oldest son of Jesse and a brother of David. Refer to 1 Sam 16:6-7.

Eliakim (e LIE uh kim) - A son of Josiah, whose name was changed to Jehoiakim by Pharaoh Necho. Refer to 2 Kings 23:34.

Eliam (e LIE um) – The father of Bathsheba, who was the wife of Uriah and then King David. Refer to 2 Sam 11:3

Eliasaph (e LIE uh saf) – (1) A priest in the time of David (1 Chron24:12. (2) A high priest in the time of Nehemiah who built the sheep gate in Jerusalem (Neh 3:1, 20-21).

Eliashib (e LIE a schib) – Aaron's descendant chosen by David for sanctuary services (1 Chron24:12); (2) High priest in the succession from Jeshua (Neh 12:10); (3) Levite and Temple singer (Ezra 10:24).

Eliel (E LIE el) - One of David's heroes. Refer to 1 Chron11:47.

Eliezer (EL ee EE zur) – (1) A servant of Abraham, from Damascus (Gen 15:2). (2) A son of Moses and Zipporah (Ex 18:4).

Elihu (ee LIE hew) – (1) The fourth of Job's visitors (Job 32:2); (2) David's eldest Brother, also called Eliab (1 Sam 16:6).

Elijah (ee LIE jah) - A Prophet of Gilead, who appeared suddenly. Refer to 1 Kings 17:1-24; 19; 2 Kings 2.

Elimelech (ee LIM ah leck) – Man from Bethlehem who took his family to Moab because of famine in Judah. Refer to Ruth 1:2, 3.

People, Titles, Positions, Nations

Eliphaz (EL ih faz) – Oldest son of Esau and father of Teman. Refer to Gen 36:4.

Eliphelet (el ah fil ET) – One of David's thirteen sons born in Jerusalem. Refer to 2 Sam 5:1.

Elisha (ee LIGH shuh) - A Prophet anointed by Elijah. Refer to 1 Kings 19:16-21.

Elisheba (ee LISH ih buh) – Wife of Aaron who bore him four sons. refer to Ex 6:12.

Elkanah (el KAY na) – (1) A son of Korah (Ex 6:24). (2) The husband of Hannah and father of Samuel (1 Sam 1:2; 2:11). (3) A doorkeeper for the ark, for David (1 Chron15:23).

Elnathan (el na THAN) – Grandfather of King Jehoiachin. Refer to 2 Kings 24:8.

Eluzai (el oo ZAY) – One of the men of Benjamin who came to join David. Refer to 1 Chron12:5.

Enoch (EE nuhk) - The eldest son of Cain and grandson of Adam. One of the few who apparently never died. God "took him" Gen 4:17; 5:24.

Enosh (ee nosh) – Seth's son and a grandson of Adam. Refer to Gen 4:26.

Epher (EE fur) – Grandson of Abraham. Refer to Gen 25:4.

Ephraim (EE fray ihm) - Joseph's youngest son. Blessed by Jacob and became one of the tribes of Israel. Refer to Gen 41:45-52.

Ephraim (EE fray ihm), tribe of – Descendants of Ephraim, one of the twelve tribes of Israel who settled in the land of Canaan. Refer to Josh 16:5-10.

Ephron (EE frawn) – Hittite from whom Abraham purchased the cave of Machpelah where Sarah, Abraham and Jacob were buried. Refer to Gen 23:8-17.

Esarhaddon (eh sar HAD un) – A son of Sennacherib, king of Assyria 681-669 BCE. He rebuilt Babylon and murdered his father Sennacherib and fled into Armenia (2 Kings19:36-37). Succeeded to the throne of Assyria.

Esau (EE saw) - The First of twin boys born to Isaac and Rebekah. Refer to Gen 25:25.

Eshbaal (esh BAYAL) – King Saul's fourth son who became Israel's king after his father's death.

Essenes (ESS seenz) - An ascetic Jewish sect whose high ideals conflicted with the evil practices in the Temple.

Esther (ES tur) - Persian name of Hadassah, Mordecai's cousin. Married King Ahasuerus and saved the lives of many Hebrews.

Ethan (EE thun) – Wise man comparable to Solomon. Refer to 1 Kings 4:31.

Eunuch (U nuck) - A castrated male. Refer to 2 Kings 9:32; Est 2:3.

Eve (EEve) - The first woman; made from the side of man and for him. Refer to Gen 2:18-25; 3-4.

Evil-Merodach (EE vul MARE ah doc) – Son and successor of Nebuchadnezzar as king of Babylon. Refer to 2 Kings 25:27-30.

Ezekiel (ih ZEE kih uhl) - A Major Prophet, carried captive to Babylon. Refer to Ezek 1:1-3.

Ezer (EE zur) – (1) Joined David at Ziklag (1 Chron12:9; (2) Jeshua's son who helped repair the Jerusalem wall (Neh 3:19).

Ezra (EZ ruh) - A scribe and priest who returned from Babylon to Jerusalem. He is considered to have settled the Old Testament canon.

F

Firstborn - The firstborn received a double portion of his father's inheritance and usually succeeded the father as head of the family. Refer to Deut 21:17; 1 kings 1:30.

G

Gabriel (GAY bree uhl) - An angel of great position, generally used by God to make announcements. Sent to Daniel to interpret a vision (Dan 8:16-27).

Gad (gad) – The son of Jacob and Zilpah, Leah's handmaid. Gad had seven sons. Refer to Gen 30:10-11.

Gad (gad), Tribe of - One of the twelve tribes of Israel, assigned territory east of the Jordan, but assisted Joshua in conquest of The Promised Land. Refer to Num32:6-34.

Gamaliel (guh MAY lee uhl) – Captain of Manasseh's tribe, chosen by Moses to help take the census in the wilderness. Num 1:10, 10:23.

Gatam (GAY tum) – Esau's grandson. Refer to Gen 36:11.

Geber (GHEE buhr) – A son of Uri and servant of Solomon in Gilead. Refer to 1 Kings 4:19.

Gedaliah (geh DAL i al) – Appointed by Nebuchadnezzar as governor over the Jews remaining in Israel to work the fields. Refer to 2 Kings 25:12, 22.

Gehazi (gea HI zuh) – Servant of Elisha who gave instructions to the prophet. Refer to 2 Kings 5:25; 4:11-17.

Gemariah (ghem ah RYE ah) – Hilkiah's son and emissary to Nebuchadnezzar from King Zedekiah. Refer to Jer 29:3.

Gentiles (JEN tiles) – Refers to all people who are not Jewish. Refer to Gen 10:5; 14:1.

Gershom or Gershon (GUR shun) – (1) The firstborn of Moses by Zipporah, daughter of Jethro (Ex 2:22); (2) The eldest son of Levi (1 Chron 6:16, 17).

Gershon (GUR shon)– Levi's oldest son who went into Egypt with Israel. Refer to Gen 46:11; Num 3:17.

Geshem (GEH shim) – Opponent of Nehemiah who derided those seeking to rebuild the walls of

People, Titles, Positions, Nations

Jerusalem. Refer to Neh 2:19; 6:1-6.

Gideon (GID ee uhn) - The powerful warrior of Manasseh, and Judge of Israel for forty years. Refer to Judg 6-9.

Gilalai (GILL ah lilh) – Musician present at the dedication of the Jerusalem wall, rebuilt during Ezra's time. Refer to Neh 12:36.

Gilead (GILL ee add) – Father of Jephthah during the period of the judges. Refer to Judg 11:1, 2.

Ginnethon (GHIN ee thun) – Priest who set his seal on Ezra's covenant during the postexilic period. Refer to Neh 10:6.

Girgashites (GUR hah shites) – The people of one of the nations in Canaan when the Israelites arrived. Refer to Josh 3:10.

Gog (GAUG) – Individual described as the prince of Meshech who ruled over the land of Magog. Refer to Ezek 38:2-21.

Goliath (go LIE uhth) - The Philistine giant who defiled the army of Israel. Refer to 1 Sam 17:4-54.

Gomer (GOAM uh) - Oldest son of Japheth (Gen 10:2-3), included in the army of Gog (Ezek 38:3, 6).

Guni (goo NIGH) – grandson of Jacob. Refer to Gen 46:24.

Habakkuk (huh BACK uhk) – A prophet of God to the Northern Kingdom of Judah. He was from the tribe of Levi. Refer to Hab 1:1.

Hadad (HAY dad) – A prince of Edom, Son of Ishmael. He fled to Egypt in fear of David. Later he returned to Edom and caused trouble for Solomon. Refer to 1 Kings 11:14.

Hadassah (ha DASS ah) – Original Hebrew name of Esther. Refer to Est 2:7

Hagar (HAY gahr) - Sarah's Egyptian bondwoman (Gen 16:1-16). She gave birth to Ishmael by Abraham.

Haggai (HAG ay igh) – The tenth of the Minor Prophets. He accompanied Zerubbabel from Babylon. He and Zechariah urged the people to resume construction of the Temple. Refer to Hag 1:1.

Haggith (HAGG ith) – One of David's wives and the mother of Adonijah. Refer to 2 Sam 3:4; 1 Kings 1:5.

Ham - One of Noah's three sons. He saw his father naked, so Noah placed a curse on him, and sent him away. Refer to Gen 5:32.

Haman (HAY muhn) – The evil prime minister of King Ahasuerus. He plotted to destroy all the Jews in the Persian empire. Refer to Est 3:1; 7:9.

Hammedatha (ham ih DAY thuh) – Father of Haman a chief adviser to the Persian king Ahasuerus. Refer to Est 3:1, 10.

Hammurapi (hahmuhr RAH pee) – A king who ruled Babylonia in the mid BCE era.

The Code of Hammurape was discovered in 1901 CE, which contained the laws from the ancient world.

Hanan (HAY nuhn) – (1) One of David's mighty men (1 Chron 11:43); (2) A Levite who assisted Ezra in reading and teaching the Law (Neh 8:7).

Hanani (hah NAH nigh) – (1) The father of Jehu the Prophet (1 Kings 16:1; (2) Nehemiah's brother (Neh 1:2).

Hananiah (han uh NIGH uh) – (1) A son of Zerubbabel (1 Chron 3:19, 21); (2) A captain of Uzziah's army, king of Judah (2 Chron 26:11); (3) A priest for the dedication of the wall of Jerusalem (Neh 12:41).

Hannah (HAN uh) – The mother of Samuel. Refer to 1 Sam 1-2.

Haran (HAIR uhn) - A son of Terah and brother of Abraham. Refer to Gen 11:29.

Harhaiah (hahr HIGH uh) – Father of Uzziel a goldsmith who worked to rebuild the wall of Jerusalem. Refer to Neh 3:8.

Harim (huh RIM) – (1) Priest whom King David appointed to duties in the Temple (1 Chron 24:8); (2) Priest who returned from the Exile with Zerubbabel (Neh 12:3).

Hariph (HAIR if) – The founder of a large family, which came to Jerusalem from Babylon with Zerubbabel. Refer to Ezra 2:32; Neh 7:35.

Harlot - A Prostitute. A type of idolatry. Refer to Gen 38:15; Isa 1:21.

Hasadiah (haus a DIE uh) – One of Zerubbabel's sons (1 Chron 3:20).

Hashabiah (ha SHA bi uh) – (1) A musician in the Temple during the reign of David (1 Chron 6:45; (2) Head of a group of Hebronites who was given the position of overseer of Israel west of the Jordan (1 Chron 26:30; (3) Priest who returned to Jerusalem from Babylon with Ezra (Ezra 8:24.

Hashem (HAY shem) – He is listed as one of David's warriors. Refer to 1 Chron 11:34.

Hashubah (ha SHOO bah) – One of Zerubbabel's sons. refer to 1 Chron 3:20.

Hathach (HATH ack) – Eunuch appointed by King Ahasuerus to wait on Esther. Refer to Est 4:5-10.

Hazael (HAZ ay el) – He stole Syria's throne by suffocating King Ben-hadad. Refer to 2 Kings 8:28-29.

Heber (HEE burr) – descendant of Jacob and the father of the Heberites. Refer to Gen 46:17; Num 26:45.

Hebrews - The nation that descended from Abraham referred to as Israelites. Refer to Gen 14:13; 32:28.

Heldai (HEL digh) – (1) A descendant of Othniel and captain in David's army (1 Chron

27:15); (2) One who returned from Babylon with gold and silver (Zech 6:10-14).

Helem (HEE lem) - One of those who assisted Zechariah in crowning Joshua the high priest. Refer to Zech 6:10, 14.

Helez (he LEZZ) – One of David's warriors, called a Paltite. Refer to 2 Sam 23:26.

Heman (HEE muhn) – (1) One of Solomon's counselors, next to him in wisdom (1 Kings 4:31); (2) A grandson of Samuel (1 Chron 15:19).

Hephzibah (heh FIZZ ah buh) – Mother of Manasseh, king of Judah. Refer to 2 Kings 21:1.

Heth (heth) – The forefather of the Hittites. Refer to Gen 10:15.

Hezekiah (hez uh KIGH uh) – (1) A king of Judah for twenty-nine years, 726-697 BCE. He reformed temple worship. The son of Ahaz, 1 Chron 3:23); (2) An ancestor of the Prophet Zephaniah (Zeph 4:1); (3) The head of a family which returned from Babylonia (Ezra 2:16).

Hezron (HEZ rahn) - A son of Reuben. Refer to Gen 46:9.

Hiel (HIGH uhl) - The man from Bethel who rebuilt Jericho in spite of the curse pronounced by Joshua. Refer to Josh 6:26; 1 Kings 16:34.

High Priest – A Chief priest, Aaron being the first. See author's list of High Priests in *Travel through The Old Testament, Vol. 2*. Refer to Ex 28:1; Num 3:32.

Hilkiah (hill KI uh) - The high priest who found a copy of the Jewish laws lost in the Jerusalem temple. Refer to 2 Kings 22:4.

Hiram (HIGH ruhm) - A king of Tyre who enlarged his city. He furnished the timber and workmen for David's house. Refer to 2 Sam 5:11.

Hittites (HIT tights) - This kingdom extended from northern Palestine to the central part of Asia Minor.

Hivites (HIGH vights) – The descendants of Canaan, son of Ham. Refer to Gen 14:6.

Hobab (HO babb) – Name associated with Moses' father-in-law, priest of Midian. Refer to Num 10:29; Ex 18:1.

Hodaviah (ho dah VIAH) – descendant of David. Refer to 1 Chron 3:24.

Hophni (HOFF nee) - A son of Eli and a brother of Phinehas. These brothers were noted for their lust and greed. They were killed while bringing the ark of the covenant onto the battlefield. Refer to 1 Sam 2:22-4:22.

Horam (HOR um) – King of Gezer who was defeated and killed by Joshua. Refer to Josh 10:22.

Hosea (ho ZAY uh) - First of the Minor Prophets. Refer to Hos 1:1.

Hoshaiah (ho shay I uh) – Prince of Judah who led a group of princes in procession at the dedication of the rebuilt walls of Jerusalem. Refer to Neh 12:32.

Hoshea (ho SHE uh) – (1) Original name of Joshua, Moses' successor. His name was changed by Moses. Refer to Num 13:8, 16; (2) King Hoshea's actions prodded Assyria to wipe Israel off the map, deporting most of the Jews. Refer to 2 Kings 15:30.

Huldah (HUHL duh) – Prophetess and wife of Shallum. She confirmed the Book of the Law. Refer to 2 Kings 22:14.

Hur (HURR) – Aaron's assistant in supporting Moses' hands until the Amalekites were defeated. Refer to Ex 17:8-13.

Hushai (who SHAY) – Friend and faithful adviser to King David. Refer to 2 Sam 15:32-37.

Hyksos (HICK soss) - A people from Asia or Mesopotamia who ruled Egypt for 100 years. Not mentioned in the Bible.

I

Ibhar (IB ar) – son born to David in Jerusalem. Refer to 2 Sam 5:15.

Ibzan (ihb Zan) – Judge over Israel for seven years. Refer to Judg 12:8-10.

Ichabod (IK uh bahd) – The son of Phinehas and grandson of Eli, the high priest. Refer to 1 Sam 4:19-22.

Iddo (IH doo) – (1) Father of Ahinadab, Solomon's official who directed the royal household (1 Kings 4:14; (2) Zechariah's son during David's reign (1 Chron 27:21).

Igal (ih GAHL) – Joseph's son (Num 13:7); (2) Nathan's son and one of David's mighty men (2 Sam 23:36).

Immer (IMM ur) – Priest in the time of David. Refer to Jer 20:1.

Ira (I rah) – Warrior among David's mighty men and became commander of one of David's military divisions. Refer to 1 Chron 11:28.

Irad (EAR odd) – Enoch's son, a member of Cain's line. Refer to Gen 4:18.

Iru (IGH roo) – Caleb's son. Refer to 1 Chron 4:15.

Isaac (I zack) – A son of Abraham. Refer to Gen 17:17-22.

Isaiah (eye ZAY uh) - A prophet in Judah in the reigns of several kings. Called the Messianic Prophet because of his many descriptions of the Messiah. Refer to Isa 53.

Ish-bosheth (ish BO sheth) - The youngest son of Saul. Refer to 2 Sam 2:8.

Ishbi-Benob (ISH bee beh NOB) – A giant who nearly killed David. Refer to 2 Sam 21:16.

Ishmael (ISH may el) – A son of Abraham by Hagar, Sarah's Egyptian maid. Refer to Gen 16:3, 15.

Ishmaiah (ISH ma I ah) - Warrior from Benjamin's tribe who

People, Titles, Positions, Nations

joined David. Refer to 1 Chron 27:19.

Ishvi (EESH vee) – Asher's third son. Refer to Gen 46:17.

Israel (the man) – The name given to Jacob after his struggle with God at Peniel. Refer to Gen 32:28; 35:10.

Issachar (IS uh car) – The ninth son of Jacob by Leah. Refer to Gen 30:17-18.

Issachar, Tribe of - The tribe made up of Issachar's descendants. One of the twelve tribes who settled the land of Canaan.

Ithamar (ITH a mar) – Aaron's fourth son, served as a priest to the tribes of Israel during the wilderness period. Refer to Ex 6:23; Num 3:2-4.

Ittai (ih TIE) – Benjaminite warrior among David's mighty men. Refer to 2 Sam 23:29.

J

Jaasiel (J see el) – Warrior among David's might men, called "the Mezobaite." Refer to 1 Chron 11:47.

Jaaziel (jay a ZEEL) – one of the men appointed to play harps when the Ark was brought up to Jerusalem by David. Refer to 1 Chron 15:18-20.

Jabal (JAY ble) – Descendant of Cain and the first son of Lamech. Refer to Gen 4:20.

Jabin (JAY bin) - A King of Hazor, defeated by Joshua at the waters of Meron. Refer to Josh 11:1-14.

Jabesh (JAY besh) – The fifteenth king of the Northern Kingdom, Israel.

Jabez (JAY bez) - An Israelite known for his prayer for success. Refer to 1 Chron 4:9-10.

Jabin (JAY bin) – King of Hazor during the period of the judges. Oppressed Israel for twenty years. Refer to Jud 4.

Jadah (JAY duh) - Ahaz's son and descendant of King Saul. Refer to 1 Chron 8:36

Jaddua (JAD oo uh) –.Leader who set his seal on Ezra's covenant. Refer to Neh 10:21

Jachin (JAY kin) – (1) A son of Simeon (Gen 46:10); (2) A priest who lived in Jerusalem after the captivity (1 Chron 3:17).

Jacob (JAY cub) – A son of Isaac, twin brother of Esau. He married Rachel and Leah. Died in Egypt. Refer to Gen 25:24-34.

Jadah (JAY duh) – Ahaz's son and a descendant of King Saul. Refer to 1 Chron 8:36.

Jael (JAY el) - Jael killed one of Israel's most feared enemies, Sisera, with a tent peg and a hammer. Refer to Judg 4:17-22.

Jahaziel (juh HAY zih uhl) – (1) A Levite and son of Hebron (1 Chron 23:19); (2) A Benjamite warrior who joined David at Ziklag (1 Chron 12:4); (3) a priest who sounded a trumpet when the ark was brought to Jerusalem for David (1 Chron

16:6); (4) a son of Zechariah (2 Chron 20:14).

Jair (JAY ur) – (1) The father of Mordecai (Est 2:5); (2) A judge of Israel for twenty-two years (Judg 10:3-5).

Jakin (YAY kun) – Priest who lived in Jerusalem after the Exile (1 Chron 9:10); (2) Descendant of Aaron and head of later priests assigned to Temple duty in David's reign (1 Chron 24:17).

Jalam - A son of Esau. Refer to Gen 36:5; 1 Chron 1:35.

Jalon (JAY lahn) – A son of Ezra. Refer to 1 Chron 4:17).

Jambres (JAM breeze) – Enemy of Moses used in the New Testament as an example. Refer to 2 Tim 3:8, 9.

Jamin (JAY min) – (1) Simeon's son (Gen 46:10; Ex 6:15); (2) One of the men who taught and explained the law to the people following Ezra's public reading (Neh 8:7).

Jannes (JAN iz) and Jambres (jam BREZ) – They were Egyptian magicians who tried to discredit Moses. Refer to Ex 7:11-12.

Japheth (JAY feth) – A son of Noah, descendants were Indo-European and Caucasian races. Refer to Gen 5:32; 10:1-5.

Japhia (juh FIGH uh) - A son of David born at Jerusalem. Refer to 2 Sam 5:15.

Jared (Jehr ed) – A descendant of Seth, and father of Enoch. Refer to Gen 5:15-20

Jarib(JAY rib) – Man who assisted Ezra in securing Temple servants before the return from exile. Refer to Ezra 8:16.

Jashen (JAY shun) – One of David's mighty men. Refer to 2 Sam 23:32.

Jashobeam (juh SHOE bih uhm) - A warrior of David. Military captain. Refer to 1 Chron 11:11; 27:2-3.

Jashub (JAY schub) – Issachar's third son, called Iob. Refer to 1 Chron 7:1; Gen 46:13.

Jason (JAY sun) – Jewish high priest who brought about the decline of the priesthood. Refer to 2 Macc 4:9.

Javan (JAY vun) – Jepheth's son whose descendants migrated by water to the west of Canaan.

Jedaiah (juh DAY uh) - Two priests who returned with Zerubbabel to Jerusalem. Refer to Neh 12:6-7.

Jediael (jay DIE el) – Benjamin's son whose descendants were warriors (1 Chron7:6); (2) Listed among David's mighty men (1 Chron 12:20).

Jeduthun (juh DOO thuhn) – (1) He was the father of Obed-edom. (1 Chron 16:38); (2) A singer of the family of Merari (1 Chron 9:16; 16:41-42.

Jehiel (juh HIGH uhl) – A son of

Jehoshaphat, slain by Jehoram. Refer to 2 Chron 21:2-4.

Jehohanan (jee hoe HAY nuhn) - A captain of Jehoshaphat. Refer to 2 Chron 1: 15.

Jehoahaz (juh HO uh has) – A king of Judah for three months, taken to Egypt, 609 BCE.

Jehoash (juh HOE ash) - (Or Joash), A King of Israel (Northern Kingdom) for sixteen years, 840-826 BCE.

Jehohanan (jay ho HAN un) – Levite who was a gatekeeper of the sanctuary during David's' reign (1 Chron 26:3); (2) Commander of thousands in King Jehoshaphat's army (2 Chron17:15); (3) Priest and family leader in postexilic Jerusalem (Neh 12:13).

Jehoiachin (juh HOY uh kin) –A king of Judah, son of Johoiakim, for three months, deported to Babylon as Nebuchadnezzar invaded Jerusalem, 598 BCE. Refer to 2 Kings 25:27-30.

Jehoiakim (juh HOY uh kim) – A king of Judah, a son of Josiah, for eleven years, rebelled against Nebuchadnezzar, 609-598 BCE. He was carried away to Babylon. Refer to 2 Kings 23:36.

Jehoiada (jih HOY uh duh) - A high priest who organized a revolt against Queen Athaliah, resulting in her death.

Jehoram (jih HOH ruhm) – The successor of Jehoshaphat as King of Israel (Northern Kingdom) for twelve years, 897-884. His wife was Athaliah, daughter of Ahab and Jezebel. Refer to 2 Kings 8:16.

Jehoshaphat (juh HAH suh fat) – A king of Judah for twenty-five years, 914-889 BCE, son of Asa. Noted for his religious reform and peace with Israel. He continued the reforms of his father King Asa. Refer to 1 Kings 22:41-42; 1 Kings 252:1-38.

Jehosheba (juh HAH shuh buh) – A daughter of Jehoram and wife of Jehoiada, the High Priest. Refer to 2 Kings 11:2.

Jehozabad (juh HOE zuh bad) – (1) One of Jehoshaphat's generals (2 Chron 17:18); (2) A son of Obed-edom, a porter at a gate of the temple (1 Chron 26:4).

Jehu (JAY hue) – A king of Israel (Northern Kingdom), son of Jehoshaphat, king for twenty-seven years, attempted reform, paid Assyria a tribute, shrewdest of all Israel Kings, 884-857 BCE. Refer to 1 Kings 19:16-17.

Jeiel (jih EYE uhl) – (1) One of the ancestors of King Saul (1 Chron 9:35); (2) One of David's mighty men (1 Chron 11:44); (3) A scribe who recorded the number of troops of King Uzziah of Judah (2 Chron 26:11); (4) One who returned with Ezra from Babylon (Ezra 8:13).

Jemimah (juh MIGH muh) – First of the three daughters born to Job following his restoration from his affliction. Refer to Job 42:14.

Jemuel (jay moo EL) – Simeon's first son. Refer to Gen 46:10; Ex 16:15.

Jephthah (JEFF thuh) – The eleventh Judge who delivered

Israel from the Ammonites. Son of Gilead. Was a famous hunter. Had to kill his own daughter because of a Promise made to God. One of the heroes of faith in Heb 11:32. Refer to Judges 10:6-12:7; 1 Sam 12:11.

Jephunneh (jay PHOON neh) – Father of Caleb, one of the twelve spies sent to search the Promised Land. Refer to Num 13:6; 1 Chron 4:15.

Jerahmeel (jih RAH mih uhl) - One of the three men Jehoiakim ordered to arrest Jeremiah and Baruch. Refer to Jer 36:26.

Jeremiah (jerr uh MY uh) - One of the Major Prophets during the reigns of Josiah, Jehoiakim, and Zedekiah.

Jeremoth (jerr uh mauth) – (1) Levite registered during David's reign (1 Chron 23:23); (2) One of Elam's descendants who was encouraged by Ezra (Ezra 10:26).

Jerimoth (JER e moth) - A Benjamite and archer who joined David at Ziklag. Refer to 1 Chron 12:5.

Jeroboam (JERR uh BO uhm) - First King of Israel (Northern Kingdom) for twenty-two years, 975-954 BCE, established shrines at Bethlehem and Dan. The son of Nebat who was an official under Solomon. The idolatry he established continued until the fall of the Northern Kingdom. Refer to 1 Kings 11:26-28.

Jeroboam II - Son and successor of Joash as fourteenth King of Israel. Beginning about 826 BCE, he reigned forty-one years. He was killed by Jehu.

Jeroham (juh ROE ham) – (1) Father of Elkanah (1 Sam 1:1); (2) Father of the chief of the tribe of Dan in the reign of David (1 Chron 27:22).

Jerubbaal (jer uh BAY uhl) - Name given to Gideon by his father, Joash. Refer to Judg 6:32.

Jeshaiah (juh SHAY uh) – A son of Athaliah and head of the house of Elam. He returned from Babylon with Ezra. Refer to Ezra 8:7.

Jeshua (JESH oo uh) – (1) A descendant of Aaron. The Family was a line of priests (1 Chron 24:1, 6); (2) A high priest who came from Babylon with Zerubbabel (Ezra 2:2); (3) A Levite who assisted Ezra in teaching the people the law (Neh 8:7, 9:4-5).

Jesse (JESS ee) - Father of David. Refer to 1 Sam 16:1-8.

Jether (JEE thur) – (1) A descendant of Judga, son of Ezra (1 Chron 4:17); (2) Gideon's first son (Judg 8:20-21).

Jethro (JETH row) - A priest of Midian and father-in-law of Moses. He helped Moses delegate responsibilities of leadership. Refer to Ex 18.

Jetur (jeh TUR) – Son of Ishmael whose descendants fought the Israelites who settled east of the Jordan. Refer to 1 Chron 5:19.

Jeuel (JOO uhl) - One of those who returned with Ezra. Refer to Ezra 8:13.

Jeush (JEE uhsh) – (1) A son of Esau (Gen 36:5, 18); (2) A son of Rehoboam (2 Chron 11:19).

Jews – (Refer to Hebrews). After captivity, the name Hebrews as in general use. Refer to Est 5:13; Dan 3:8-12.

Jezebel (JEZZ uh bell) – A Phoenician princess, daughter of Ethbaal. Wife of Ahab who became the power behind the throne. Instilled worship of Baal, killed the Prophets of Jehovah. Refer to 1 Kings 16:32-33, 18:4-13.

Jeziel (jay ZEEL) – Warrior from Benjamin's tribe who joined David in his struggle against King Saul. Refer to 1 Chron 12:3.

Jezrahiah (jez ruh HIGH uh) – Leader of the Temple singers who participated in the dedication of the rebuilt Jerusalem wall. Refer to Neh 12:42.

Jezreel (JEZ reel) – (1) A descendant of Hur of Judah (1 Chron 3:3); (2) A son of Hosea the Prophet (Hos 1:4-5).

Joab (JOE ab) – A son of Zeruiah, the half sister of David. A companion of David and commander of his troops. Refer to 2 Sam 8:16.

Joah (JOE uh) – (1) a son of Obed-edom (1 Chron 6:2); (2) a son of Asaph, King Hezekiah's recorder (2 Kings 18:18, 26); (3) son of Joahax and recorder under Josiah (2 Chron 34:8).

Joash (JOE ash) - King of Judah for forty years, son of King Ahaziah. He was hid in the temple by High Priest Jehoiada, became king at age seven, repaired the temple, 879-839 BCE (2 Kings 11:1-20); 2 Chron 23:10-21); (2) A son of King Jehoahaz of Israel. Supported the worship of calves as King during his sixteen-year reign. Succeeded by his son Jeroboam II (2 Kings 14:8-16). Also called Jehoash.

Job (JOHB) - The wealthy patriarch of Uz, the central person of the Book of Job in the Old Testament, who withstood an attack from Satan.

Job's comforters – The three persons who came to Job to reason with him. Three cycles of debates took place, followed by a fourth person's strong accusations.

Jobab (JOE bab) – (1) A son of Zerah of Bozrah, a king of Edom (Gen 10:29; 1 Chron 1:23); (2) One of the kings that formed the northern confederacy against Joshua who defeated him in battle (Josh 11:1; 12:19).

Jochebed (JOCK uh bed) - Wife of Amran and mother of Moses and Aaron. Refer to Ex 6:20.

Joel (JO uhl) – (1) A contemporary with Uzziah (Joel 2:28; Acts 2:16-18); (2) Oldest son of Samuel the prophet (1 Sam 8:2-5); (3) Nathan's brother and one of David's mighty men (1 Chron 11:38); (4) Levite who participated in the royal procession that brought the Ark of God to Jerusalem (1 Chron 15:7-11).

Joelah (joe EE luh) – One of David's warriors at Ziklag. Refer to 1 Chron 12:7.

Joezer (JO zer) – Warrior who joined David in his struggle against King Saul. Refer to 1 Chron 12:6.

Johanan (jo HAN un) – (1) A contemporary of Jeremiah (2 Kings 25:23; Jer 40:8); (2) eldest son of King Josiah of Judah (1 Chron 3:15); Warrior who joined David's special men at Ziklag (1 Chron 12:4); (3) Priest under Joiakim (Neh 12:22).

Johoahaz (jo HO a hasz – A king of Judah (Northern Kingdom) for seventeen years, 857-840 BCE.

Joiada (jay OH ah dah) – Levite and high priest in Jerusalem during the postexilic era and the great-grandson of Jeshua. Refer to Neh 12:10-11.

Joiakim (JO ah kim) – Levite high priest in a family of high priests. Refer to Neh 12:10-12.

Joiarib (jo are ibh) – (1) One of the Jewish leaders whom Ezra set to gather Levites and Temple servants. Refer to Ezra 8:16; (2) Zechariah's son (Neh 11:5).

Jokshan (JAHK shan) – Son of Abraham and father of Sheba. Refer to Gen 25:2-3.

Jonadab (JOE nuh dab) – David's nephew, the son of his brother Shimeah. Refer to 2 Sam 13:3-5.

Jonah (JOE nuh) – (1) The father of Peter the apostle (Matt 16:17); (2) A prophet of Israel, son of Amittai (2 Kings 14:25).

Jonathan (JAHN uh thun) – The eldest son of Saul and friend of David. Refer to 1 Sam 13:2-3; 2 Sam 1:17-27. At least fourteen others are named Jonathan in the OT.

Joram (JOHR uhm) – The successor of Jehoshaphat as King of Judah. He was also called Jehoram. Reigned eight years. Refer to 1 Chron 3:10-11; 1 Kings 22:50.

Joseph (JOE zif) – The eleventh son of Jacob, sold into slavery, rose to high position in Egypt. The first child of Rachel, and his father's favorite son. It is noted that he preserved the line of Christ. Refer to Gen 30:24; 37:21; Gen cps 37-50.

Joshaphat (JAHSH uh fat) - A priest who served as a trumpeter at the time the ark was brought to Jerusalem. Refer to 1 Chron 15:24). Sometimes referred to as Jehoshaphat.

Joshua (Jahsh oo uh) – The successor to Moses and the man who led the nation of Israel to conquer and settle the Promised Land.

Josiah (joe SIGH uh) - King of Judah, son of Amon for thirty-one years, 640-609. He became King at age eight. He was influenced under the care of Hilkiah, the high priest. Killed in battle at Megiddo. Refer to 2 Kings 22:1-2; 23:29-30.

Jotham (JOE thum) – (1) A king of Judah, son of Uzziah (or Azariah) for sixteen years, 758-742 BCE (2 Kings 15:5, 32-33); (2) The youngest son of Gideon. He spoke on Mount Gerizim (Judg9:1-21).

Jozabad (JOHZ a bahd) – One of the Levites who assisted with the administration of the Temple contributions during King Hezekiah's reign. Refer to 2 Chron 31:13

Jubal (JOO buhl) – A son of Lamech. He was a musician, father of all those who play the harp and flute. Refer to Gen 4:21).

Judah (JOO duh) – (1) The fourth son of Jacob, and a son of Leah (Gen 38:1-10; 38:11); (2) One who officiated when the wall of Nehemiah was dedicated (Neh 12:34).

Judah (JOO duh), tribe of – The tribe founded by Judah. Judah was the southernmost tribe of the Israelites. Together with the tribe of Benjamin, formed the southern kingdom of Judah.

Judith – One of Esau's wives. Refer to Gen 26:34.

Jush-Hesed (JUSH ab hess ed) - One of Zerubbabels's seven sons. refer to 1 Chron 3:20.

K

Kadmiel (cad mi EL) – Head of a Levite family who returned from the Exile with Zerubbabel. Refer to Ezra 2:40.

Kassites – A people of the ancient Near East who controlled Babylonia after the fall of the Old Babylonian Empire.

Kedar (KEE der) – Second son of Ishmael, Abrahams' son. Refer to Gen 25:13.

Kedorlaomer (kee dor LAY omer) – King of Elam who participated in a campaign against five cities near the southern end of the Dead Sea plane. Refer to Gen 14.

Kemuel (KEM yoo uhl) - A prince of Ephraim who assisted in the division of the Promised Land. Refer to Num 34:24.

Kenan (KEE none) – Fourth generation descendant of Adam, in Luke's genealogy of Christ. Refer to Gen 5:9-14.

Keren-Happuch (KEE wren HAP puch) – Job's third daughter at the time of his restoration. Refer to Job 42:14.

Keturah (keh TUR uh) – The wife of Abraham following the death of Sarah. Refer to Gen 25:1.

Keziah (kee ZIGH uh) – Job's second daughter, born after his restoration. Refer to Job 42:14.

Kileab (ki LEEB) – David's second son, and the first born to him by Abigail. Refer to 2 Sam 3:3.

Kilion (KILL ee hon) – One of the two sons of Elimelech and Naomi. Refer to Ruth 1:2.

Kish (kish) – (1) The Benjamite Father of King Saul. (1 Sam 9:1; 10:11, 21); (2) An ancestor of Mordecai, a Benjamite (Est 2:5).

Kohath (CO hath) – son of Levi,

father of Amram. Refer to Gen 46:11; Ex 6:18.

Korah (KOH ruh) – (1) A son of Esau (Gen 36:5, 14); (2) A son of Eliphaz and grandson of Esau (Gen 33:16); (3) A Levite who conspired against Moses and Aaron (Num 16:1; 26:10).

L

Laban (LAY buhn) – A son of Bethuel and grandson of Abraham's brother, Nahor. Jacob stayed with him and eventually married his two daughters. Refer to Gen 24:10, 15; 29:16-28.

Ladan (LAY duhn) – Member of Ephraim's tribe who was Joshur's ancestor. Refer to 1 Chron 7:26.

Lamech (LAY mek) – The Father of Noah. Refer to Gen 5:28-32.

Leah (LEE uh) – A daughter of Laban who was passed off on Jacob instead of her younger sister. Refer to Gen 29:16.

Lemuel (LEM u el) – King credited with writing Proverbs 31:1-9.

Levi (LEAVE eye) – The third son of Jacob by Leah. Refer to Gen 29:34.

Levites (LEE vytes) – The descendents of Levi. The priestly tribe in charge of religious affairs. Refer to Num 35:2.

Lo-Ammi (loe AM eye) – symbolic name given by the prophet Hosea to his son. Name had meaning of "Not My People." Refer to Hos 1:9.

Lot (lath) - A Shemite, son of Haran, and nephew of Abraham. He came with Abraham to Canaan, and then went with him to Egypt. Refer to Gen 11:341, 13:1.

Lot's wife – The wife of Lot, Abraham's nephew. She did not follow the angels' orders and looked back at Sodom. Her disobedience resulted in her being turned into a "pillar of salt." Refer to Gen 19:26.

Lucifer (Loo sih fur) – The name only appears in the Bible one time. Used as a name/description of Satan. Refer to Is 14:12.

Lud (luhd) – The fourth son of Shem. Refer go Gen 10:22.

M

Maacah (MAY ah kah) – (1) A wife of David and mother of Absalom (2 Sam 3:3); (2) A granddaughter of Abishalom, wife of Rehoboam King of Judah and mother of Abijan (1 Kings 15:2); (3) A wife of Machir the son of Masasseh (1 Chron 7:15-16); (4) A wife of Jehiel, the father of Gibeon, and ancestress of King Saul (1 Chron 8:29).

Maasai (muh SI) – Priest who returned to Jerusalem with Zerubbabel after the Exile. Refer to 1 Chron 9:12.

Maaseiah (mass I uh) – (1) One of the singers appointed to accompany David when he brought the Ark to Jerusalem. (1 Chron 15:18-20; (2) Officer who served King Uzziah by helping to organize the king's army (2 Chron 26:11); (3) Ezra's helper when he read the law to the people (Neh 3:23); (4) Father of Zephaniah the priest (Jer 21:1, 2) At least fifteen others with the same name. (2 Chron 28:7; Ezra 10:30; Jer 21:1-20

Maaziah (may uh ZYE uh) – Levite who served in the Temple during David's reign. Refer to 1 Chron 24:18.

Maccabees (MACK uh bees) – The surname of one of the sons of Mattathias. This heroic family revolted from Antiochus Epiphanes II, which led to independence for a short period.

Machir (MAY kir) - The son of Manasseh. Refer to Num 32:39-40.

Madai (muh DIE) – Third of Japheth's seven sons. Refer to Gen 10:2.

Mahalath (muh HAY lath) – Daughter of Ishmael, Esau's third wife. Refer to Gen 36:3-17.

Maharai (muh HAR ih) – One of David's mighty men. Refer to 2 Sam 23:28.

Magicians - People who practiced illusion or sleight of hand. Refer to Gen 41:8; Dan 1:20.

Maher-Shalel-Hash-Baz (MAY ur SHALL uhl HASH bahs) – The longest name in the Bible, son of Isaiah. Refer to Isa 7:1; 8:1, 3.

Mahlon (MAY lun) – Son of Elimelech and Naomi. Refer to Ruth 1:2.

Mahol (MAY hall) – Father of three wise men during the era of Solomon. Refer to 1 Kings 4:31

Makir (may KERR) – Joseph's grandson and the firstborn son of Manasseh. Refer to Gen 50:23.

Malachi (MAL uh kigh) – The last of the Minor Prophets.

Malkijah (mal KI jah) – (1) Appointed by David to serve as a Temple musician (1 Chron 6:40); (2) Priest who served in the time of David (1 Chron 9:12); (3) Goldsmith who worked under Nehemiah to repair the Jerusalem wall (Neh 3:31).

Malkishua (mal KISH u ah) – King Saul's third son. Refer to 1 Sam 14:49.

Manasseh (muh NASS uh) – (1) The first son of Joseph (Gen 41:51); (2) A king of Judah for fifty-four years 697-642 BCE. His reign was evil and full of idolatry. He killed Isaiah.

Manasseh, Tribe of - One of Israel's twelve tribes, the only tribe to split in two.

Manoah (muh NOH uh) – The Danite father of Samson (Judges 13:1-25), an angel promised him the birth of Samson.

Mara (MAY ruh) – A name which Naomi gave to herself when she returned as a widow to Judah. A meaning of "bitter." Refer to Ruth 1:20.

Mareshah (muh REE shuh) – Caleb's first-born and the father of Hebron. Refer to 1 Chron 2:42.

Mash (mash) – Aram's fourth son, a descendant of Shem. Refer to Gen 10:23.

Massa (MAGH suh) – Ishmael's seventh son and Abraham's grandson (Gen 25:14.

Mattaniah (mat uh NYE uh) –(1) A son of King Josiah (2 Kings 24:17); (2) A son of Heman in David's time, who was a singer (1 Chron 25:4, 16); (3) A singer among the Levites, descended from Asaph (1 Chron 9:15).

Mebab (MAY bab) – Eldest of Saul's two daughters. Refer to 1 Sam 14:49.

Medes – A highly civilized people in Asia, linked with the Persians politically. Refer to Ezra 6:1-2.

Melatiah (ma LAT I ah) – Descendant of Gideon who helped repair the Jerusalem wall. Refer to Neh 3:7.

Melchizedek (mel KIZ uh deck) - The king-priest of Salem (Jerusalem). Met Abraham and blessed him. He received tithes from Abraham. Refer to Gen 14:18; Ps 119:4.

Melech (mel ECK) – Micah's son. Refer to 1 Chron 8:35.

Melatiah (mel uh TYE uh) – Descendant of Gideon who helped repair the Jerusalem wall. Refer to Neh 3:7.

Menahem (MEN ah him) – A king of Israel (Northern Kingdom) for ten years 772-762 BCE. He paid tribute to Assyria when they invaded Israel.

Mephibosheth (me FIB oh sheth) – (1) A son of King Saul, slain by the Gibeonites (2 Sam 21:8-9); (2) The son of Jonathan who was crippled by falling from his nurse (2 Sam 4:4; 16:1-4).

Meraioth (meh RAY yawth) - A son of Aaron and head of a priestly house. Refer to 1 Chron 6:3, 6, 7.

Merib-baal (MER ib BAY uhl) – The son of Jonathan, also referred to as Mephibosheth. Refer to 1 Chron 8:34; 2 Sam 21:8-9.

Merodach-baladan (MEHR oh dack BAL ah dahn) – He seized the throne of Babylon in 722 BCE when Israel was overthrown by Assyria. He reigned for eleven years, submitted to Sargon in 710. Refer to 2 Kings 20:12-19.

Mesha (ME shuh) - A king of Moab who paid tribute to Ahab, king of Israel. Refer to 2 Kings 3:4.

Meshach (MEE shak) – The Babylonian name of Mishael, One of Daniel's companions. Daniel and his companions refused to bow down to an image. Refer to Dan 1:6-7.

Meshech (MEE shek) – (1) son of Japheth and Grandson of Noah (Gen 10:2); (2) Shem's son (1 Chron 1:17).

People, Titles, Positions, Nations

Meshullam (meh SHUHL um) – (1) A son of Zerubbabel (1 Chron 3:19); (2) An overseer of the temple repairs in the reign of Josiah (2 Chron 34:12); (3) One who stood by Ezra when he read the law (Neh 8:4); (4) A priest who signed the covenant (Neh 10:7). At least twenty others in the OT with the same name.

Meshullemeth (meh SHULL eh meth) – Mother of Amon, king of Judah. Refer to 2 Kings 21:19.

Methuselah (mih THYOO zuh luh) – Son of Enoch, grandfather of Noah; oldest of those who lived before the flood. Refer to Gen 5:21-27.

Mibsam (MIB sam) – One of Ishmael's sons. refer to Gen 25:13.

Micah (MY kuh) - One of the Minor Prophets.

Michael (MY kuhl) – (1) An archangel or an angel of high rank (Dan 10:21; 12:1; Rev 12:7); (2) One mentioned in the family tree of King Saul of Benjamin (1 Chron 8:16); (3) A warrior from the tribe of Manasseh who joined David at Ziklag (1 Chron 12:20).

Michaiah (my KYE uh) – (1) The daughter of Uriel, wife of King Rehoboam of Judah, and mother of Abijah (2 Chron 13:2); (2) A priest and trumpeter (Neh 12:41).

Michal (MY kuhl) – The daughter of Saul, given conditionally to David. She helped David escape from her father. Saul gave her to another man when David was away. Refer to 1 Sam 18:27-28, 19:11-17.

Midian (MID ee un) – A son of Abraham. Isaac's younger half-brother. Refer to Gen 25:2; Ex 3:1.

Midianites – The descendants from Midian.

Mighty Men - David's group of skilled warriors. Refer to 2 Sam 23:8-39.

Mijamin (mi JA min) – (1) Priest who ministered during the time of David (1 Chron 24:9); (2) One of the priests who signed Ezra's covenant during the postexilic period (Neh 10:7).

Milalai (MILL ah lye) - Participant in the dedication of the rebuilt Jerusalem wall (Neh 12:36.

Milcah (MILL kuh) – The daughter of Haran and wife of Nahor, Abraham's brother. Refer to Gen 11:29; 22:20.

Miriam (MEAR ee uhm) – the sister of Aaron and Moses. She took a timbrel and sang a song of triumph after crossing the Red Sea. She was smitten with leprosy, Moses prayed and she was healed. Refer to Ex 15:20-21; Num 12:1-16.

Mishael (MISH ih uhl) – (1) A companion of Daniel whose name was changed to Meshach (Dan 1:6-7); (2) One who was with Ezra when he instructed the people (Neh 8:4).

Mishma (mishma) – Son of Ismael, and Abraham's grandson. Refer to Gen 25:14.

173

Mishmannah (mish ma NIAH) – Warrior who joined David at Ziklag against King Saul. Refer to 1 Chron 12:10.

Mithredath (MITH reh dath) – Treasurer of King Cyrus of Persia, in charge of the sacred vessels as the Exiles prepared to return to Jerusalem. Refer to Ezra 1:8.

Moab (MO ab) - Son of Lot by his daughter.

Moadiah (mo ah DIAH) – head of a family of postexilic priests. Refer to Neh 12:17.

Molech (MO lek) – One of the many pagan gods mentioned in the Bible.

Mordecai (MORE dih kigh) – (1) A son of Jair, a Benjamite carried to Babylonia in the second group of captives. Close relative of Esther (Est 2:7); (2) A Jew who returned to Jerusalem (Ezra 2:2).

Moses (MO ziss) - The great leader and lawgiver of the Israelites. He was the son of Amran, a Levite. He was called by God to lead the exodus from Egypt. Refer to Ex 2, 10-11.

Moza (MOE zuh) – Caleb's son by his concubine Ephah. Refer to 1 Chron 2:46.

N

Naamah (NAY ah muh) – (1) Daughter of Zilla and Lamech, descendants of Cain (Gen 4:22); One of Solomon's wives (1 Kings 14:21).

Naaman (NAY uh muhn) – (1) A son of Benjamin (Gen 46:21); (2) A Syrian commander of the army of Benhadad, king of Damascus who had leprosy (2 Kings 5:1-27).

Nabal (NAY bull) - The shepherd from Carmel who refused to give food to David and his men. Nabal's wife was Abigail (1 Sam 25:3). Refer also to cp. 25 of 1 Sam.

Naboth (NAY both) - An owner of a vineyard that King Ahab of Israel wanted to buy, but refused to sell. Ahab's wife, Jezebel killed Naboth and his sons. Refer to 1 Kings 2:1:1-24; 2 Kings 9:26.

Nachon (NAY kon) - His threshing floor was where Uzzah was struck dead when he placed his hand on the ark. Refer to 2 Sam 6:6.

Nadab (NAY dab) – (1) A king of Israel (Northern Kingdom) for two years, 954-953 BCE; (2) Eldest son of Aaron. Died because he and his brother offered "strange fire" to the Lord. Refer to Ex 6:23; Lev 10:1-2.

Nahamani (nay ha MANNY) – One of the leading officials who returned with Zerubbabel following the Exile. Refer to Neh 7:7.

Nahash (NAY hash) – (1) A king of the Ammonites who demanded a price for peace or every man would lose his right eye (1 Sam 11:1-11); (2)

Probable father of David's sisters (2 Sam 17:25).

Nahor (NAY or) – (1) Abraham's grandfather (Gen 11:22-25; (2) Son of Terah and Abraham's brother (Gen 11:26-29.

Nahum (NAY hum) – The author of the Book of Nahum whose prophecy pronounced God's Judgment against the nation of Assyria.

Naomi (nay OH me) - Wife of Elimelech and mother of Mahlon and Chilion. She returned to Bethlehem with her daughter-in-law Ruth. Refer to Ruth 1-4.

Naphish (NA fish) – One of Ishmael's sons, warred against the tribes east of Jordan.

Naphtali (NAF tuh lie) – The fifth son of Jacob. Refer to Num 1:43; 26:50.

Nathan (NAY thuhn) – (1) A son of David born in Jerusalem, and ancestor of the family of Jesus (2 Sam 5:14; Luke 3:31); (2) A prophet in the reign of David and Solomon who rebuked David for his sin with Bathsheba (2 Sam 7:1-17; 12:1-15); (3) The brother of Joel who was one of David's mighty men (1 Chron 11:38).

Nathan-melech (NAY thun MEH leck) – Official during King Josiah's reign. Refer to 2 Kings 23:11.

Nazarite (nazz uh right) - One bound by a temporary or permanent vow of separation from worldly things and to consecrate himself to God. Refer to Num 6:1-21; Amos 2:11-12.

Nebaioth (nee BAY oath) – firstborn of Ishmael's sons. Refer to Gen 25:13.

Nebuchadnezzar (neb uh cud NEZ ur) – The king of the Babylonian Empire who brought the Empire to its greatest height. He captured Jerusalem, destroyed the Temple, and carried the people of Judah into captivity. He defeated Pharaoh-Necho. Refer to Jer 46:2-26.

Necho, King of Egypt (NEE koh) – A Pharaoh of Egypt who defeated Josiah in the Valley of Megiddo. Then, King Necho was defeated by King Nebuchadnezzar of Babylon. Refer to 2 Chron 35:20.

Nehemiah (nee uh MY uh) – (1) A leader who returned with Zerubbabel from Babylon (Ezra 2:2; Neh 7:7); (2) The governor of Jerusalem who helped rebuild the wall of the city and led many social reforms including emphasis on true religion (Neh 1:1-3; 10:1).

Nephilim (NEFF ih lem) – The offspring of marriages between the "sons of God" (fallen angels) and "the daughters of men." Scripture makes it clear that these angels fell because of their desire for women. Refer to Gen 6 and Jude 6.

Ner (nur) – Father of Abner and brother of Kish. Uncle of Saul. Refer to 1 Sam 14:51; 2 Sam 2:8.

Neriah (neh RI uh) – Father of Baruch the scribe. Refer to Jer 32:12.

Nethanel (neh THAN el) - (1) David's brother and son of Jesse

(1 Chron 2:14); (2) One of the musicians, a priest when the ark was brought to Jerusalem (1 Chron 15:24); (3) son of Obed-edom in the time of David (1 Chron 26:4); (4) A priest in the time or Joiakim (Neh 12:21).

Nethinim (NEHTH uh neam) - A name given to those working in the sanctuary. They were temple servants, founded by David. Refer to Ezra 2:58; Neh 7:60.

Nimrod (NIM rod) - The son of Cush and a mighty hunter. Refer to Gen 10:8-10; Micah 5:6.

Nimshi (NIM she) – Father of Jehoshaphat and grandfather of Jehu. Refer to 1 Kings 19:16.

Noah (NO uh) – The ninth in descent from Adam, saved from the flood with his three sons. He and his family built an ark on which they were preserved from the flood. He was alive in the late years of Adam. Refer to Gen 5:28-32; 7-10.

Nogah (NO guh) – One of the sons of David born in Jerusalem after David was established in his kingdom . Refer to 1 Chron 3:7.

Nun – Father of Joshua. Refer to Ex 33:11.

Obadiah (oh buh DIE uh) – (1) An officer in the court of Ahab who hid a hundred prophets when Jezebel was persecuting prophets (1 Kings 18:3-4); (2)The son of Jehiel who came with Ezra from Babylon (Ezra 8:9); (3) A priest who signed the covenant with Nehemiah (Neh 10:5); (4) A Prophet of Judah and author of a Bible book (Oba 1).

Obed (OH bed) – (1) The son of Boaz and Ruth, and grandfather of David (Ruth 4:17, 21-22); (2) One of David's mighty men (1 Chron 11:47); (3) The father of Azariah (2 Chron 23:1).

Obed-edom (OH bed EE dum) – (1) The Ark was placed in his house (2 Sam 6:10-12); (2) A gatekeeper who was part of the procession bringing the ark into Jerusalem (1 Chron 15:18-24); (3) A Levite musician who ministered in the tabernacle in Jerusalem (1 Chron 16:5).

Og (AHG) - One of the last kings of Bashan and one of the last giants. Refer to Deut 3:11.

Ohad (OH had) – Simeon's son. Refer to Gen 46:19.

Oholah (oh HOH lah) and Oholibah (o HOLE ih bah) – Ezekiel's names for the northern and southern kingdoms in his allegory concerning the unfaithfulness of God's people. Refer to Ezek 23.

Oholiab (o HO lee ab) – Man assigned by Moses to assist Bezalel in the construction of the Tabernacle. Refer to Ex 31:6.

Oholibamah (o ho LIB ah ma) – Essau's wife who bore Korah. Refer to Gen 36:2.

Omar (OH mer) – Son of Eliphaz, grandson of Esau and the great-

People, Titles, Positions, Nations

grandson of Abraham. Refer to Gen 36:11, 15.

Omri (um rih) – (1) The commander of Israel's army who became king. Practices of idolatry were prevalent during his reign (1 Kings 16:25; Mi 6:16); (2) A son of Michael and prince of the tribe of Issachar (1 Chron 27:18).

Onan (OH nan) - A son of Judah. His mother was a Canaanite. Refer to Gen 38:4-10.

Orpah (OR puh) – The daughter-in-law of Naomi, wife of Chilion, a Moabitess. She was persuaded to remain in her homeland. Refer to Ruth 1:4, 11, 15.

Othniel (AHTH nee el) - One of the Judges in Israel. Refer to Judg 1:13; 3:9.

Paarai (puh AIR ih) – One of David's mighty men. Refer to 2 Sam 23:35.

Pahath-moab (PAY hath MO ab) – Head of a family who returned with Zerubbabel to Jerusalem. Refer to Ezra 2:6; Neh 7:11.

Palal (pa LAUL) – Uzai's son who helped rebuild the Jerusalem wall. Refer to Neh 3:25.

Pallu (PAL oo) – Reuben's son and father of Eliab. Refer to Gen 46:9; Ex 6:14.

Palti (Pal tee) – One of the twelve spies Moses sent to explore the land of Canaan. Refer to Num 13:9.

Parosh (pa ROSH) – Head of a family who returned to Jerusalem with Zerubbabel. Refer to Ezra 2:3; Neh 7:8).

Parshandatha (par shan DA tha) – One of the sons of Haman slain by the Jews. Refer to Est 9:7.

Pashhur (PASH ur) - A priest who sealed the covenant with Nehemiah. Refer to Neh 10:3.

Pedaiah (pih DAY uh) – (1) The father of Joel, prince of Manasseh (1 Chron 27:20); (2) One who stood by Ezra as he taught the people (Neh 8:4).

Pekah (PEE kuh) – A king of Israel (Northern Kingdom) for eleven years 759-739 BCE.

Pekahiah (pek uh HIGH uh) – A king of Israel (Northern Kingdom) for two years, 761-760 BCE.

Pelaiah (peh LIE yuh) – (1) One who helped explain the law to the people as Ezra read it aloud (Neh 8:7); (2) A Levite who sealed the covenant (Neh 10:10).

Peleg (PEE leg) – A son of Eber and descendant of Noah through Shem. Refer to Gen 10:25.

Pelet (PEE let) – Warrior who joined David at Ziklag against King Saul. Refer to 1 Chron12:2, 3.

Perez (PIR ez) – Son of Judah. Refer to Gen 38:29.

Perizzites (PIR eh zights) – A people never conquered by Joshua. Ref to Gen 13:7; Josh 9:1.

Pethahiah (pee thuh HIAH) – Levite who assisted Ezra at the Feast of Tabernacles. Refer to Neh 9:5.

Pethuel (peh THU el) – Father of the prophet Joel. Refer to Joel 1:1.

Pharaoh (FAY roh) - The title of the kings of Egypt, meaning "great house." Refer to Ex 1:81; 1 Chron 4:18; Jer 37:5-8.

Phicol (FI cole) – Commander of Abimelech's army. Refer to Gen 21:22, 32.

Philistines (fih LIS teens) - A people who endangered Israel during the reign of Saul. David broke their power when he defeated Goliath. Refer to 1 Sam 14:52; 17:38.

Phinehas (FIN ee huhs) – A grandson of Aaron and wicked son of Eli. Refer to 1 Sam 1:3; 14:3.

Pildash (PILL dash) – Son of Nahor and Milcah; Nephew of Abraham refer to Gen 22:22.

Poratha (poor AHTHA) – one of the sons of Haman killed by the Jews. Refer to Est 9:8.

Potiphar (PAUT uh fur) - Captain of Pharaoh's guard. Refer to Gen 37:36; 39.

Potiphar's wife – She became attracted to Joseph and attempted to seduce him. When he rejected her advances, she falsely accused him and had him imprisoned. Refer to Gen 30:6-19.

Proselyte (PROS eh lite) - A convert to the Jewish faith. Refer to Deut 10:18-18.

Puah (POO ah) – (1) Issachar's son who went with Jacob to Egypt (Gen 46:13); (2) One of two Hebrew midwives ordered by Pharaoh to kill Hebrew males at birth (Ex 1:15).

Pul (PULL) – Name give to Tiglath-pileser the Assyrian ruler when he became king of Babylon. Refer to 2 Kings 15:19; 1 Chron 5:26.

Put (put) – Third of Ham's sons, who most likely settled in northern Africa and perhaps the forefather of the peoples of Egypt. Refer to Gen 10:6.

Putiel (POO tih uhl) – The father-in-law of Eleazar, Aaron's son. Refer to Ex 6:25.

Raamah (RAH ma) – One of Cush's sons and a descendant of Ham's line. Refer to Gen 10:7.

Rachel (RAY chuhl) - Laban's younger daughter whom Jacob loved. She had two sons, Joseph and Benjamin, but died giving birth to the latter in Canaan. Her burial place is near Bethlehem. Refer to Gen 30:22-25; 35:16-18.

Raddai (rad DIE) – One of Jesse's seven sons and the brother of David. Refer to 1 Chron 2:14.

Rahab (RAY hab) - A harlot who lived in Jericho in a house on a

People, Titles, Positions, Nations

wall. She concealed the spies sent by Joshua, then lowered them down the wall. She is listed with the heroes of faith (Heb 11), and was part of the genealogy of Jesus. Refer to Josh 2:1-24; 6:22-25.

Ram (ramm) – Ancestor of King David. Refer to Ruth 4:19.

Rameses, Pharaoh (RAM uh sees) – King of Egypt well after the Israelites left the land. The name actually referred to the fertile district of Egypt in the Nile Delta. Refer to Gen 47:11.

Rebekah (ruh BECK uh) – A daughter of Bethuel and sister of Laban. She met the servant of Abraham at a well. She was the wife of Isaac and mother of Esau and Jacob. Buried in the cave of Machpelah, the same place where Abraham, Isaac, Jacob, Sarah, and Leah were also buried. Refer to Gen 24:1-67; 25:28; 27:1-28:5.

Regem-melech (ree guhm MEE lek) – One of the delegation sent to ask if fasting should continue. Refer to Zech 7:2.

Rehoboam (ree huh BOH uhm) - First King of Judah, son of Solomon. During his reign of seventeen years, 975-959 BCE, he increased the taxes on the people. He experienced the dividing of the United Kingdom into Judah and Israel. Refer to 1 Kings 11:43, 14:21; 1 Kings 14:21-31.

Rehum (REE huhm) – (1) One who returned with Zerubbabel from Babylon (Ezra 2:2); (2) He wrote Artaxerxes, King of Persian, denouncing the building of the temple (Ezra 4:8-9).

Remaliah (re MAL ih ah) – Father of King Pekah of Israel. Refer to 2 Kings 15:25-37.

Rephaiah (rih FAY uh) – Descendant of Solomon (1 Chron 3:21); (2) Hur's son who worked on the Jerusalem wall with Nehemiah. (Neh 3:9).

Rephaim (REF ih yuhm) - A race in Palestine before the time of Abraham. Refer to Gen 14:5; Josh 17:15.

Reuben (RHOO ben) – The eldest son of Jacob's first wife, Leah. Reuben saved the life of his brother, Joseph, when the other brothers wished to kill him. Refer to Gen 29:31-32; 46:8.

Reuben, Tribe of (ROO ben) – The ancestors of Reuben who requested their land east of the Jordan River. They were conspirators against Moses claiming legal right to leadership as descendants of Jacob's oldest son. Refer to Num 1:5; 16:1-3.

Rhesa (REE suh) – Descendant of Zerubbabel and ancestor of Christ. Refer to Luke 3:27.

Rizpah (RIZ puh) – a concubine of Saul. She bore two sons to Saul.

Rosh (rahsh) – One of Benjamin's sons. Refer to Gen 46:21.

Ruth - A Moabite who embraced the Jewish religion, married Boaz, and was an ancestress of Christ. Refer to Ruth 1:1.

Sabtah (SAB tuh) – One of Cush's sons and a descendant of Noah through Ham's line. Refer to Gen 10:7.

Sabteca (SAB tuh kuh) – One of Cush's five sons and a descendant of Noah. Settled in Arabia. Refer to Gen 10:7; 1 Chron 1:9.

Sacar (SAY kahr) – (1) The father of Ahiam and one of David's men (1 Chron 11:35): (2) A son of Obed-edom (1 Chron 26:4).

Sallai (sal LAY) – One of the Benjaminites who lived in Jerusalem during the postexilic period. Refer to Neh 11:8.

Salmon (SAL muhn) - Father of Boaz, the husband of Ruth. He was an ancestor of the family of Jesus. Refer to Ruth 4:18-21.

Samaritans (suh MAR ih tuhns) – Inhabitants of Samaria, a region in Central Canaan. Location of Mount Gerizim and Mount Ebal. Samaria, built by Omri and Ahab became the capital of the Northern Kingdom. Jews labeled them as ceremonially unclean and shunned them. Refer to 1 Kings 12:25; 2 Kings 17:24.

Samson (SAM son) – A son of Manoah and Judge of Israel. He is noted for his great strength. Samson married, then deserted his wife. He killed himself by pulling down the pillars of the building in which his enemies were feasting. Refer to Judg13:3-25; Ex 34:16; Judg16.

Samuel (SAM you uhl) - Faithful Prophet dedicated by his mother to the Lord's service. When he was an old man, Samuel anointed Saul and then David, as Israel's first two kings. Refer to 1 Sam 1:11; 3:1.

Sanballat (san BAL uht) - A man who had considerable influence in Samaria and served Artaxerxes (Neh 2:10, 19; 4:2).

Saph (saf) – Descendant of the giants. Refer to 2 Sam 21:18.

Sarah (SAIR uh) – The beautiful wife and half-sister of Abraham (Gen 20:12). She was promised to give birth to a special son, but questioned God. However, in spite of the expressed doubt, she gave birth to Isaac. Her name was changed from Sarai. Refer to Gen 16: 1-16; 17:1-19. She is listed in the heroes of faith (Heb 11).

Sargon (SAHR gahn) – (1) A king of Akkad in Mesopotamia, extending this kingdom to the Mediterranean Sea. The first true world empire in history; (2) Two other Sargons were kings of Assyria and Babylonia. Sargon II was well known, leading military campaigns, defeating Samaria and Egyptian.

Sargon II, King of Assyria - One of the greatest of Assyrian kings. Shalmaneser IV had besieged Samaria for three years (2 Kings 17:3-6) but Sargon claimed the victory in 722 BCE.

Saul (King) - (SAWL) - The first king of a united Israel. The Spirit departed him when he sought advice from a witch. He committed suicide. Refer to 1 Sam 28:8; 31:3.

Scribe – A secretary or recorder for kings, priests, and prophets. Refer to 2 Sam 8:17.

Seir (SEE ur) – Father of seven sons and a descendant of Abraham through Esau's line. Refer to Gen 36:20, 21.

Semites (SEM ights) – An ancient reference to any people speaking any ancient Semitic language (includes Hebrew, Aramaic, etc).

Sennacherib (suh NAK uh rib) - Son of Sargon, king of Assyria. He invaded Judah, capturing forty-six towns, and 200,000 residents. He attacked Jerusalem, saying God was not powerful enough to save the city. The angel of the Lord killed 185,000 Assyrian solders forcing Sennacherib to return home. He later destroyed much of Babylon. He was killed by two of his sons. Refer to 2 Kings 18:17-19:37; 2 Chron 32:21).

Serah (SEE rah) – Asher's daughter. Refer to Gen 46:17.

Seraiah (sih RAY uh) – (1) A scribe in the reign of David (2 Sam 8:17); (2) A chief priest, son of Azariah during the period of Nebuchadnezzar (2 Kings 25:18-21; Jer 52:24-27); (3) A son of Asiel and father of Josibiah, ancestor of Jehu (1 Chron 4:35); (4) An ancestor of Ezra (Ezra 7:1).

Seraphim (SER uh fim) - An order of celestial beings, pictured in Isaiah's vision. Refer to Isa 6:2-7.

Seth (seth) – The third son of Seth and head of the line, which led to Jesus Christ. Refer to Gen 5:6-8; Luke 3:38.

Shaaph (shaef) – Son of Caleb by his concubine. Refer to 1 Chron 2:49.

Shabbethai (SHAB uh thigh) - A chief Levite of Jerusalem after the exile. An overseer of the temple interpreter of the law. Refer to Ezra 10:15; Neh 8:7, 11:16.

Shadrach (SHAD rak) – The name given to Hananiah, Daniel's companion. Refer to Dan 1:7; 3:12-30.

Shallum (SHAL uhm) – (1) The fifteenth King of Israel (Northern Kingdom) for one month, 772 BCE. The son of Jabesh (2 Kings 15:10); (2) The son of Josiah, king of Judah, also called Jehoahaz (2 Kings 23:30-34); (3) A grandson of Simeon (1 Chron 4:25).

Shalmaneser (SHALL muh NEE zur) – One of five rulers of Assyria with this name. Shalmaneser I restored Assyrian power. Shalmaneser IV was responsible for what we call the "ten lost tribes of Israel. Only Shalmaneser V is mentioned in the Bible (2 Kings 15:19).

Shamgar (SHAM gahr) – A son of Anath and third Judge of Israel. He delivered Israel with an ox-goad in battle. Refer to Judg 3:31.

Shammah (SHAM uh) - A son of Jesse and brother of David (1 Sam 16:9).

Shammua (sha MOO uh) - David's son by Bathsheba. Refer to 2 Sam 5:14; 1 Chron 3:5.

Shaphan SHAY fuhn) – (1) A scribe and secretary of King Josiah of Judah (2 Kings 22:8-14; Jer 26:24, 39:14); (2) The father of Ahikam who stood by Jeremiah saving his life (Jer 26:24).

Shaphat (SHAY fat) – The father of Elisha. Refer to 1 Kings 19:16; 2 Kings 3:11.

Sharezer (shuh REE zur) – A son of Sennacherib the king of Assyria. He and his brother murdered their father. Refer to 2 Kings 19:37; Isa 37:38.

Shaul (shahl) – (1) A son of Simeon the head of a tribal family (Gen 46:10; 1 Chron 4:24; Num 26:13); (2) A Levite descended from Korah (1 Chron 6:24).

Shavsha (SHAV shuh) - A scribe of David and Solomon. Refer to 1 Chron 18:16.

Shealtiel (shee AL tih uhl) – A son of Jeconiah, father of Zerubbabel. Ancestor of the family of Christ. Refer to 1 Chron 3:17; Ezra 3:2, 8.

Shear-jashub (sheer josh ub) – Isaiah's son. Refer to Isa 7:3.

Sheba (SHE buh) – (1) A grandson of Cush (Gen 10:7; 1 Chron 1:9); (2) A son of Joktan. His descendants were founders of the Kingdom of Sheba in Arabia.

Shebaniah (sheb uh NIGH uh) - A Levite who blew the trumpet when the ark was brought by David to Jerusalem. Refer to 1 Chron 15:24.

Sheber (SHE burr) – Caleb's son by his concubine Maacah. Refer to 1 Chron 2:48.

Shecaniah (shek uh NIGH uh) – (1) A descendant of David (1 Chron 3:21-22); (2) A descendant of Aaron during the time of David (1 Chron 24:1, 6, 11); (3) A son of Jahaziel who returned with Ezra from Babylon (Ezra 8:5).

Shechem (SHEC kem) – One of Gilead's sons, a descendant of Joseph. Refer to Num 26:31.

Sheerah (SHE ur ah) – Daughter of granddaughter of Ephraim. Refer to 1 Chron 7:24.

Shelemiah (sheh luh MITH uh) – (1) A porter of the tabernacle in David's time (1 Chron 26:14); (2) The father of one who helped build the wall of Jerusalem (Neh 3:30); (3) A priest appointed to distribute the tithes (Neh 13:13); (4) One sent to ask Baruch to read the roll of Jeremiah (Jer 36:14; (5) One ordered to arrest Baruch and Jeremiah (Jer 36:26).

Shelomith (shih LOE mith) – (1) A daughter of Zerubbabel (1 Chron 3:19); (2) A descendant of Eliezer the son of Moses. He was a temple treasurer in David's time (1 Chron 26:25-26); (3) A son or daughter of Rehoboam (2 Chron 11:20); (4) An ancestor of a family that returned from captivity with Ezra (Ezra 8:10).

People, Titles, Positions, Nations

Shem (shem)– The firstborn son of Noah; received a blessing from his father. He was the father of Arphaxad and the ancestor of Abraham and the family of Jesus. Refer to Gen 5:32; 9:23-37; Luke 3:36.

Shemaiah (shih MAY uh) – (1) A prophet in the reign of Rehoboam who directed him to stop fighting the Northern Kingdom (1 Kings 12:22-24); (2) A son of Joel (1 Chron 5:4); (3) A tabernacle gatekeeper in David's time (1 Chron 26:L6-7; (4) A Levite who assisted Nehemiah in building the wall of Jerusalem (Neh 11:15). At least twenty-five others with the same name in the OT (1 Chron 3:22; 15:8-11; Ezra 10:31; Neh 12:34).

Shemariah (shem uh RIGH uh) also called Shamariah – (1) A son of Rehoboam (2 Chron 11:19); (2) A warrior who joined David at Ziklag (1 Chron 12:5).

Shemer (SHE murr) – Owner of the hill of Samaria, which King Omri brought as the site of his capital city. Refer to 1 Kings 16:24.

Shephatiah (shef uh TIGH uh) – (1) A son of David born at Hebron (2 Sam 3:4); (2) The head of the tribe of Simeon (1 Chron 27:16); A son of Jehoshaphat of Judah (2 Chron 21:2).

Sherebiah (share ah BIAH) – (1) One who helped the people understand the law read by Ezra (Neh 8:7); (2) One of the leaders of the Levites who led the songs of praise and thanksgiving (Neh 12:24).

Shethar-bozenai (SHEE thahr BAHZ us nigh) – Persian official in a province west of the Euphrates River who helped in writing the letter to King Darius. Refer to Ezra 5:3, 6.

Sheshbazzar (shesh BAZ ur) - The prince of Judah who brought the golden vessels from Babylon and helped to lay the foundation of the second temple. Refer to Ezra 1:8 11; 5:14-16.

Sheva (SHEE vuh) – Caleb's son. Refer to 1 Chron 2:49.

Shimea (SHIM ih uh) – (1) David's brother and third son of Jesse (2 Sam 13:3); (2) A son of David by Bathsheba (1 Chron 3:5).

Shimei (SHIM ih uh) – (1) Solomon's purveyor in the territory of Benjamin (1 Kings 4:18); (2) A brother of King Zerubbabel (1 Chron 3:19); (3) A son of Gog (1 Chron 5:4); (4) A Levite in the time of Ezra who divorced his foreign wife (Ezra 10:38); (5) A brother of David and the father of Jonathan (2 Sam 21:21). At least twenty others with the same name in the OT (Zech 12:13; 1 Sam 16:9; 1 Kings 1:8; 1 Chron 23:9; Est 2:5). :

Shimron (SCHIM ron) – Issachar's son. Refer to Gen 46:13.

Shishak (SHIGH shak) - A king of Egypt, invaded Judah and Israel. He conquered many cities. Refer to 2 Chron 12:2-9; 1 Kings 14:25-26.

Shitrai (SHIT righ) – David's chief shepherd in charge of his flocks in Sharon. Refer to 1 Chron 27:29.

Shobal (SHOE bigh) – One of Judah's five sons. refer to 1 Chron 4:1-2.

Shuah (SHOO a) – One of the sons borne to Abraham by Keturah. Refer to Gen 25:2.

Shuni (SHOO nih) – one of Gad's sons. refer to Gen 46:16.

Shuthelah (SHOO thuh lah) – Ephraim's son, and an ancestor of Joshua. Refer to Num 26:35.

Sidon (SIGH dun) – Canaan's firstborn son. Refer to Gen 10:15.

Sihon (SIGH un) – The king of the Amorites when the Hebrews arrived in the Promised Land. Refer to Num 21:21.

Sisera (SIS ur uh) – A captain of King Jabin's forces when defeated by Barak. Refer to Judg 4-5.

Solomon (SAH luh muhn) - Last of David's sons by Bathsheba. Followed his father to the throne of Israel. Refer to 1 Kings 1:13-53; 2 Chron 1-9.

Soothsayer - One who claimed to be able to foretell future events. Refer to Dan 2:27.

T

Tahan (TAY han) – (1) Ephraim's son (Num 26:35); (2) Telah's son and a descendant of Ephraim (1 Chron 7:25).

Tahpenes (TAH puh neez) – Egyptian queen during the reigns of David and Solomon. Refer to 1 Kings 11:8-20.

Tahrea (tuh REE uh) – a descendant of King Saul. Refer to 1 Chron 8:35.

Tamar (TAY mar) – (1) The mother of Perez and Zarah (Gen 38:6-30); (2) The sister of Absalom (2 Sam 13).

Taphath (TAY fath) – Solomon's daughter and the wife of Ben-abinadab. Refer to 1 Kings 4:11.

Tebah (TEE buh) – son of Abraham's brother Nahor. Refer to Gen 22:24.

Telem (TEE lem) – One of the gatekeepers counseled by Ezra. Refer to Ezra 10:24.

Tema (TEE muh) – Son of Ishmael. Refer to Gen 25:15.

Taphath (TAY fath) – Solomon's daughter and the wife of Ben-abindab. Refer to 1 Kings 4:11.

Tappuah (TAP yoo uh) - A son of Hebron of the line of Caleb. Refer to 1 Chron 2:43.

Tebah (TEE buh) – son of Abraham's brother Nahor. Refer to Gen 22:24.

Teman (TEE muhn) - Son of Eliphaz, grandson of Essau. Refer to Gen 36:11.

Terah (TAIR uh) - Father of Abraham, from Ur, an idolater. Refer to Josh 24:2.

Tibni (TIBB nie) - Tibni is sometimes listed as sixth King of Israel (Northern Kingdom), rival king with Omri during a total of twelve years, set up idols of Baalism, 929-918 BCE.

Tiglath-pileser (TIG lath puh LEE zur) – He ruled Assyria and led them during a period of expansion and military greatness. Captured many of the towns of Israel. Refer to 2 Kings 15:19-20.

Tiglath-pileser II – A weak king of Assyria, powerless to prevent invasions. Refer to 2 Kings 17:6.

Tiglath-pileser III – The second Assyrian king who came in contact with the Israelites. Ahaz paid him tribute of silver and gold from the Temple. Refer to 2 Kings 16:8.

Tirhakah (tur HAY kuh) – Ethiopian king who marched north to fight the Assyrian army. Refer to 2 Kings 19:9; Isa 37:9.

Tobadonijah (tahb ad uh NIGH juh) – One of the Levites under Jehoshaphat who taught the law in the cities of Judah. Refer to 2 Chron 17:8.

Tobiah (toe BIGH uh) – Ammonite who opposed Nehemiah when he arrived in Jerusalem. Refer to Neh 2:10, 19.

Tobijah (toe BIGH juh) –Levite sent by King Jehoshaphat to teach the law in the cities of Judah. Refer to 2 Chron 17:8.

Togarmah (toe GAHR muh) – third son of Gomer, a descendant of Japheth. Refer to Gen 10:3.

Tola (TOE luh) – (1) A Judge of Israel after Abimelech (Judg10:1-2); (2) One of the sons of Issachar, among the descendants of Jacob who migrated to Egypt (Gen 46:13).

Tubal (TOO buhl) – A son of Japheth. Refer to Gen 10:2; 1 Chron 1:5.

Tubal-cain – Son of Lamech by his wife Zillah. The forger of all instruments of bronze and iron. Refer to Gen 4:22.

Twelve spies – Moses sent twelve men into the land of Canaan to gather information about its manpower, defenses, etc. Because of their lack of faith in God, the Hebrew people were forced to wander for forty additional years in the wilderness. Refer to Numbers cps 13-14.

U

Uri (YOU rye)– One of the Temple gatekeepers who obeyed Ezra's request. Refer to Ezra 10:24.

Uriah (yoo RIGH uh) – (1) One of David's mighty men, a Hittite, Husband of Bathsheba. He was killed when placed at the front of battle by David (2 Sam 23:39); (2) A priest in the time of Ezra (Ezra 8:33).

Uriel (YOU righ ehl) – Levite who officiated over the moving of the Ark to Jerusalem (1 Chron 15:5-11); (2) Grandfather of King Abijah of Judah (2 Chron 13:2).

Uthai (YOU thigh) – One who returned to Israel following the Exile. Refer to 1 Chron 9:4.

Uz (uhz) - A grandson of Shem. Refer to Gen 10:23; 1 Chron 1:17.

Uzza (UHZ uh) – (1) The owner of the garden where King Manasseh of Judah and his son, Amon were buried (2 Kings 21:18); (2) A descendant of Ehud (1 Chron 8:7); (3) the head of a family, some of whom returned with Zerubbabel (Ezra 2:49).

Uzzah (uz ZIGH uh) - He put forth his hand to steady the Ark on its way to Jerusalem and was struck dead. Refer to 2 Sam 6:3-8.

Uzzi (UHZ eye) – Descendant of Eliezer who was in the direct line of high priests, though he never served in thatt capacity. Refer to 1 Chron 6:5, 6.

Uzzia (you ZIGH ah) – One of David's mighty men. Refer to 1 Chron 11:44.

Uzziah (uz ZIGH uh) – A righteous King of Judah for fifty-two years, 810-758 BCE. Refer to 2 Chron 26:1-23.

Uzziel (uz ZEE al) – (1) A kinsman of Aaron (Lev 10:4); (2) The father of David's overseer (1 Chron 27:25); (3) A man of Judah who lived in Jerusalem after the captivity (Neh 11:4).

Vajezatha (vah JEZ ah thah) - One of the sons of Haman. Refer to Est 9:9.

Vashti (VASH tee) – The queen of the king of Persia, deposed because she flouted the king's command. Refer to Est 1:9-2:17.

Vophsi (VAHF sigh) – Man from Naphtali's tribe appointed to spy out the land of Canaan. Refer to Num 13:14.

Xerxes of Persia (ZURK sees) (see Ahasuerus) -

Zabad (ZAY bad) – (1) One of David's warriors (1 Chron 2:31-37); (2) One of the two assassins of King Joash of Judah (2 Chron 24:26); (3) The name of three Hebrews in the time of Ezra who were persuaded by Ezra to divorce their pagan wives (Ezra 10:27, 33, 43).

Zabbai (ZAB ay eye) - Father of Baruch. Refer to Neh 3:20.

Zabdi (ZAB die) - David's officer over the produce of the vineyards. Refer to 1 Chron 27:27.

Zaccur (ZACK coor) – One of the twelve spies sent into Canaan. Refer to Num 13:4.

Zachariah (zak uh RIGH uh) - King of Israel (Northern

People, Titles, Positions, Nations

Kingdom) for six months, 772 BCE.

Zadok (ZAY doc) – (1) He held the office of high priest when David became king of all Israel (2 Sam 8:17); (2) The father of Jerusha the wife of King Uzziah of Judah (2 Kings 15:33); (3) A priest who labored on the wall of Jerusalem (Neh 3:29).

Zalmon (ZAL muhn) - One of David's warriors. Refer to 2 Sam 23:28.

Zebadiah (zebb ah DIE AH) – (1) One whom allied with David at Ziklag (1 Chron 12:7); (2) One appointed by Jehoshaphat to teach the law to the people of Judah (2 Chron 17:8); (3) One who returned to Babylon with Ezra (Ezra 8:8).

Zebidah (zebb ah DIE ah) – Mother of Jehoiakim, king of Judah. Refer to 2 Kings 23:36.

Zebulun (ZEB yoo luhn) - The youngest of the sons of Jacob by Leah. Refer to Gen 30: 19-20.

Zechariah (zech uh RYE uh) – (1) The last king of the Jehur dynasty of Israel, son of Jeroboam II. He reigned six months, assassinated by Shallum (2 Kings 14:29; 25:20); (2) Uncle of Saul (1 Chron 9:37); (3) A Levite who played music when the Ark was brought to Jerusalem by David (1 Chron 15:18-20; 16:5); (4) A son of Jehoiada a high priest (2 Chron 24:20-22). At least thirty others with the same name in the OT (2 Kings 18:2; 1 Chron 9:37; 2 Chron 29:1; Neh 11:4; Isa 8:2.

Zedekiah (zed uh KI uh) - King of Judah for eleven years, 597-586 BCE. He was the last King of Judah. His reign was evil.

Zephaniah (ZEF uh NI uh) – (1) An ancestor of Samuel (1 Chron 6:36-38); (2) One of Jeremiah's loyal friends who served as a messenger (Jer 21:1; 29:25, 29); (3) A Prophet living at the time of King Josiah (Zeph 1:1).

Zerubbabel (zuh RUHB uh buhl) - One who with the high priest, Jeshua, led the first group of Jewish exiles from captivity in Babylon to Jerusalem. He was a descendant of David in the direct line to Jesus. He was the prime builder of the Second Temple referred to as "Zerubbabel's Temple." Refer to Ezra 2:1-2; Hag 2:21.

Ziba (zie BAH) - A servant of King Saul, had a large family. Brought Jonathan's crippled son, Mephibosheth, to David. Refer to 2 Sam 9:9-12.

Zilpah (zill PAH) - A Syrian given by Laban to his daughter Leah as an attendant. Mother of Gad and Asher. Refer to Gen 29:24; 30:9-13.

Zimri (ZIMM rye) - Fifth King of Israel (Northern Kingdom), seven days (shortest of Israel dynasties), 929 BCE. Refer to 1 Kings 16:8-18.

Zipporah (zip POH ruh) - Daughter of Jethro, priest of Midian, who married Moses. Refer to Ex 2:21.

Zophar (ZOH far) - One of the "friends" who debated with Job. Refer to Job 2:11; 20:1; 42:9.

BOOK OF OLD TESTAMENT BIBLE LITERACY

THREE

COLLECTION/DICTIONARY of Places in the Old Testament or in Bible History

Abana River (AB ah nah) – A river of Syria that flowed through the city of Damascus. Refer to 2 Kings 5:12.

Abarim (AB ah rim) – A mountainous area east of the Jordan and Dead Sea. One of the encampments of the Israelites. Refer to Num 21:11.

Abel-meholah (A bell me HOE lah) - The home of Elisha, on the west side of the Jordan. Refer to Judg 7:22; 1 Kings 19:16.

Abel-shittim (A bell SHIT tihm) - Also called Shittim. The final stopping place of the Israelites just before crossing the Jordan. Refer to Num 25:1; Josh 2:1.

Achor (A kore) - A valley south of Jericho on the northern boundary of Judah. Refer to Josh 7:24-26; 15:7.

Accad (ACK add) – See Akkad. One of four cities built by Nimrod in the land of Shinar, which were "the beginning of his kingdom." Refer to Gen 10:10.

Adadah (ADD a dah) - A town in the southern part of Judah. Refer to Josh 15:22.

Addan (ADD un) - A place in Babylonia where certain persons lived before they returned to Israel. Refer to Ezra 2:59.

Adoraim (ad oh RAY em) - A city of Judah fortified and rebuilt by Rehoboam, son of Solomon. Southwest of Hebron. Refer to 2 Chron 11:9.

Ahava (a HAH vuh) - The river which was a gathering point for those who returned to Jerusalem with Ezra on the second expedition. Refer to Ezra 8:15.

Ahlab (A lub) - A town of the tribe of Asher from which the Canaanites were not expelled. Refer to Judg 1:31.

Ai (A eye) - A town east of Bethel where Joshua was defeated because of sin in his camp. Refer to Josh 7:2; 8:11.

Aijalon (A jah lon) - A valley over which the moon stood still at the command of Joshua. Refer to Josh 10:12.

Akkad (ACK kad) One of the four towns in Shinar which formed the kingdom of Nimrod. Refer to Gen 10:10. Formed by Sargon the Great and located near modern Baghdad.

Alexandria Egypt (al ex AN dree uh) - Named after Alexander the Great who founded it in 332 BCE. It was here that the Hebrew Scriptures were translated into Greek, called the Septuagint.

Alush (A luhsh) - A place between Egypt and Sinai where the Israelites camped during the wanderings. Refer to Num 33:13-14.

Amarna (a MAR nuh) - A city in Egypt where important archeological discoveries of clay tables of letters of Canaanite

Places in the Old Testament or Bible History

Kings to Egyptians. This was during the Israelite invasion of Canaan under Joshua.

Anathoth (AN uh thoth) – A village about three miles north of Jerusalem, the birthplace of the prophet Jeremiah. Refer to Jer 1:1.

Aphek (A fek) – (1) A city of the Canaanites (Josh 12:18); (2) A city of Asher near Sidon (Josh 19:30); (3) A place where the Philistines captured the Ark (1 Sam 4:1); (4) A city east of the Sea of Galilee (1 Kings 20:26).

Ar (R) – A chief city of Moab in the valley of Arnon. Refer to Num 21:15; Deut 2:18.

Arab (A rab) - A town of Judah in the hill country. Refer to Josh 15:52.

Arabah (AIR ah bah) The valley on both sides of the Jordan River, from Mount Herman to the Red Sea. Refer to Josh 18:18.

Arad (A rad) – A city in the southern wilderness of Judah whose inhabitants fought against the Israelites at Mount Hor. Joshua defeated them. Refer to Josh 12:14.

Ararat, Mount (AIR uh rat) - Usually identified as the mountain of Noah, 17,000 feet above sea level.

Argob (AR gob) – a district included in Solomon's' kingdom. Refer to 1 Kings 4:13.

Armageddon (are muh GED un) - The great plain of Megiddo lying between the "Galilean hills" and the mountains of Israel. It is notable as the location of many battles. Refer to Judg 5:19.

Arnon River (R nahn) – A swift river that runs through the mountains of Transjordan and empties into the Dead Sea. Refer to Num 21:24.

Arumah (a ROO mah) - A town near Shechem, once the residence of Abimelech. Refer to Judg 9:41.

Ashdod (ASH dodd) - One of five Philistine cities, this one twenty miles from Gaza. The captured Ark of the Covenant was placed here in the temple of Dagon. Refer to Josh 13:3; 1 Sam 5:1-8.

Ashkelon (ASH kah lawn) - One of the five cities of the Philistines; located on the Mediterranean north of Gaza. Refer to Josh 13:3; Judg 1:18.

Ashtaroth (ASH tah rahth) –The capital of King Og of the remnant of the giants. Refer to Josh 12:4; 13:12.

Asia Minor (AY sha) - The peninsula, which is modern Turkey.

Assyria (uh SEER ee uh) - The land lying on the Tigris between Padanaram, Babylon, Armenia, and Media. The Assyrians originated in Babylon (Gen 10:11); Under Shalmanesar, they invaded Israel and carried many captive into Assyria, 722 BCE. (see the author's book, *The Chronological History of the Bible Lands.*

Ava (AY vah) – An Assyrian city whose citizens settled in

B

Baal-Hazor (BAY uhl HAY zor) – the place where Amnpn was murdered by Absalom's servants concerning the rape of Tamar. Refer to 1 Sam 13: 14, 29.

Baal-perazim (BAY uhl PER uh zem) – a place in Palestine where David defeated the Philistines. Refer to 2 Sam 5:18-20.

Baale (BAY uh leh) - A town of Judah from which David brought the ark to Jerusalem. Refer to Josh 15:9-10; 2 Sam 6:2.

Babel (BAY bull) - Location of the brick tower built in the plain of Shinar. It brought confusion and dispersion. Refer go Gen 11:4-9.

Babylon (BABB uh lawn) - Capital city of the Babylonian empire. Once the capital of Assyria. Reached great splendor under Nebuchadnezzar. Refer to Gen 10:10; Isa 14:1-3. Jer 51:41.

Babylonia – a powerful nation in Mesopotamia that carried the Jewish people into exile. Refer to Jer 25:26; Isa 11:11.

Bashan (BAY shun) - A district east of the Jordan extending from Gilead to Hermon. Taken when Israel crossed the Jordan. Assigned to the tribe of Manasseh. Refer to Deut 3:10, 13, 14.

Beer (Beer) – A place in the land of Moab where the Israelites camped during their wanderings. Refer to Num 21:16-18.

Beersheba (beer SHE buh) - The ancient capital in the Negev Desert, home of Abraham. Refer to Gen 28:10.

Beth anath (beth AY nath) - A fortified city of Naphtali from which the Israelites did not drive the Canaanites. Refer to Josh 19:35, 38; Judg 1:33.

Beth Car (beth CAR) - The place where the Philistines were driven after their defeat at Ebenezer. Refer to 1 Sam 7:11.

Beth-diblathaim (beth dib lah THAY em) - A city of Moab denounced by Jeremiah. Refer to Jer 48:21-22.

Bethel (BETH uhl) – An ancient city west of Ai where Abraham pitched his tent. (Gen 13 :3). The Canaanites called it Luz, Jacob named it Bethel (Gen 28:19; 35:1-15).

Bethlehem (BETH le hem) – The birthplace of Jesus Christ, five miles south of Jerusalem. David was anointed as Saul's successor in this city. Refer to 1 Sam 16:1, 13; Mic 5:2.

Beth-horon (beth HOE run) – Twin towns in the territory of Ephraim, important military outposts. Refer to 2 Chron 8:5.

Beth-peor (beth PEA oar) - A town of the tribe of Reuben on the east side of Jordan. Moses

Places in the Old Testament or Bible History

was buried near here. Refer to Deut 3:29; 34:6; Josh 13:20.

Beth-shan (BETH shan) – A philistine city where King Saul's corpse was displayed. Refer to 1 Sam 31:10-13.

Beth-shemesh (beth SHEH mesh) – A border town between Judah and Dan, taken by the Philistines. Refer to 1 Sam 6:1-7:2.

Beth-zur (BETH zur) - A town in the hill country of Judah fortified by Rehoboam. Following the return from Babylon, the people from Bethzur responded to Nehemiah and assisted in the rebuilding of the wall of Jerusalem. Refer to Josh 15:58; 2 Chron 11:7; Neh 3:16.

Beulah (BUE luh) - A symbolic name for the land of Israel. Refer to Isa 62:4.

Bezer (BEE zur) – A fortified city in the territory of Reuben designated as one of the six cities of refuge. Refer to Josh 20:8.

Bozrah (BAHZ ruh) – The ancient capital city of Edom. Refer to Isa 63:1.

#

Calneh (KAL neh) – An ancient city built in Mesopotamia by Nimrod. Refer to Gen 10:9-10.

Canaan, Land of (KAY nuhn) - The country between the Jordan River and the Mediterranean Sea, given by God to the Israelites. Refer to Ex 6:4; Zech 2:13.

Carchemish(KARR kem ish) – a city west of the Euphrates river in north Mesopotamia. The ancient capital of the Hittites, later a fortified city of the Assyrians. Refer to 2 Chron 35:20; Jer 46:2.

Carmel, Mount (CAR mull) - A mountain in northern Israel where the Prophet Elijah demonstrated the power of God in an encounter with the priests of Baal. Refer to 1 Kings 18:17-39; 1 Sam 15:12.

Chaldea (cal DEE uh) - The wide plain formed by the deposits of the Tigris and Euphrates Rivers. Refer to Jer 50:10; Ezek 1:3.

Chariot Cities – The cities where Solomon stored his chariots and forces. Refer to 1 Kings 9:19.

Chebar (KEE bahr) – A canal of Babylonia where Jewish captives settled during the Exile. Refer to Ezek1:3.

Cherith (KEE rith) – A brook where the prophet Elijah hid and was fed by ravens. Refer to 1 Kings 17:3-5.

Chinnereth or Gennesaret (CHIN uh reth) - Fresh water lake fed by the Jordan river. The early name of the Sea of Galilee.

Cities of Refuge – Six cities offering safety to those committing an involuntary crime. Refer to Num 35:9-14; Ex 21:13.

City of David – A title applied to Bethlehem and Jerusalem because of David's close association with these cities. Refer to Neh 3:15.

Cush (KOOSH) - Land bordering the Gihon River, named after the son of Ham. Refer to Gen 2:10-14.

Cuth (kooth) – A city of district of Babylonia that provided for those from the Northern Kingdom. Refer to 2 Kings 17:30.

D

Damascus (duh MASS cuss) - The oldest continually inhabited city in the world. The current capital of Syria. It was founded by Uz, grandson of Shem (Gen 5:32; 10:21).

Dan - The northernmost city of Israel. Refer to Judg 18:29.

David, city of - David captured the small city of Jerusalem (2 Sam 5:6-9). David, Solomon and many later kings were buried there (1 Kings 2:10, 11; 14:31; 25:8, 24).

Dead Sea - Called by this name in the early 2nd century CE. Earlier called the Salt Sea.

Den of Lions – A deep cavern where lions were kept by Persian kings. Refer to Dan 6:16-24.

Dor (dor) - A Canaanite town on the Mediterranean Sea, north of Caesarea. Joshua defeated its king. Refer to Josh 11:2; 12:23.

Dothan (DOE thun) - A town north of Samaria where Joseph was cast into a pit. Refer to Gen 37:17; 2 Kings 6:13.

Dura (DEW ruh) – A plain in Babylonia where the golden image of King Nebuchadnezzar was set up. Refer to Dan 3:1.

E

Ebal, Mount – A Mountain in Samaria known as the "Mount of Cursing." Refer to Deut 27:13-26.

Ebenezer (ebb un EE zur) – site of Israel's defeat by the Philistines. Refer to 1 Sam 5:1.

Eden, Garden of (EE den) - Eden (EE den) – The name of the first home of Adam and Eve. Possibly located between the two rivers of Tigris and Euphrates in Mesopotamia. Refer to Gen 2:10-14.

Edom (EE duhm) - The territory of the descendants of Esau. Refer to Gen 32:3-19.

Eglon (EGG lon) – An Amorite city, one of the five allied cities that attacked Gibeon. It was later conquered by Joshua. Refer to Josh 10:3.

Egypt (EE jipped) - Northeastern country of Africa. Ps 105:23 calls it "the land of Ham." Israelites were in bondage in Egypt. It is still noted for the Nile River. Refer to Ex 1-14.

Ekron (ECK ron) - One of the five chief cities of the Philistines. The ark was sent here and then returned to Israel. Refer to 1 Sam 5:10; 6:16-17.

Elah Valley (EE lah) – A valley in Judah where David Killed

Places in the Old Testament or Bible History

Goliath. Refer to 1 Sam 17:2; 21:9.

Elam (EE luhm) - A country of western Asia. It is now part of Iran.

Elath (EE lath) - A town on the northeast arm of the Red Sea. The Israelites passed it in their forty-year wanderings. Refer to Deut 2:8.

Eloth (E luth) – An Edominte seaport captured by David. Refer to 1 Kings 9:16.

Elkosh (EL kosh) - The residence and probably birthplace of the Prophet Nahum. Refer to Nah 1:1.

Endor (EN dorr) - A town in Manasseh where the witch lived whom Saul consulted the night before his death. Refer to 1 Sam 28:7.

En-gedi (en GED dee) – A town on the western shore of the Dead Sea. Refer to 1 Sam 23:29.

Ephes Dammin (EE fez DAM im) - A place in Judah where the Philistines were encamped when David killed Goliath. Refer to 1 Sam 17:1.

Ephraim (EE fray im) - Joseph's younger son, born in Egypt. Refer to Gen 41:45-52.

Ephraim, Tribe of (EE freh em) – The descendants of Ephraim who were one of the twelve tribes of Israel. There were an influential force in Israel, being commended by Gideon. Refer to Josh 16:5-10; Judg 8:2.

Ephrath (EE frath) - A town by which Bethlehem was originally known. Rachel was buried here. Refer to Gen 35:19; 48:7; Ruth 4:11.

Eridu (AIR ih doo) – The oldest city in ancient Mesopotamia.

Esek (EE seek) – A well in the valley of Gerar over which the servants of Isaac and Abimelech quarreled. Refer to Gen 26:20.

Eshcol (ESH cuhl) - A valley near Hebron renowned for its great clusters of grapes. The twelve spies brought a cluster of grapes from here. Refer to Num 13:24.

Eshtaol (ESH tuh ole) - A town between Judah and Dan. Samson was born near here. Refer to Judg 13:24-25.

Ethiopia (EEth ee O pee uh) - A territory in the upper Nile Valley called Cush by the Hebrews (2 Chron 16:8).

Euphrates River (you FRAY tees) - A great river, which rises in northeast Turkey and flows to the Persian Gulf, some 1,780 miles. Refer to Gen 15:18; 2 Sam 8:3.

Ezion-gaber (EE zih on GHEE bur) – A place on the coast of the Red Sea where the Israelites camped during the wilderness wandering. Refer to 1 Kings 9:26.

Fertile Crescent - A crescent-shaped area of fertile land in the Middle East extending from the eastern Mediterranean coast through the valley of the Tigris and Euphrates Rivers to the Persian Gulf.

Fish Gate – A gate in the wall of Jerusalem. Refer to Neh 3:3.

Gaash, Mount (GAY ash) – A mountain in the hill ocountry of Ephraim where Joshua was buried. Refer to Josh 24:30.

Garrison – A fortified military post. Refer to 2 Sam 23:14.

Gath (gath) - A city of the Philistines and home of large stature men. One of these men was Goliath. Refer to Josh 13:3; 1 Sam 17:4; 1 Chron 18:1.

Gath-hepher (gath HEE fur) – The home of Jonah. Refer to 2 Kings 14:25.

Gaza (GAH zah) - One of the five main cities of the Philistines, located on the Mediterranean Sea. Samson's career was mostly in this location. Refer to Judg 16:23-31; 1 Sam 6:17.

Gehenna (guh HEN uh) - A valley south of Jerusalem notorious as a place of child sacrifice to Molech. King Josiah wiped out this dreadful practice. It later became a garbage dump. Refer to 2 Chron 28:3; 33:6; 2 Kings 23:10.

Gerar (GEE rar) – An ancient wealthy Philistine city in southern Palestine. During a famine, Abraham and his wife Sarah journeyed to Gerar. Refer to Gen 10:19; 20:1.

Gerizim, Mount (GEH ruh zim) - A mountain in the district of Samaria, southwest of Mount Ebal.

Gerzites (GEHZ rites) - A Canaanite nation raided by David during the time he was running from Saul. Refer to 1 Sam 27:8.

Gezer (GEEZ ur) – An ancient Canaanite city west of Jerusalem that was conquered by Joshua. Refer to Josh 10:33; 12:12.

Gibeah (GIB ee uh) – A city belonging to Benjamin. The birthplace of Saul and capital of his kingdom. Refer to Judg19:14; 1 Sam 14:16; 15:34.

Gibeath Elohim (GIB ee ath el oh HEEM) - The hill where Samuel told Saul that the Spirit of the Lord would come upon him. Refer to 1 Sam 10:5.

Gibeon (GIB ee uhn) - The people of Gibeon made an agreement with Joshua to escape being destroyed. Refer to Josh 9:3-15.

Gihon (GUY Hahn) - One of the rivers of Eden. Refer to Gen 2:13.

Gilboa, Mount (gill BOW ah) - A mountain near the city of Jezreel where the forces of Israel under Saul were defeated by the Philistines. Saul and his sons died here. Refer to 1 Sam 31:1; 2 Sam 1:6.

Gilead (GILL ee uhd) - The mountainous region east of the Jordan. Refer to Gen 31:21, 25.

Gilgal (GILL gal) - The first camp of the Israelites after they

Places in the Old Testament or Bible History

crossed the Jordan. Refer to Josh 4:19-20; 5:9-10.

Golan (GO lawn) - A city in an area of ancient Bashan. One of the Cities of Refuge. Refer to Deut 4:43; Josh 21:27.

Gomorrah (guh MORE uh) - One of the cities destroyed by fire from heaven. Refer to Gen 19:23-29.

Goshen (GO shun) - The district in Egypt in which the Israelites lived prior to their exodus.

Gozan (GOE zan) – A town or river of Mesopotamia to where the people of the Northern Kingdom were deported. Refer to 2 Kings 18:11.

Hades (HAY deez) – the Greek word for hell. See Sheol. See Hell.

Halah (HAY luh) - A place in Assyria to which Israelite captives were deported after the fall of Samaria. Refer to 2 Kings 17:6.

Hamath (HAY math) – a Hittite city north of Damascus. Refer to Josh 13:5.

Hara (HAIR uh) – A site in Assyria where some of the Northern Kingdom captives were settled. Refer to 1 Chron 5:26.

Haran (HAIR uhn) - A city of Mesopotamia in which Abraham settled after leaving Ur. Refer to Gen 28:10; 29:4.

Harod, Spring of – A spring near the mountains of Gilboa by which Gideon and his soldiers camped before they defeated the Midianites. Refer to Judg 7:1.

Hazeroth (HAH zuh rahth) - A place in the wilderness where the Israelites camped after leaving Sinai. Refer to Num 11:35; Deut 1:1.

Hazor (HAH zohr) - The capital of the Canaanites in the northern part of Palestine. It was destroyed by Joshua. Refer to Josh 11:1-13; 19:36.

Hebron (HEE bruhn) - A town in the hill country of Judah, the oldest town of Palestine. Refer to Gen 13:18; Num 13:22.

Hell – The place of eternal torment reserved for unbelievers. A Hebrew word *Sheol*. The Greek word *Hades*.

Hena (HEN uh) - A town which fell to the Assyrians. Refer to 2 Kings 18:34; Isa 37:13.

Hermon, Mount (HUR mon) – Located in the territory taken by the Israelites from the Amorites. The high mountain on which Christ was transfigured. Refer to Deut 3:8; Josh 11:3, 17.

Hiddekel (HID uh kel) - One of the four rivers of Eden. Refer to Gen 2:14.

High Places - Altars and temples, originally built on high ground. Refer to Gen 12:8; Judg 6:25; Isa 65:7.

Hinnom, Valley of (HIN ahm) - Horrible rites including human sacrifices and burning children were performed here. Refer to 1 Kings 11:7; Lev 18:21.

Hor, Mount (hoer) - The mountain near Petra where Aaron died. Refer to Num 20:25-29.

Horeb (HOHR eb) - Alternate name for Sinai. Refer to Ex 3:1.

Horse Gate – A gate in the old wall of Jerusalem. Refer to Neh 3:28.

I

Idumea (id you ME uh) - (see Edom)

Israel (IZ ray el) – The land given to the Hebrews. At various times in history, it was under the domination of Persia, Syria, Egypt and others.

Iye-abarim (igh ee AH buh rim) - One of the encampments of the Israelites on the border of Moab. Refer to Num 21:11; 33:44.

J

Jabbok River (JAB bock) - A stream flowing west through the mountains of Gilead. Refer to Josh 12:2.

Jabesh-Gilead (JAY besh GIL ih add) – A city of Gilead, south of the Sea of Galilee. Saul defended this city. Refer to 1 Sam 11:1-11.

Jabneel – A city near Mt. Baalah, close to the Mediterranean Sea, thirteen miles south of Joppa. Refer to Josh 15:11; 2 Chron 26:6.

Jacob's Well – Although unknown as to being dug by Jacob, he did purchase the land. Refer to Gen 33:19; Josh 24:32.

Jahaz (JAY haz) - The place in the plain of Moab where the Israelites defeated the Amorites. Refer to Num 21:23; Deut 2:32.

Jazer (JAY zur) - A city of Gilead east of the Jordan River from which the Amorites were driven by the Israelites. Refer to 2 Sam 24:5; Num 21:32.

Jearim, Mount (JEE uh rim) - A mountain marking the northern boundary of Judah. Refer to Josh 15:10.

Jebus (JEE buhs) - A name for Jerusalem in use when the city was in possession of the Jebusites. Refer to Josh 15:63; Judg 19:10.

Jehoshaphat, Valley of (juh HAH shuh fat) - The valley between Jerusalem and Mount of Olives. Also called the valley of the Kidron and the valley of Decision.

Jericho (JERR uh koh) – An ancient city of Canaan, west of the Jordan River. It was fortified, but conquered by Joshua. Refer to Josh 6:1; 1 Kings 16:34.

Jehovah-Shammah (jih HOE vuh Shah mah) – The name of a city of the future envisioned by Ezekiel. Refer to Ezek 48:35.

Jerusalem (jih ROO suh lem) - Called "Salem" in Abraham's

Places in the Old Testament or Bible History

day, later captured by David, became the worship center and capital of Israel.

Jezreel (JEZ reel) – (1) A town of the district of Judah (Josh 15:56); (2) A town in the territory of Issachar near Mount Gilboa. The Israelites camped here in Saul's last battle with the Philistines (1 Sam 29:1).

Jezreel Valley (JEZ reel) – The valley that separates Samaria from Galilee. A major corridor through the rugged Palestinian hills, and a crossroads of two major ancient routes.

Jokmeam (JAHK mee uhm) - A town south of Hebron in the mountain region of Judah. Refer to Josh 15:56.

Jokneam (JAHK nee uhm) - A city of the border of the territory of Zebulun. Refer to Josh 12:22.

Joktheel (JAHK thih uhl) - A town in the lowlands of Judah. Refer to Josh 15:33, 38.

Joppa (JOP uh) - A town and shipping center on the Mediterranean cost in the area of Dan. Refer to Josh 19:46-47.

Jordan River (JOR dun) – The main river of Palestine, enlarging into the Sea of Galilee, and emptying into the Dead Sea. Refer to Gen 13:10; Josh 2:7; 2 Sam 10:17.

Judea (joo DEE uh) - The Greek and Roman name for the land which was once the kingdom of Judah.

K

Kadesh-Barnea (KAY desh bar NEE uh) - An ancient town located in the wilderness of Zin, where the Israelites were to enter the Promised Land. However, fear prevented the entrance. Refer to Num 13:3, 26; 27:14.

Keilah (kee EYE luh) - A town of Judah delivered from the Philistines by David. Refer to Josh 15:44; 1 Chron 4:19.

Kerioth (KER ih ahth) - A border town in the south of Judah, quite possibly the birthplace of Judas Iscariot.

Kidron Valley (KID run) - A location between Jerusalem and the Mount of Olives. It must be crossed in order to go from Jerusalem to Bethany and Jericho. Refer to 2 Sam 15:23.

Kirjath Jearim (KIR jath JEE uh rim) - A town of the Gibeonites on the boundary between Judah and Benjamin. It fell to Judah. The ark remained here twenty years after the Philistines sent it back to the Israelites. Refer to Josh 9:71; 1 Sam 6:19-7:2.

Kish – Ancient city in Sumer, Mesopotamia

Kishon River (KISH on) - A river of Palestine, next to the Jordan in importance. The river empties into the Mediterranean. Refer to Judg 5:19-21; Ps 83:9.

L

Lachish (LAY kish) - A city in Judah which was taken by Joshua. King Amaziah of Judah fled to this city and was slain. It was besieged by Sennacherib and Nebuchadnezzar. Refer to Josh 10:3-35; 2 Kings 14:19; 2 Kings 18:14.

Laish (LAY ish) - A city north of Palestine given to the tribe of Dan and renamed Dan. Refer to Josh 19:47; Judg 18:7-29.

Lebanon (LEB uh nuhn) - A mountain range along the northwestern boundary of the Promised Land. Refer to Deut 11:24; Josh 1:4; 13:5.

Lehi (LEE hi) - A place in Judah where Samson slew one thousand Philistines. Refer to Judg 15:9, 14, 16.

Levitical Cities — Forty-eight cities assigned to the tribe of Levi instead of one specific territory. Refer to Num 35:2-7.

Libya (LIB ih uh) - The African nation west of Egypt. Also called Phut in Ezek 27:10. Refer to Ezek30:5; Acts 2:10.

Lo Debar (low DEE bahr) - Probably the same as Debir, a town east of the Jo9rdan River. Refer to Josh 13:26; 2 Sam 9:4-5.

Lowland - The low geographical area between Philistia and the Mediterranean Sea. Refer to 1 Kings 10:27.

Luz (LUHZ) - An ancient town of the Canaanites, which was later, called Bethel. Refer to Gen 28:19; 35:6; Josh 18:13. See Bethel.

Lydia (LID ih uh) - A province of Asia Minor (modern Turkey) on the Mediterranean Sea. Its fertile land produced figs, grain, and olives. Ezekiel mentioned them as "men of war." Refer to Ezek 27:10.

M

Machpelah (mahk PEE lah) - A field purchase by Abraham. He made a burial place for his wife, Sarah. Also buried here were Abraham, Isaac, Rebekah, Jacob, and Leah. Refer to Gen 13:18; 23:9; 25:9-19; 35:29.

Magog (MAY gahg) - A country of which Gog was the prince. A northern country, hostile to Israel. They were skilled horsemen and experts in warfare. Associated with the final apocalyptic encounter at the end of this age. Refer to Ezek 38:2, 15.

Mahanaim (may huh NAY im) - A place east of the Jordan where Jacob was met by angels. Refer to Gen 32:2.

Mamre (MAM ree) - A town of Hebron where Abraham made a covenant with Lot. Refer to Gen 13:6.

Marah (MARR uh) - A place in the wilderness where the Israelites found springs of bitter water. Refer to Ex 15:23.

Masada (muh SAH duh) – An ancient fortification in southern Israel situated on top of an isolated rock plateau.

Mediterranean Sea (MED uh tur RAIN ee uhn) – A large sea

Places in the Old Testament or Bible History

bordered by many important nations of the ancient world including Palestine. Called "the Great Sea," the Western Sea," and "the Sea of the Philistines" in the Bible. Refer to Num 34:6; Deut 34:2; Ex 23:31.

Megiddo (mih GIDD oh) - A walled city in Palestine. All major traffic went through the city. A military stronghold where many major battles were fought.

Memphis, Egypt (MEM fuss) - The capital of Egypt, built by Menes the first king of Egyptian history.

Mesha (ME shuh) – A boundary of the territory in Arabia. Refer to Gen 10:30.

Meribah (MEHR ih bah) - Two different places where water came from a rock to satisfy the thirsty Israelites. Refer to Ex 17:1-7; Num 20:2-13; Deut 32:51.

Mesopotamia (MESS uh puh TAY me uh) - The country between the Tigris and Euphrates rivers. See the author's book *The Chronological History of the Bible Lands* for a detailed view of ancient Mesopotamia. Refer to Gen 24:10; Judg 3:8-10; Acts 2:9.

Michmash (MICK mash) – A city of Benjamin northeast of Jerusalem. It figured prominently in the early history of Saul's reign. Refer to 1 Sam 13:2.

Midian (MID ee uhn) – The land east of the Jordan River inhabited by the descendants of Midian.

Migdol (MIG dahl) - A frontier fortress in Egypt on the route the Israelites traveled during the exodus. Refer to Ex 14:2; Num 33:7.

Millo (MILL oh) – (1) A stronghold at Shechem (Judg 9:6, 20); (2) A fortress tower built by David near Jerusalem (2 Sam 5:9).

Mizpah (MIZ puh) - Territory inhabited by Hivites. They were defeated by Joshua. Refer to Josh 11:3.

Moab (MO ab) - The land on the east side of the Dead Sea. God placed Judgment upon Moab because of their idolatry.

Modin – The hometown of the Maccabean family.

Moreh (MORE uh) - The first resting place of Abram after entering Canaan. Refer to Gen 12:6.

Moriah (mo RYE uh) - A mountain peak in Jerusalem where Abram took Isaac to be sacrificed. It was also the site of Solomon's Temple. Refer to Gen 22:2; 2 Sam 24:18.

Mosera (moh SEE ruh) – A place in the wilderness where the Israelites camped on their way to Canaan. Refer to Deut 10:6.

Naioth (NAY oth) – A place in Ramah where David fled from King Saul and where Samuel lived. Refer to 1 Sam 19:18-20.

Nebo (NEE boh) - A town of the Moabites near Mount Nebo. Refer to Deut 32:49; Num 32:3.

Negev (NEG ev) – A term used for the southern desert of Judah. Abraham journeyed in the Negev. The twelve spies went up by the way of the Negev. Refer to Gen 12:9; Num 13:17, 22.

Netophah (neh TOE fuh) - A town of Judah near Bethlehem where a number of people returned from Babylon with Zerubbabel. Refer to Ezra 2:22; Neh 7:26.

Nile River (NI uhl) - The great river of Egypt, worshipped as a god. The name is not mentioned in scripture, however alluded to as "the river." Refer to Gen 12:1; Ex 2:3.

Nineveh (NIN uh vuh) – The ancient capital of Assyria, founded by Nimrod. It was captured by the Medes. Refer to Gen 10:11; Jonah 3:5-10.

No (Thebes) – An Egyptian city on both sides of the Nile River, capital of Upper Egypt, destroyed in 81 BCE.

Nob (knob) - A Levitical city near Jerusalem where David fled to escape King Saul. Refer to Isa 10:32; 1 Sam 21:1-6.

Nod (nahd) - The land east of the Garden of Eden, to which Cain fled after he murdered his brother. Refer to Gen 4:16.

Northern Kingdom of Israel – The ten tribes who broke away from the united kingdom of Solomon. They retained the name of Israel.

Olives, Mount of - A hill consisting of a series of four peaks located east of Jerusalem. It was once thickly wooded with olive trees (Neh 8:15). David fled here, from Absalom (2 Sam 15:11). Also, refer to Zech 14:4.

Ophir (OH fur) – A region from which David and Solomon obtained gold. Its exact location remains a mystery. Refer to 1 Kings 9:28; 1 Chron 29:4.

Orontes (oh RAHN tez) – The major river of Syria. Refer to 2 Kings 23:33.

Padan-Aram (PAD uhn AH rem) - The country lying to the northeast of Palestine. Haran was located in Padan-aram. Refer to Gen 11:31; 24:10; 28:2, 5.

Palestine (PAL ess tyne) – The land promised by God to Abraham and his descendants. The Hebrew people conquered and lived here. Refer to 1 Sam 13:19.

Paran (PAY ran) - A wilderness between Sinai and Canaan where the Israelites wandered for 38 years. Refer to Gen 21:21; Num 10:12; 12:16.

Places in the Old Testament or Bible History

Pas Dammin (pass DAM mim) - A place where David's mighty men defeated the Philistines. Refer to 1 Chron 11:13-14.

Pathros (PATH rahs) - The name of upper Egypt (southern Egypt) where some Jews moved after the fall of Judah. Refer to Isa 11:11; Jer 44:1, 2.

Peniel (pen NI el) – A place where Jacob wrestled with an angel. Refer to Gen 32:30; Judg 8:17; 1 Kings 12:25.

Peor (PEE ohr) - The mountain in Moab to which Balak took Balaam. Refer to Num 23:28.

Persia (PURR zhuh) - Originally the country around the head of the Persian Gulf. It became a great empire, including all western Asia and parts of Europe and Africa. It was conquered by Alexander the Great. Refer to Ezek 38:5; 2 Chron 36:20-23.

Pethor (PEE thohr) – A town in northern Mesopotamia near the Euphrates River. Refer to Num 22:5-7.

Petra (PET ruh) - A unique red rock city located south of the Dead Sea. Many buildings were carved into the huge red rock cliffs.

Phenice (fuh NIH seh) – A Mediterranean coastal region including Tyre and Sidon. Refer to 2 Sam 5:11.

Philistia (fih LIST ih uh) - A coastal country in southwestern Palestine. Refer to Ps 60:8; 87:4.

Phoenicia (fho NISH ih uh) - A narrow strip of land on the eastern shore of the Mediterranean. The Prophets mentioned its lush vegetation. The cedars of Lebanon were treasured. Refer to Hos 14:5-7.

Pisgah, Mount (PIZ guh) - The high place in Moab where Moses viewed the Promised Land. Refer to Num 21:10; Deut 3:27; 34:1.

Pison (PIE shahn) – One of four rivers that flowed out of the Garden of Eden. Refer to Gen 2:10-14.

Pithom (PIE thuhm) – An Egyptian city build by Hebrew slaves. Refer to Ex 1:11.

Promised Land - The land of Canaan, which God gave to the Hebrews.

Qumran (KOOM ron) - The ruins of a community of Essene Jews. The community collected and saved the famous Dead Sea Scrolls.

Rabbah - A strong chief city and capital of the Ammonites east of the Jordan. They joined with the Arameans to fight against Israel. Refer to Deut 3:11; 2 Sam 12:26.

Ramah (RAY mah) – A City of Benjamin on the frontier between Israel and Judah. Refer to Josh 18:25.

Ramoth Gilead (RAY moth GIL ee uhd) - A town in the territory of Gad, one of the cities assigned by Moses as a City of Refuge. Refer to Deut 4:3.

Red Sea - The long narrow body of water, which separates Arabia from Egypt. It is approximately 1300 miles long. In the Bible, the Hebrews used it to flee from the Egyptians. Refer to Ex 14:16; Num 33:8; Deut 11:4.

Refuge, Cities of - Six cities set apart for the temporary escape of involuntary killers. Refer to Num 35:6; Deut 10:7-9; Josh 20:2-8.

Rehoboth (rih HOE buhth) - A well dug by Isaac in the Valley of Gerar. Refer to Gen 26:22.

Riblah (RIB luh) - The military outpost between Jerusalem and Babylon where Nebuchadnezzar and his staff established a headquarters. Refer to 2 Kings 25:1-6.

Rome (RHOME) – It has been called the "eternal city." Rome controlled all the countries bordering on the Mediterranean Sea during a period of the first 600 years of the CE.

S

Salem (SAY luhm) - The city over which Melchizedek was king. Thought to be the city of Jerusalem. Refer to Gen 14:18.

Salt Sea – A body of water at the southern end of the Jordan Valley, Gen 14:3. Also called the "Dead Sea" of Deut 4:48; "Salt Sea" of Deut 3:17; "East Sea" of Ezek 47:18; "The Sea" of Ezek 47:8.

Salt, City of - A town near the Dead Sea believed to be Khirbet Qumran, the city near where the Dead Sea Scrolls were found.

Salt, Valley of – A valley where King David was victorious in battle. Refer to 2 Sam 8:13.

Samaria (suh MAIR ee uh) - Synonymous with the kingdom of Israel. Located north of the kingdom of Judah. Refer to 1 Kings 13:32; 2 Kings 18:9-12.

Seir, Mount (SEE ur) - The mountain range of Edom running south from the Dead Sea. The land was taken by the descendants of Esau. Refer to Gen 36:21; Num 24:18; Deut 2:12; Josh 24:4.

Sela (SEE luh) - The capital of Edom, later the site of Petra. Refer to 2 Kings 14:7.

Sepharvaim (she fur VAY uhm) – A city whose residents were sent to colonize the Northern Kingdom after Samaria was captured. Refer to 2 Kings 17:24:31.

Sheba (SHEE buh) – A mountainous country in Arabia identified as the land of "the queen of the South." She came to investigate Solomon's fame and wisdom. Refer to 1 Kings 10:1-13.

Shechem (SHECK uhm) – An ancient fortified city in central

Places in the Old Testament or Bible History

Canaan and the first capital of the northern kingdom of Israel. The city has been destroyed and rebuilt several times through the centuries. Gen 12:1-3; Gen 33:18 -20.

Sheol (SHE ole) – Hebrew word for a place or state to which one's body goes after death. In Greek, it is Hades. Many references such as Gen 42:38; Job 17:13-16; Ps 9:17; Pro 15:24.

Shiloh (SHY low) - A small Old Testament village north of Jerusalem. The religious center for the Hebrew people during the period of the Judges before the kingdom was united under David. Refer to Judg 18:31; 1 Sam 3:1-10.

Shinar (SHIGH nahr) - A second name for the area between the Tigris and Euphrates, known as Chaldea. Refer to Gen 10; 11:2; Dan 1:2.

Shittim (SHI tum) - The last encampment of the Israelites in the plains of Moab. The location of the event concerning Balaam. The second census of Numbers was taken here. Refer to Num 22-25. Josh 2:1.

Shual (SHOO al) - A district near Bethel invaded by the Philistines. Refer to 1 Sam 13:17.

Shunem (SHOO nuhm) - The Philistines camped here before their victory over Saul. Refer to 1 Sam 28:4.

Shur (SURE) - A place on the border of Egypt mentioned in connection with Abraham, Hagar, and the sons of Ishmael. Refer to Gen 16:7; 20:1; 25:18.

Shushan (SHOO shan) - A wealthy and powerful city where Persian kings lied and where Esther interceded for her people (Susa). Refer to Est 1:2.

Sidon (SI duhn) - A city of Phoenicia, north of Tyre. It is called Zidon in the Old Testament. Refer to Gen 49:13; Josh 19:28.

Siloam Pool (si LOW uhm) - A pool of Jerusalem also called the upper pool and It was probably identical with the king's pool. Refer to Isa 7:3; Neh 2:14.

Sin, Wilderness of – A wilderness region between the Red Sea and Sinai where manna and quail were given. Refer to Ex 16.

Sinai (SIGH nih eye) – (1) A large peninsula forming a natural bridge between Africa and the Middle East; (2) The wilderness of the Exodus of the Israelites (Ex 19:1); (3) The mountain on which God met Moses and gave him the law (Ex 19).

Siphmoth (SIF mahth) – A place in Judah where David hid from King Saul. Refer to 1 Sam 30:26-28.

Sodom and Gomorrah (SOD uhm, go MORE uh) - The two cities known for wickedness, destroyed by the Lord. Refer to Gen 13:13; 18:20; Isa 3:9.

Sorek (SOW reck) - A valley west of Jerusalem through which the ark was taken to Beth Shemesh where Delilah resided. Refer to 1 Sam 6; 7-13; Judg 16:4.

South Ramoth (RAY mahth) – A place in southern Judah where

David hid from King Saul. Refer to 1 Sam 30:26-27.

Southern Kingdom of Judah – One of the two nations into which the united kingdom of Israel was divided following King Solomon's death. Judah consisted mostly of the tribes of Judah and Benjamin, although Simeon apparently was included later.

Succoth (SUCK uhth) - The place of the first encampment of the Israelites after leaving Egypt. Refer to Ex 12:37; Num 33:5-6.

Sumer (SOO mehr) - The fertile area between the Tigris and Euphrates Rivers. In the time of Abraham, this area was called Shinar. They developed the first high civilization in history. See the author's book *The Chronological History of the Bible Lands*. Refer to Gen 10:10; Isa 11:11.

Susa (SU suh) – the ancient capital of Elam in Iran. It existed long before the time of Abraham and centered on worship of the Elamite gods.

Syria (SEER ee uh) – A major nation that served as a political threat to the nations of Judah and Israel.

T

Tabor, Mount (TAY buhr) - A notable mountain north of Mount Gilboa. The forces of Barak gathered here for the conflict with Sisera. Refer to Ps 89:12; Judg 4:6; 8:18-19.

Tadmor (TAD mohr) - A city built by Solomon in the wilderness as a part of his northeast border. Refer to 1 Kings 9:18; 2 Chron 8:4.

Tahpanhes (TAH puh neez) – An Egyptian city on the Nile river to which many in Judah fled to after the fall of Jerusalem. Refer to Jer 43:7-10.

Tarshish (TAR shish) - A city with which the Phoenicians traded. Refer to Jer 10:9; 1 Kings 0:26.

Tekoa (tuh KOH uh) - A town of Judah close to Bethlehem, fortified by Rehoboam after the division of Israel. Refer to 2 Chron 11:6; 20:20.

Thebes (THEEBZ) – The royal city of southern Egypt. It was of major importance from the time of Abraham until it was sacked by the Assyrians. Refer to Jer 46:25.

Tigris River (TIE griss) - One of the four rivers which watered the Garden of Eden. Refer to Gen 2:14; Dan 10:4.

Timnah (TIM nuh) – A city in northern Judah allotted to the tribe of Dan (Josh 15:10); (2) A city in the hill country of Judah (Josh 15:57).

Timnath serah (Tim nath SIR uh) – A town in the territory of Ephraim given to Joshua, where he was later buried. Refer to Josh 24:29-30.

Transjordan - The area on the east side of the Jordan River usually referred to as "beyond

Places in the Old Testament or Bible History

the Jordan." Refer to Gen 50:10-11.

Tyre (TIRE) - Ancient city of Phoenicia. It was mentioned many times along with another Phoenician city, Sidon. Refer to Isa 23:1-17.

U

Ur (URR) - A city where Abraham lived before moving to Canaan. Ur was a bustling metropolis in Abraham's day. Refer to Gen 11:28, 31; 15:7.

Urik – Ancient city in Mesopotamia.

Uz (UHZ) - The home of Job. Its exact location is unknown, probably east of the Jordan and south of Damascus. Refer to Job 1:1.

V

Valley of Dry Bones – A vision of the prophet Ezekiel; the bones representing Israel's exile. Refer to Ezek 37:1-14.

Z

Zarephath (ZAIR uh fath) - A town near Sidon where the widow who sheltered Elijah lived. Refer to 1 Kings 17:9-6.

Zeboim (Zeh BOY yim) – One of the five cities destroyed along with Sodom and Gomorrah. Refer to Gen 14:8.

Ziklag (ZIKK lag) - A town in Judah eventually given to Simeon. David fled here from Saul, and where he later pursued the Amalekites. Refer to 1 Chron 4:30; 1 Sam 27:6; 30:1-31.

Zin, Wilderness of (zihn) - The Israelites passed through here in their wandering. It is near the southern boundary of Canaan. Refer to Num 13:21; 27:14; Deut 32:51.

Zion (ZIE uhn) - One of the hills on which Jerusalem was built. Refer to 2 Sam 5:6-9.

Zoar (ZOH ahr) - One of the five cities of the plain, originally called Bela. The city was spared because of Lot's prayer. Refer to Gen 14:2, 8; 19:20-22; Isa 15:5.

Zorah (ZOOR uh) - A town of Judah inhabited by Dan. Samson was born and buried here. King Rehoboam of Judah fortified it. Refer to Josh 15:33; Judg 13:2, 25; Neh 11:29.

FOUR

COLLECTION/DICTIONARY of Important Old Testament-Related Words And Phrases

Old Testament Words and Phrases

Aaron's Rod - Mentioned on two dramatic occasions in the Old Testament. Refer to Ex 7:12-20; Num 17:1-10.

Abib (A bibb) - The first month of the Hebrew calendar. March-April. Refer to Ex 13:4, 23:15.

Abide - To trust God and live for Him. Refer to Ps 91:1; John 12.

Abomination — Description of a detestable and vile act. Usually used to describe something vile in the eyes of God. Refer to Lev 11:43; Deut 7:26.

Abomination of Desolation - A despicable misuse of the Temple foretold by Daniel. Refer to Dan 11:31 and 12:11.

Abstain, Abstinence - To refrain from eating or drinking harmful substances of from participating in sinful actions. Refer to Gen 9:4; Lev 11; Acts 15:29; 1 Thess 5:22.

Accountability - A biblical principle that we are answerable to God for our actions and words. Not directly found in the Old Testament. Ref to Rom 3:19, 23; Eph 4:25.

Adjuration - The urging or advising by a person in authority. Refer to 1 Sam 14:24; 1 Sam 14:24.

Adoration - The act of paying respect and honor to God. Refer to Gen 17:3; Ps 95:6.

Adversary - An opponent or an enemy. It is often used of Satan. Refer to Deut 32:43.

Advocate - A helper or intercessor. A word for the Holy Spirit. Not directly found in the Old Testament. Refer to John 14:16; 16:7.

Affliction - Any condition that causes pain or suffering. Refer to Job 36:15; Ps 25:18; Jer 16:19.

Aleph - The first letter of the Hebrew alphabet. It is the heading of verses 1-8 of Psalm 119.

Allegory - A symbolic representation of a truth about human experience. Refer to Ps 80:8-19.

Ambassador - A person who represents one government at the seat of another. Refer to Num 20:14; Josh 9:4.

Amen - A word used to fix the stamp of truth upon a statement. Refer to Num 5:22.

Amulet - An ornament usually assumed to have supernatural powers. Does not appear in the Bible; however see Is 3:20.

Anathema (ah NATH a mah) - Accursed or separated. Refer to Deut 7:23-26; Josh 7:1.

Ancient of Days - A name for God used by Daniel. Refer to Dan 7:9, 13, 22.

Angel of the Lord — A heavenly being sent by God to human beings. Considered to be Jesus Christ or One representing God. Refer to Gen 16:L7-12.

Annunciation - Announcement by Gabriel to Mary of the coming birth of Jesus. Not directly found in the Old Testament. Refer to Luke 1:26-38.

Anoint - To pour oil on a person for a specific purpose. For example, as an act of healing. Refer to Gen 28:18.

Antitype (AN tih type) - Fulfillment or completion of an earlier truth revealed in the Bible. Noah was a type of one's salvation. Refer to 1 Pet 3:21.

Apocalyptic Literature (a pock uh LIP tik) - A type of Jewish and Christian literature written in Egypt and Palestine. It was a particular type of literature to reveal mysteries concerning heaven and earth, angels, righteousness and evil. Certain literary style set it apart from other literature. It is rich in symbolism.

Apostasy - A renunciation of one's faith. Refer to Jer 5:6; 1 Sam 15:11.

Apocrypha (A POCK rih fuh) - A group of books written during a time of turmoil in the history of the Jewish people. There are fifteen Old Testament, and several New Testament writings.

Archangel - A chief angel, or one higher in rank than normal angels. Refer to Dan 10:13; 12:1.

Ark of the Covenant - The sacred portable chest that was the most important sacred object of the Israelites. Refer to Josh 6:11; 1 Sam 3:3.

Armageddon (ahr muh GED uhn) – The site of the final battle of this age in which God intervenes to destroy the armies of Satan. The word is not directly found in the Old Testament; however, reference is made to the event.

Armor of God - An expression that symbolizes the combat equipment of a Christian soldier who fights against spiritual wickedness. Not directly found in the Old Testament. Refer to Eph 6:11, 13.

Ascension of Christ - Jesus' return to God after His resurrection. Refer to Ps 68:18.

Ascents, Song of - A phrase that occurs in the titles of fifteen Psalms, 120-134. Sung by those "going up" to Jerusalem. Refer to 1 Sam 1:3; Is 30:29.

Atonement, Day of - The expiration of sin and propitiation of God by the incarnation, life, suffering, and death of Christ. Refer to Ex 29:36; 1 Chron 6:49.

Avenger of Blood - A responsibility of a relative for avenging an injury to a member of his family. Refer to Deut 19:6; 2 Sam 14:11.

Baal – See chapters Two and Six.

Backslide - To revert to sin or wrongdoing. Refer to Jer 2:19; 31:22.

Old Testament Words and Phrases

Balm of Gilead - Highly prized balsam used as a cosmetic. A plant Product of Gilead. A sweet smell. Refer to Gen 37:25; Jer 8:22; Ezek 27:17.

Barren – A woman unable to bear children. Refer to Gen 11:30; 29:31.

Begotten, Only - A New Testament phrase that describes Christ as the only Son of His heavenly Father. Not directly found in the Old Testament. Refer to John 1:14. 18; 3:16-18.

Beth - The name of a Hebrew letter and prefix used in Hebrew names. Refer to Judg 7:22; Amos 1:5; Josh 21:20-22.

Betrothal - A mutual promise of contract for a future marriage. Refer to Deut 20:7.

Binding and Loosing - A phrase describing the authority and power that Jesus assigned to believers, allowing them to forbid or allow certain kinds of conduct. Not directly found in the Old Testament. Refer to Matt 16:19.

Birthright - The firstborn son enjoyed the right of great dignity and a double portion of the estate. Refer to Gen 49:3; Deut 21:17.

Bitter Herbs – Herbs eaten by the Hebrew people during their celebration of the Passover. Refer to Ex 12:8.

Blasphemy - The act of cursing or slandering God. An act of contempt or lack of respect. Refer to Lev 24:15-16; Ex 20:7.

Bondage - The state of being held against one's will. Refer to Ex 1:14; Ezra 9:9.

Book of Life - A heavenly book in which the name of the righteous are written. Refer to Rev 20:11-15; Ex 32:32-33.

Books of Moses - Generally considered the first five books of the Bible. Book of the Law. Refer to Deut 31:9-11.

Branch – Used literally only twelve times in the OT of a bud or an offshoot of a plant or tree. The metaphorical meaning is that of the land of Israel (Isa 4:2). Refer to Jer 23:5, 33:15; Zech 3:8.

Brass Serpent – A serpent cast from metal and raised up by Moses in the wilderness on a pole. Refer to Num 21:9.

Breastplate - Worn by the high priest, adorned with twelve precious stones. Refer to Ex 28:15; 28:12-29.

Breath of God – A phrase that portrays God as the source of Life. Refer to Job 33:4; 2 Sam 22:14-16.

Brimstone – A bright yellow mineral usually found near active volcanoes. Large deposits of the substance are found in the Dead Sea region. Refer to Gen 19:24.

Bul (bool) - The eighth month of the Hebrew calendar. Oct/Nov. Refer to 1 Kings 6:38.

Bulrush – A reed-like plant that grew in marshy areas of the Nile River. Used for making papyrus. Refer to Ex 2:3.

Burning Bush - The flaming shrub at Mount Horeb through which Moses became aware of the presence of God. Refer to Ex 3:2-4.

C

Calf, Golden – An idol built by the Israelites as they waited for Moses. Refer to Ex 32:1-4.

Cankerworm - A variety of caterpillar. Also used as locust. Refer to Joel 1:4; Nah 3:15-16.

Canon – Word means a "rod" used for measuring. It came to be used as the collection of books accepted to be of God's direction.

Capstone - The uppermost stone in a building. Refer to Zech 4:7.

Carnal - Worldliness, desires of the flesh. Not directly found in the Old Testament. Refer to Lev 18:20; Rom 8:6; 2 Cor 10:4.

Chariot of Fire – The chariot that came between Elijah and Elisha as Elijah was taken into heaven. Refer to 2 Kings 2:11.

Cherub (CHAIR ub) – The guards of the mercy seat, imaged on wood or gold. Refer to Ex 25:18; 36:5.

Cherubim (CHAIR oo beam) - Winged angelic beings associated with worship and praise of God. Refer to Gen 3:24; Ex 25:17-22.

Chosen People - A name for the Israelites as well as the Christian church. Refer to Deut 14:2.

Circumcision – The removal of the foreskin of the male sex organ, performed shortly after the birth. Refer to Lev 12:3.

Cistern - An artificial reservoir for storing liquids.

Clay Tablets - One of the world's oldest known writing materials originating in Mesopotamia.

Codex (COE dex) - The forerunner of the modern book. Sheets of papyrus folded in the middle and sewed together.

Concubine - A secondary wife according to accepted custom. Refer to Gen 21:14; 25:6; Ex 21:7.

Concupiscence – A strong, passionate desire especially lust. Not directly found in the Old Testament. Refer to Rom 7:8; Col 3:5.

Condemnation - The declaration of a person as guilty. Not directly found in the Old Testament. Refer to Luke 23:40; John 5:24; James 5:12.

Consecration - the act of setting apart or dedicating for God's use. Refer to 2 Chron 7:5-9; Ezra 6:16-17.

Contrite - The kind of spirit or heart pleasing and acceptable to God. Refer to Ps 34:18.

Corban - A word applied to a gift or offering in the Temple dedicated to God in a special

Old Testament Words and Phrases

sense. The word is not directly found in the Old Testament, however the act is clearly identified. Refer to Mark 7:11-13.

Cornerstone - A stone placed at the corner or the intersecting angle where two walls come together.

Covenant- An agreement between two parties. Could be God and Abraham. Could be the covenant of law. Covenant with Moses. Covenant through Christ. Refer to Gen 9:15; Ex 20:24.

Covenant, Book of the - A name for the code of laws in Ex 20-23. Refer to Ex 24:7.

Covenant, New - The new agreement God has made with mankind based on the death and resurrection of Jesus Christ. Refer to Jer 31:31-34.

Covenant People - A name used for Abraham's descendants. Refer to Gen 12:1-3. Also, see a better covenant, Luke 22:20; 2 Cor 3:6.

Covetousness - A desire to possess something that belongs to another person. Refer to Ex 20:17; Deut 5:21.

Crown of Thorns - A mock symbol of authority fashioned and placed on Jesus' head before He was placed on a cross. Not directly found in the Old Testament, however referred to in prophecy. Refer to Matt 27:29; John 19:2, 5.

Cuneiform (kyu NAY uh form) - A system of early writing developed in Mesopotamia, Probably by the Sumerians.

Cupbearer – A royal servant who tasted wine before it was served to the king. Refer to Neh 1:11.

Day of Atonement – The holiest day in the Jewish calendar, called Yom Kippur. It is marked by a total fast, prayer, and reflection for twenty-four hours. Yom Kippur is repentance of wrongdoing, pleas for divine forgiveness, and determination for self-improvement.

Day of the Lord – A special day/period at the end of time when God's will and purpose for mankind and His world will be fulfilled. Refer to Amos 5:18-20; Isa 13:6, 9; Jer 46:10. See Day of the Lord detailed in chapter Six.

Dayspring - A poetic way of speaking of the dawn.

Debauchery - Moral corruption. Not directly found in the Old Testament, however the idea is found there. Refer to Rom 13:13; Gal 5:19.

Decree - An official order issued by a king or person of authority. Refer to Ezra 1:1; Amos 4:5.

Defiled - Contamination or to make something impure. Refer to Gen 34:2; Ezek 43:8.

Degrees, Songs of – The fifteen psalms of the book of Psalms. Means "goings up." Refer to Ps 120-134.

Depression - State of extreme sadness or remorse. Refer to Ps 43:5; 127:2.

Diadem (DIE uh dem) - A band around the turban of a king or his queen signifying their authority. Refer to Lev 8:9; Ezek 21:26.

Diaspora – the term used to describe the scattering of Jews following the fall of Israel to Assyria in 586 BCE. One example would be the one million Jewish residents in Alexandria.

Discern - To weigh all the facts and make a wise decision. Refer to Eccl 8:5; Luke 12:56; 1 Cor 12:10.

Discerning of spirits - A gift of the Holy Spirit that enables one to judge whether another who speaks in tongues or performs miracles does so by the power of the Holy Spirit or by a false spirit. Not directly found in the Old Testament, however the experience is found there. Refer to 1 Cor 12:10; 14:12, 26.

Discipleship – the training or leading of one "to follow." The word means "learner, pupil." Not directly found in the Old Testament.

Dispensation - a period under which mankind is answerable to God for how it has obeyed from the revelation of God revealed.

Dispersion of the nations – The dividing and scattering of the people of the earth after the flood and the Tower of Babel. This was done through the three sons of Noah. Refer to Gen 10:32.

Divination – Occult practices such as fortune telling and witchcraft, which were common among the pagan nations of the ancient world. Refer to Deut 18:10-11.

Doctrine - A body of beliefs about God, Christ, etc. considered worthy of acceptance by members of the community of faith.

Doxology - A declaration of praise to God expressing His power and glory.

Elect - A person or group chosen by God for special favor. Not directly found in the Old Testament, however the chosen people are there. Refer to 1 Pet 2:4, 6; Rom 8:33.

Elul (ee LOOL) - The sixth month of the Hebrew year (Aug-Sept).

Enmity - Animosity or hatred. Not directly found in the Old Testament, however the action is found there. Refer to Rom 8:7.

Ephod - A vest worn by the High Priest when he presided at the altar. Refer to Ex 28-4-14; 39:2-7.

Eschatology - See End Time Events in chapter Six.

Eternal life – A person's new and redeemed existence in Jesus Christ that is granted by God as a gift to all believers.

Refer to Dan 12:2; Matt 19:16-21.

Ethanim - The seventh month of the Hebrew calendar. Sep/Oct).

Eunuch (YOO nuck) – A male servant of a household in Bible times, emasculated by castration. Refer to 2 Kings 9:32; Est 2:15.

Evil one – Often used to refer to Satan/devil. One of many New Testament titles to identify Satan. Not directly found in the Old Testament, but this angel is referred to by many names. Refer to Matt 13:19, 38; 2 Cor 6:15; Eph 6:16.

Feast of Booths – A festival, also known as the *Feast of Ingathering,* observed annually during the harvest season. Refer to Ex 23:16; Num 29:12.

Feast of Harvest – An annual Jewish feast commemorating the end of the harvest. Also known as the *Feast of Weeks.* Refer to Ex 34:22.

Feast of Ingathering – See Feast of Booths.

Feast of Lights – A festival commemorating the Jewish victories that restored the temple. Also known as the *Feast of Dedication* or *Hanukkah.*

Feast of Unleavened Bread – A Jewish festival that commemorated the Exodus from Egypt. Also Passover. Refer to Josh 5:10.

Feast of Weeks – See Feast of Harvest.

Familiar Spirit – The spirit of a dead person that a sorcerer calls back in order to communicate with that person. refer to Deut 18:11.

Fetters - Shackles or chains attached to the ankles of prisoners to restrain movement. Refer to Ps105:18.

Firstborn - The first offspring of human beings or animals. Refer to Ex 13:11-13; Num 18:16.

Firstfruits - The firstborn of the flocks and the first vegetables and grains to be gathered at harvest time. Refer to Num 28:26; 2 Chron 31:5.

Foreknowledge – Refer to chapter Five.

Former Rain – The first rain of the growing season. Refer to Joel 2:23.

Frontlet (or Phylacteries) – Small square leather boxes containing four strips of parchment inscribed with quotations from the Pentateuch. They were worn by every male Israelite above thirteen years of age. Refer to Ex 13:1-10; Deut 6:4-9.

Fullness of time – A phrase used to describe the divine working of God leading to the second coming of Christ. The phrase is not directly found in the Old Testament. It appears in different context in Gal 4:4.

G

Gallows - A platform on which a person was executed. Refer to Est 2:23; 7:9; 9:25.

Gate, East – Refer to 1 Chron 26:14; 2 Chron 31:14.

Gate, Fish – Refer to 2 Chron 33:14; Neh 3:3.

Gate, Fountain - A gate in the wall of Jerusalem. Refer to Neh 12:37.

Gate, Sheep – A gate in the wall of Jerusalem repaired under Nehemiah. Refer to Neh 3:1, 32.

Gates of Jerusalem - The gates in the city wall of Jerusalem and the Temple area. Refer to Acts 3:10; Zech 14:10; Neh 8:16.

Graveclothes - Strips of cloth wrapped around a corpse in preparation for burial. Not directly found in the Old Testament. Refer to John 11:44

H

Hammurapi, Code of (hah muhr RAH pee) - Ancient law code named after the king of Babylonia. This is valuable to Bible students because the Code is so similar to the Law revealed to Moses.

Handbreadth - A linear measurement based on the width of the palm, four fingers closely pressed together. Refer to Ps 39:5.

Hardness of Heart - Stubbornness in opposition to God's will. Refer to 1 Sam 6:6; Ex 4:21; 7:3.

Hexateuch - A term for the first six books of the Old Testament viewed as a unit.

High Places – Elevated or hilltop sites dedicated to worship of pagan gods. The well-known step pyramids called Ziggurats were built in Mesopotamia. These were generally forbidden by the Israelites. Refer to Gen 11-9; 1 Sam 9:12-14; 1 Kings 3:4-15.

Holy of Holies – The most sacred inner room in the Tabernacle and the Temple, where only the High Priest was allowed to go. Refer to Lev 16.

Host of Heaven - Heavenly beings created by God and associated with Him in His rule over the world. Refer to Is 1:9 Ps 103:18-9-21.

I

Idolatry - The worship of something created as opposed to the worship of the Creator.

Image of God - The characteristics of humankind with which God endowed them at creation. Refer to Gen 1:26-27; 1 Cor 11:7.

Immorality - Behavior contrary to established moral principles. Refer to Ezek 23:8, 17.

Immortality - Exemption from death; living forever.

Old Testament Words and Phrases

Immutability - See Chapter Five.

Imputation - Charging or reckoning something to a person's account. Not directly found in the Old Testament. Refer to Rom 5:12-19; Phil 18.

Incarnation - The coming of God's Son into the world as a human being. Not directly found in the Old Testament. Refer to Rom 8:3; Eph 2:15; Col 1:22.

Infinity - See Chapter Five.

Innocence - Blamelessness; freedom from sin and guilt. Refer to Gen 20:5; Ps 26:6; Hos 8:5; Rom.

Inquire of the Lord - To seek God's counsel and guidance. Refer to Gen 25:22; 2 Sam 2:1.

Intercession - The act of petitioning God or praying on behalf of another person. Refer to Gen 18; Ex 8:28; 15:25.

J

Justification - The Process by which sinful human begins are made acceptable to a holy God. See Chapter Five.

K

Kenosis (keh NOE sis) - A term expressing the dual nature of Jesus as fully human and fully divine. (see Chapter Five).

Kingdom of God – God's rule of grace in the world, generally used of a future period foretold by the Prophets and Jesus. Not directly found in the Old Testament. Refer to Matt 4:17; 12:28.

Kinsman-Redeemer – A close relative who had first option to buy back or redeem freedom or property that had been forfeited by members of the clan. Refer to Lev 25:48-49; Ruth 4.

L

Lamb of God - Used by John the Baptist to describe Jesus (John 1:29, 36). Not directly found in the Old Testament, however it is alluded to. Refer to Acts 8:32; 1 Pet 1:19; Rev 5:6.

Leaven – A substance used to produce fermentation in dough and make it rise. Prohibited in food offerings dedicated to the Lord by fire. Refer to Ex 12:15, 19-20; Lev 2:11.

Leper – A person who suffers from a slowly progressing and incurable disease. Refer to Lev 13:45-46; 2 Kings 5:7.

Lewdness - Preoccupation with sex and sexual desire; lust. Refer to Judg 20:6; Hos 2:10.

Licentiousness - Undisciplined and unrestrained behavior. Not directly found in the Old Testament. Refer to Mark 7:22; 2 Cor 12:21.

Living Creatures - Heavenly beings mentioned in the visions of Ezekiel and John. Refer to Ezek 1:1-28; Rev 4:6-9.

Loincloth – A material covering the hip area and abdominal region of the body.

Longsuffering - Refers primarily to God's patient endurance. Refer to Ex 34:6; Rom 2:4, Eph 4:31-32.

Lots, Casting of - A way of making decisions in Bible times. The guidance of God was trusted. Similar to drawing straws or casting of dice. Refer to Lev 16:8-10.

Lukewarm - Mildly warm; neither hot nor cold; lacking in conviction. Not directly found in the Old Testament. Refer to Rev 3:14-22.

M

Manna – The food provided by God for the Israelites in the wilderness during their Exodus from Egypt. Refer to Ex 16:15, 31, 33.

Mene Mene (MEE nih) - , **Tekel (TEE kl)** - , **Upharsin (yoo FAR sin)** – Words which appeared on the wall of the palace of King Belshazzar of Babylon. Daniel was summoned and deciphered the message and told the king what it meant. Refer to Dan 5:1-29

Mercy Seat – The golden lid or covering on the Ark of the Covenant, regarded as the resting place of God. Refer to Ex 25:17-22; 1 Chron 28:11.

Midwife – A woman who helped other women give birth to their children. They were sometimes relatives of friends. Refer to Gen 35:17; Ezek 16:4.

Millennium, The – Refer to End Time Events, chapter Six.

Millstone – Usually in pairs, used to grinding grains. The two "stones," one concave the other the other convex.

Mishna (MISH nah) - The first and basic part of the Talmud. The written basis of religious authority for traditional Judaism.

Monotheism - Worship of one supreme God; the characteristic of the worship system of the Hebrew people. Refer to Chapter Five.

Most Holy Place – (see Holy of Holies).

Nazarite (NAZZ uh right) - A person who took a vow to separate from certain worldly things and to consecrate himself to God. Refer to Num 6:1-8.

Nephilim (NEFF ih lem) - The offspring of marriages between angelic beings and human females. Refer to Gen 6:4; Num 13:33.

Northern Kingdom – See Chapter Three.

O

Obelisk (AHB uh lisk) - A stone monument or pillar. Generally associated with Egyptian religion. Refer to Gen 35:20; 2 Sam 18:18; Jer 43:13.

Old Testament Words and Phrases

Old Testament - The first of two sections in the Bible. Old Testament history closes about 400 years before the physical birth of Jesus Christ.

Omnipotence (om NIP oh tunce) – God has ALL power.

Omnipresence (om nih PRES ence) – God is everywhere at the same time.

Omniscience (om NISH unce) - God has ALL knowledge.

Oracle (OR uh cull) - A Prophetic speech or declaration. Refer to Num 23, 24; Josh 13:22.

Ordinance – Protestant term for religious practices. Baptism and Communion are two.

Ox Goad – A spike used to drive oxen. Refer to Judg 3:31.

Pagan - A follower of a false god or religion. Refer to Ezra 10:2, 10-18; Neh 13:26-27, 30.

Palmerworm – A caterpillar of locust that ate vegetation. Refer to Joel 1:4.

Papyrus (puh PIE russ) - A paper made from the pith of papyrus. Papyrus plants of northern Africa along the Nile River valley. The plant is almost unknown today in Egypt. Refer to Ex 2:3; Job 8:11.

Parable - A short, simple story designed to communicate a spiritual truth. Refer to 2 Sam 12:1-4.

Parchment – The ancient writing material made from the skins of cattle, sheep, etc

Parousia (puh ROO sih ah) - A Greek word that refers to the second Coming or the return of Jesus Christ at the end of this age. Not directly found in the Old Testament. Refer to Titus 2:13.

Passover – The first of the three great festivals of the Hebrew people. It referred to the sacrifice of a lamb in Egypt when the people of Israel were slaves. Refer to

Patriarch – **(PAY trih ark)** – The name usually refers to the tribal leaders of Israel who lived before the time of Moses. Specifically it is used of Abraham, Isaac, Jacob, and Joseph.

Pentateuch - Refers to the first five books of the Old Testament. Also, refer to "Torah" or "Book of the Law."

Pentecost – Refers to the Feast of Weeks in Ex 13:3-10, Lev 23:15-21, and 2 Chron 8:13. It is also known as the Feast of Harvest.

Perdition - Destruction, ruin, or waste. Not directly found in the Old Testament. Refer to Heb 10:39; 2 Pet 3:7.

Phylacteries (fie LACK tuh rees) - Small square leather boxes containing four strips of parchment inscribed with quotations from the Pentateuch. Refer to Ex 13:1-10; 13:11-16; Deut 6:4-9.

Pillar - Upright standing stones with religious significance, used by both the Canaanites and the Israelites. Refer to Gen 31:45; Ex 24:4; 2 Kings 17:10.

Pillar of Fire and Cloud - The phenomenon by which God guided the Israelites during their travels through the wilderness. Refer to Ex 13: 21-22; 14:24.

Potsherd (POTT shurd) - A fragment of broken pottery. Refer to Job 2:8; Ps 22:15.

Profane - To treat anything holy with disrespect. Refer to Is 56:6.

Propitiation (Pro pish ee Ay shun) - The atoning death of Jesus on the cross, through which He paid the penalty demanded by God for people's sin. Not directly found in the Old Testament. Refer to 1 John 2:2.

Providence - The continuous activity of God in His creation by which He preserves and governs. Refer to Ps 103:19; 1 Sam 2:9.

Provocation - Anything that Provokes or incites. Refer to Heb 3:8, 15; Ex 17:1-7.

Pseudepigrapha - A collection of Jewish books written by pious Jews living in Palestine or Egypt.

Purin (POOR im) – A Jewish holiday observed a month before Passover. It commemorates the deliverance of the Jews by Esther and Mordecai. Refer to Est 3:&; 9:24-32.

Q

Q - Refers to a hypothetical document that contained material such as the sayings of Jesus.

R

Rapture - See Chapter Five. Refer to End Time Events in chapter Six.

Reconciliation - See Chapter Five.

Redemption - See Chapter Five.

Regeneration - See Chapter Five.

Remission - See Chapter Five.

Repentance - See Chapter Five.

Reprobate - One who fails to pass a test and is rejected. Refer to Jer 6:30.

Resurrection - Being raised from the dead. Refer to 1 King 17:20-24.

Retribution - The act of receiving what one deserves. Refer to 2 Chron 6:23.

Righteousness - See Chapter Five.

S

Sabbath (SAB buhth) - The practice of observing one day in seven as a time for rest and worship. Refer to Ex 20:3-11.

Sackcloth - A rough, coarse cloth, or a baglike garment made of this clothe and worn as a symbol of mourning. Refer to Gen 37:34; Est 4:1-4; Job 16:15.

Sanctification – See Chapter Five.

Scapegoat - A live goat over whose head Aaron confessed all the sins of the people of Israel. The goat was sent into the wilderness, symbolically taking away their sins. Refer to Lev 16:8, 10, 26.

Scepter - The official staff of a ruler, symbolizing his authority. Refer to Mic 17:14; Ezek 19:11, 14.

Scripture - The Old and New Testaments, which make up the Bible. Considered to be God's Word. Refer to 2 Tim 3:16.

Scroll – A roll of papyrus, leather, or parchment on which an ancient document such as the Bible was written. It was rolled up on a stick, usually thirty-five feet in length. Refer to Ezra 6;2.

Seal - A device such as a signet ring engraved with the owner's identity. Impressed on wax or clay to leave the owner's mark. Refer to Ex 28:11; Jer 22:24.

Second Coming - See Chapter Five.

Sepulchre – A natural cave or place carved out of rock where bodies were buried. Refer to Gen 23:6-9.

Septuagint – **(SEP too uh jint)** – The oldest Bible translation in the world. It was completed in Alexandria, Egypt where six scholars from each of the twelve tribes, worked as individual groups in the translation. It is known as LXX, the rounded number of the translators.

Seraphim (SER uh fim) – Angelic or heavenly beings associated with Isaiah's vision of God in the Temple. Isaiah 6:1-7 is the only verse that mentions them.

Sheep Gate – see Gate.

Shewbread – Unleavened bread kept in the temple for ceremonial purposes. Refer to Num 4:7.

Southern Kingdom – See chapter Three.

Spiritual Gifts - Special gifts bestowed by the Holy Spirit. Not directly found in the Old Testament.

Standard – A banner, flag, or streamer to identify groups or tribes. Refer to Num 2:2, 34.

Store City – A city or a supply depot in a city for the storage of food and weapons. Refer to 2 Chron 8:4.

Storehouse – A building for storing food. Refer to Gen 41:48

Stumblingblock – A hindrance to belief of understanding. Refer to Jer 6:21; 18:15.

Supplication – The act of asking for something earnestly or humbly. Refer to Ps 4:1; 5:8.

Swaddling Clothes – These were long, narrow strips of cloth wrapped around a newborn infant to restrict movement. Refer to Job 38:9.

T

Talent – The largest unit of silver, shaped in pellets or rings, with approximately the value of one ox.

Tapestry – An expensive curtain of cloth embroidered with artwork. Refer to Pro 7:16; 31:22.

Taskmaster – One responsible for controlling and managing a group of people or a task. Refer to 2 Chron 2:8.

Tell – A mound of rubble that marks the site of an ancient city. Refer to Jer 49:2.

Tent of Meeting – Tabernacle. Refer to Ex 40:1-8.

Teraphim (TEHR uh fim) Figurines of images in human form used in the ancient world as household gods. Refer to Gen 31:19; 1 Sam 15:23; Hos 3:4; Zech 10:2.

Terrestrial – Its Latin root means "earth." Pertaining to the earth and its inhabitants rather than "extraterrestrial."

Testament - A written document that provides for the disposition of one's personal property after death. Also refers to either of the two divisions of the Bible.

Theocracy (thee OCK rih see) - The direct government of the nation of Israel by God.

Theophany (thee AHF ih knee) - Any direct, visual manifestation of the presence of God. Refer to Ex 3:1-6; Ex 13:21-22.

Thummin (THUHM im) – see Urim.

Tithe - The practice of giving a tenth of one's income or Property as an offering to God. Refer to Gen 14:17-20; Heb 7:1-10.

Torah (toe RAH) – Used to refer to the Mosaic code given at Sinai. It also includes the entire spectrum of God's teaching. In recent times, it has come to refer to the first five books of the Bible.

Tree of Knowledge of Good and Evil - One of two special trees planted by God in the Garden of Eden. Symbolized all moral knowledge. Refer to Gen 2:17; 3:5.

Tree of Life – The second tree in the center of the Garden of Eden. Adam and Eve were free to eat from this tree until they disobeyed God. Refer to Gen 2:0, 16.

Tribulation – A great trouble. Not directly found in the Old Testament. Refer to Mat 13:21, Act 14:22.

Tribulation, The Great – A time of unprecedented trouble when the wrath of God will be poured out on sinful humans. Not directly found in the Old

Testament. Refer to Mark 13:14-23.

Trinity – Not directly found in the Old Testament. See Chapter Five.

Triumphal Entry – The entry of Jesus into Jerusalem during His final week on earth. Not directly found in the Old Testament. Refer to Matt 21:1-9; John 12:12-16.

Urim – The Urim and Thummim were gems carried by the high priest and used by him to determine God's will in specific matters. They were perhaps used as dice. Refer to Ex 28:16; Lev 8:8.

Usury - Interest on money loaned. Refer to Lev 25:36, 27.

Watchman – One or more soldiers posted to keep guard Neh 4:9; 12:25.

Watchtower – An observation tower upon which a guard or lookout was stationed to keep watch. Refer to 2 Kings 17:9; Isa 21:8.

Wilderness – A land not suited for farming because it was too dry, rough, or rocky. Referred to as "desert." John the Baptist and Jesus both were in a wilderness at one time. Refer to Matt 3:1; Mark 1:12. In addition, the Israelites wandered in a wilderness for many years. Refer to Ex 15:23; Num 11:3.

Wisdom Literature – One of four categories of Old Testament Scripture consisting of Job, Psalms, Proverbs, Ecclesiastes, and Song of Songs (Solomon).

Wormwood – any of several aromatic plants that yield a bitter, dark green oil. Refer to Deut 29:18.

Year of Jubilee – It took place every forty-nine years and followed seven Sabbatical years. Servants were set free and houses and lands could be redeemed. Refer to Lev 23:15-16; 27:14-24; Jer 34:8; Isa 61:1-2.

Yoke – A type of harness that connected a pair of animals to a plow or similar tool. Also used as a symbol of burden or oppression. Refer to 1 Sam 11:7; Luke 14:9; 1 Kings 12:4-14.

Ziv (zihv) - The second month of the Hebrew calendar. April/May. Refer to 1 Kings 6:1, 37.

FIVE

Bible Theology Terminology For OLD and NEW Testament Study

Bible Theology Terminology

●─────────●

Partially extracted from the author's book *"Essence of Christian Belief,"* a thorough work on theology, doctrine, and Christian belief. Definitions are lengthy because of the nature of this topic. Many of these terms are included in this work for explanatory reasons

●─────────●

Abomination – Something that is opposing God. Usually includes hatred and evil. Refer to Lev 18:18-30; Deut 24:1-4; Pro 6:16-19; 11:20.

Absolution - A term used by Roman Catholics of the remission of sins given through the church. The Scriptures maintain that only Christ can forgive sins.

Adoption - A frequently used term in the Scriptures, usually by Paul, showing how any human being may become a child of God.

Age of Accountability - The chronological stage in a person's life when he is responsible for his conduct before God. This is a time of the knowing of good and evil, and the personal presenting of one's life to God.

Agnosticism - A term generally used for the view that one does not know whether there is a God or not. "Agnostic" comes from the Greek "not know."

Allegory - An attempt to express truth in a pictorial form. (i.e. Israel as a vine; Jesus as the Good Shepherd). Two uses of the term are found in theology. (1) Literary, "a figurative expression by which something is said other than what the word used normally means"; (2) Hermeneutical, using Scripture for the biblical interpretation by going back to pre-Christian times in search of their meaning.

Almighty – a reference to El Shaddai, one of the names of God. Refer to Ex 6:3.

Angelology - The study of the spiritual beings of angels, demons, and Satan.

Antiochene Theology – A type of theology influential in Asia Minor until the time of the Arab conquests. It was fearful of Christology, believing it would lead to the denial of the full humanity of Jesus.

Anthropology - The study of God's summit of God's creation, humans.

Anthropomorphism - The practice of describing God in human terms such as having arms, feet, etc. Refer to Matt 18:10; Ex 24:10.

Anthropopathism - The practice of describing God as if He displayed human emotions such as jealousy, anger, etc. Refer to Ex 20:5; Ps 103:8.

Antichrist - The term occurring in John's letters, referring to the archenemy of Jesus Christ. The *anti* carries the meaning of "against."

Anti-Semitism – The expressed hatred and persecution of Jews.

Apocalyptic - A term applied to a book containing revelations of events toward the end of the world as we know it and usher in the final "heaven on earth."

Apocrypha - Books collected during the years of the formation of the accepted canon of Scriptures, which never had any serious claim to be included. There are both Old Testament and New Testament collections of such books. See Pseuderpigrapha

Apologetics - A somewhat misunderstood term in our day. This is a defense of the Christian faith and not associated with the idea of apology. To defend has nothing to do with an apology. It is a subdivision of Christian theology offering a systematic defense of various topics. This is also referred to as "evidences."

Apostasy - A deliberate repudiation of one's Christian faith.

Arminianism - Liberal Christian doctrine viewed in the John Wesley belief, differing from the Luther-Calvin tradition. It stresses Scripture alone as the highest authority for doctrines, and justification is by grace alone. He defended his view in his commentary on Romans 9. He argued against both John Calvin and Theodore Beza. Their view being that before the fall, indeed before man's creation, God had already determined the destiny of each person. Arminianism teachers that indeed, believers may lose their salvation and be eternally lost.

Articles of Faith - Concise statements of Christian belief or confessions considered basic to theology.

Assurance - The sense of confidence and trust that the believer and the faithful have toward the Promises, fidelity, and pledges of God.

Atheism - From the Greek word *atheos* meaning "without God." It refers to the deepest state of heathen misery.

Armageddon – The site of the final battle of this age. God will destroy the armies of Satan and cast Satan into the bottomless pit. See End Time Events in chapter Six Refer to Rev 16:16.

Ascension of Christ – the departure of the risen Christ from His earthly ministry. This occurred forty days after the resurrection. Refer to Mark 16:19; Acts 1:9-11.

Atonement - A term usually found in Exodus, Leviticus, and Numbers. It represents the sacrifice that man needs because he is a sinner. Thus, the burnt offering was made "to make atonement." An expansion of the truth occurs in the New Testament. It emphasizes the sacrifice of Christ on a cross to save any individual who accepts Him.

Author Criticism - A sub category of Literary Criticism. This attempts to determine whether the writers of the books of the Bible used earlier sources of information and whether those sources were oral or written.

Authority – the power or right to do something. God's authority over everything is absolute and unconditional. Refer to Ps 29:10; Isa 40; Acts 1:7.

B

Backslide – To revert to sin or wrongdoing in the practice of morality or religion. Refer to Jer 2:19; 31:22.

Biblical Criticism - An *umbrella* term covering various techniques for applying general literally historical principles in analyzing, studying, and evaluating the Bible and its textual content. The word "criticism" is not to be taken in the negative sense of attempting to degrade the Bible, although this motive is found in its history. Technically, biblical criticism simply refers to the scholarly approach of studying, evaluating, and critically assessing the Bible as literature in order to understand it better. It asks when and where a particular text originated, how, why, by whom, for whom, and in what circumstances it was Produced. The principles of biblical criticism are based on reason rather than revelation. It also involves the quest for validation of Jesus Christ. Older terms to describe this same research were "rationalism" and "Higher criticism." See **Form Criticism, Historical Criticism, Literary Criticism,** and **Textual Criticism.**

Biblical Theology - A narrow center of attention drawing its information from the Bible while considering historical events during a specific era of the biblical passage. Biblical theology is exegetical in nature. Biblical and Systematic theologies are similar but separate in that both have a foundation on Scripture. However, systematic theology also includes sources outside the Bible. Biblical theology expresses the thoughts of a biblical writer from biblical passages and historical events; systematic theology seeks conclusions from all sources of information. Biblical theology considers the writers of Scripture, the historical setting of the recipients of their writings, and the circumstances that led them to write. It takes its material from the Old and New Testaments, stressing the historical circumstances in which the doctrines were formulated and arrives at a theology. Biblical theology attempts to place the findings historically in the development of the doctrine.

Born Again – An inner spiritual renewal as a result of the power of God. Jesus used the phrase in John 3:3, 7.

C

Calvinism - Calvin's theology was formulated in "Scripture only." He was a biblical theologian, trained in the techniques of exegesis, the purpose being to discover what the Scriptures clearly said. He referred to Deut. 29:29 many times, believing the Bible reveals God and His purposes to us, yet there is a dimension of the divine being, which no man can understand. His theology was the result of his belief that the Scriptures were the Word of God and therefore were the final authority for Christian belief.

Christian Ethics - The result of systematic theology in a Christian believer's life. While the emphasis of systematic theology is God's statements on a topic and what a person is to understand, the emphasis on Christian ethics is on what that person to do and be. I use the term "see and be" in explaining this. The theology allows us to "see" the Truth of God, the "be" demands an action on what is seen.

Christology - The study of the Son of God, one of the Persons of the Trinity.

Church – An assembly of believers. It is not a building, rather the Christians who gather in it; the Body of Christ. Refer to 1 Cor 4:17; Rom 16:5.

Communion – Used to describe the Lord's Supper. Refer to 2 Cor 6:14; 1 Cor 10:16

Condemnation – Guilty or wrong. Believers who follow Christ can be confident that God does not condemn them. Refer to Rom 8:1; Ps 34:22.

Confess – Openly admit and confess to God a wrongdoing. Refer to Matt 3:6.

Conscience – That part of one, which leads to feel an obligation. Refer to John 8:9; Rom 2:14-15.

Constructive Theology - A 1970s theological liberalism with the objective of discrediting and reshaping the traditional orthodox faith. Christianity is mysterious; Scripture does not hold authority in spiritual understanding, discredits the problem of evil, and deconstructs biblical faith.

Conversion – Turn from sin to God. Refer to Ps 51:13; Acts 9:1-22.

Convict of sin – The work of the Holy Spirit upon one's heart and mind concerning sin. God wants one to turn away from sin. Refer to John 8:9; Jude 15.

Covenant - A contract or agreement between two parties binding them to each other. Theologically, it denotes a gracious undertaking entered into by God for the benefit and blessing of man.

D Document - One of the possible literary sources (J.E.D.P.) of the Pentateuch. D derives from the book of Deuteronomy and other passages in the Pentateuch. Seems to have been composed about the time of the fall of the Northern Kingdom, Israel (722 BCE)

Deism. There is no personal God to whom man can relate. God separated Himself from the human race, leaving man alone in the created world. Beliefs include a denial of the Trinity, the incarnation, the divine authority of the Bible, miracles, any elect people such as Israel, and any redemptive act.

Depravity – Moral infection that draws a person toward evil action. Refer to Rom 1:29; 2 Pet 2:19.

Discern – Able to separate the things from God and the things not from Him. Also a gift for the "discerning of spirits" in 1 Cor 12:10. Refer to Job :30; Ezek44:23.

Dispensation - The Greek meaning "to manage, regulate, administer, and plan the affairs of a household." Used to refer to God's plan of the unfolding of various stewardship periods throughout history. Generally, there are seven stages of revelation. Dispensationalism derived from the teaching of John Nelson Darby, later popularized by C.I. Schofield, is based on the belief that God deals with the human race in different ways at different times.

Doctrine – Teaching about God and how to live for Him. Refer to Titus 12:1; John 7:1-17.

Dogmatic Theology - The study of a specific theological system of a denomination or theological group. A *dogma* refers to a decree, decision, or command.

E

E Document. One of the possible literary sources (J.E.D.P.) of the Pentateuch. E derives from the Hebrew divine name *Elohim*.

Ecclesiology - The study/theology of the church, the body of Christ, the corporate saved people.

Empirical Theology - An American development, arising out of an emphasis on experience. It developed during the rise of the scientific method as a way of testing conclusions. It accepts religious statements, but should be verifiable by asking questions. It thus remains open when stating conclusions. One of its founding thinkers is Alfred North Whitehead.

Epistemology - A branch of philosophy that is concerned with the theory of knowledge. It is an inquiry into the nature and source of knowledge, the bounds of knowledge, and the justification of claims to knowledge.

Eschatology - The study of "last things"—death, Judgment, heaven, hell, etc. The events of what God will do in the future as revealed in the Scriptures. See End Time Events in chapter Six.

Eternal Life - As described by Jesus Christ in John 17:3, it is *knowing* God and having fellowship *with* God through the Son. It is in contrast to physical life.

Eternity - God's infinity in relation to time. Describes God's transcendence of limitations of duration. It is an exaltation of God above all temporal limitations of the universe.

Ethics, Biblical - All biblical theology has moral implications, whether in Judaic or Christian thought. The development of ethics began in the "book of the covenant" (Ex. 20:22-23:19).

Everlasting Life - Life without end. It must not be conceived of as an exclusively future possession. It includes the fullness of life after one accepts salvation through Christ. It is a possession that can never perish. (John 10:28).

Exegesis - The applying of the rules of Biblical Hermeneutics (see definition below) to the meaning of a passage of Scripture. It is a reproductive Process of interpreting the thoughts of God as expressed in Scripture. It demands the analysis of the biblical text using literal, historical, and grammatical methods. The study of Biblical Archaeology, Biblical Hermeneutics, Biblical languages, and Biblical Theology are utilized. The importance of how words have been used historically is invaluable in Proper exegesis. Exegetical Theology is a careful, analytic study of the Scriptures classifying them into doctrinal topics. This leads to biblical theology which results in systematic theology. Exegesis concerns the meaning of the Scripture. Theology uses exegesis to systematize the topic under consideration.

Existentialism - Not a body of doctrines, rather a way of philosophy that believes the most important characteristic of a human being is freedom. What one becomes is the result of one's free choice. The free person is the authentic human being, while those who compromise their freedom are living inauthentically or in bad faith.

Fate, Fatalism - Considered to be an unseen power that rules over human destiny. Pervades much of the thought of Hinduism, Buddhism, and Islam.

Faith - Best described in Heb 11:1. The writer of Hebrews goes further in the following verses to describe examples of those who believed the Word of God regardless of contrary circumstances.

Fall - Used to describe Adam and Eve's disobedience and commission of sin. This resulted in the inheritance of sin for all human beings.

Foreknowledge - God prescience or foresight concerning future events. One aspect of God's omniscience.

Forgiveness – The fact of only God completely forgiving sin upon confession by an individual.

Form Criticism – Form criticism is concerned with what oral precursors (stories, legends, myths, etc.) - are discernible behind the text. It breaks the Bible down into sections (*pericopes*, stories) - which are analyzed and categorized by genres (Prose or verse, letters, laws, court archives, war hymns, poems of lament, etc.) - . It begins with the recognition that a portion of a text may have a history of its own, independent of the larger work in which it is located. It includes an attempt to discover the way in which a portion of Scripture made the transition from oral to written form and ultimately into the Bible canon

Fullness of time - Twice in the New Testament (Gal 4:4; Eph 1:10). To encompass the totality of God's redemptive plan in history.

Fundamental Theology – Theology that teaches God is revealed in Christ.

Glorification – Refers to the time when those who died in Christ and the living believers will be given the resurrection of the body. See Immortality. See Rapture. See End Time Events in chapter Six.

Gnosticism – Considered the Product of Greek philosophy and Christianity. They are said to mislead Christians astray by the manipulation of words and the twisting of Scriptural meanings. They claimed to have a higher knowledge, which one must subscribe to.

Glory - See Light in cp Six

Gospel - Basic meaning of "good tidings." Refers directly to the good news of the Kingdom of God.

Hamartiology - The study of sin.

Heal - The restoration of health, making whole whether physically, mentally, or spiritually.

Heaven – (1) The region above the earth (Gen 14:19); (2) The place of God's presence from whence Christ came and to which He returned (Ps 80:14; Jo 3:13). To the Jews, the seventh heaven of God's presence.

Hermeneutics (Biblical) - The science of interpretation and explanation, using various modes. It derives from the Greek word *ermeneuo*, meaning to interpret and to explain. It establishes and classifies the rules and methods used to interpret the meaning of the author's language. These rules change depending on the nature of the work under consideration. Every form of human expression demands a different set of rules. The rules for Bible interpretation depend upon the type of writing being studied. **Biblical Hermeneutics** is the science of interpretation and explanation of the Bible by establishing and classifying the rules and methods of the individual authors. The various modes used could include archaeology, canonical, historical, rhetorical etc.

Hell -See Hades, Sheol in cp Six
Hermeneutics (hur meh NEWT icks) - The principles and methods used to interpret Scripture.

Higher Criticism - The term describes the study of Scripture from the standpoint of various forms of literature contained therein. This is opposed to "lower criticism," which deals with the direct text of Scripture. Higher criticism has led to many results producing contradictions in understanding the Bible. Attacks on the authorship of certain books, as well as the suggestion that the Scriptures contain errors, attempt to remove our Christian understanding. See **Biblical Criticism.** Peeling away the layers of thought, which produced the Bible, includes the three literary tools of source criticism, form criticism, and historical criticism.

Historical Criticism - A sub category of Biblical Criticism. The examination of the Bible in light of its historical setting. Very important because it was written over a period exceeding one thousand years. When was the book written? When did the events happen?

Historical Theology - The study of theology by drawing from the development and unfolding of the entire realm of the subject. It includes the study of the development, conclusions, and Pronouncements by church councils. It traces the history of God's people since the time of Christ, organizing the spread of religion into sub-topics including Church History, Mission History, Biblical History, and History of Doctrine. It includes how Christians in various time periods understood the topic.

Holy Spirit - See author's book *The Essence of Christian Belief* for detailed treatment of Holy Spirit (Pneumatology).

Hypocrite - One who's life reflects antagonism to what is sacred. Majority of OT occurrences are in the book of Job. Also may be understood as one who forgets God.

I

Illumination - The divine element to understanding the truth of God. The Holy Spirit aids every Christian Believer in the quest of understanding Him.

Imminence - The belief that Christ can return at any moment and that no predicted event must intervene before that return.

Bible Theology Terminology

Immortality - (see Chapters Four and Five).

Immutability - A characteristic of God signifying that He does not change. Refer to Mal 3:6; James 1:17.

Incarnation - The act whereby the Son of God took union with Himself and human nature. He was born a human being by the Father's act.

Inerrancy/Infallibility - The Bible is error-free, ***The law of the Lord is perfect*** (Psalms 19:7); ***But one who looks intently at the perfect law*** (James 1:25). Not one error has been found in the writings of the authors of the Bible; the many copies of the originals have proven its perfection. We state that the Bible in its original autographs is entirely true and never false in all it affirms. There are no important omissions of the identical truths of God's Word in thousands of versions from the copies. The treatment of the sciences in the Bible has been found free of error. Examples include, *Botany* (hundreds of plants are mentioned in the Bible, all with a proven existence) and *Astronomy* with its improved telescopes tell the Biblical story of creation. Also, a myriad of Biblical facts concerning animals, birds, music, art, architecture, mysteries of the human body, and things in the natural world such as rain, water, winds, evaporation, clouds, thunder and lightning have been recorded in the Scriptures. The Lausanne Covenant in 1974 declared the Bible "inerrant in all that it affirms" and included fifteen statements, which are the basis for most doctrinal statements in modern Evangelical Christianity. The International Council on Biblical Inerrancy in its 1978 Chicago statement affirmed inerrancy in a brief statement that the "Scripture is without error or fault in all its teaching..." Then followed nineteen articles to further describe and explain inerrancy.

Infinity - A term implying that God is not bound by time and space. Refer to Col 1:15; Heb 1:3.

Inspiration - Inspiration comes for the Greek word *theopneustos,* which literally means "God-breathed." It is that power of the Holy Spirit upon the minds and spirits of specific men that enabled them to write God's will to man. Paul wrote to Timothy ***All Scripture is inspired*** (is God-breathed) ***by God and Profitable for teaching, for reproof, for correction, for training in righteousness; so that the man of God may be adequate, equipped for every good work*** (2 Timothy 3:16-17 NASU parenthesis added for emphasis). In addition, we read ***[Yet] first [you must] understand this, that no Prophecy of Scripture is [a matter] of any personal or private or special interpretation (loosening, solving) - . For no Prophecy ever originated because some man willed it [to do so — it never came by human impulse], but men spoke from God who were borne along (moved and impelled) - by the Holy Spirit*** (2 Peter 1:20-21).

J

J Document. One (J.E.D.P.) - of possible early sources of sections of the Pentateuch.

Justification - God pardons and accepts believing persons. To Pronounce, accept, and treat as just. It is a legal term declaring a verdict of acquittal, and thus excluding all possibility of condemnation. It is Proof of man's acceptance to God.

K

Kenosis - A Greek term taken from Phil. 2:7 where Christ is spoken of as having "emptied Himself" and taken human form. The preexistent Son became man.

Knowledge (to know God) - Merriam-Webster defines knowledge as *the sum of what is known: the body of truth, information, and principles acquired by humankind.* Concerning this work on theology, let us amplify this definition from the Bible story of an educated man named Nicodemus. His first words after he came to Jesus were **Rabbi, we know** (John 3:2a). Nicodemus listed a few things he knew, and Jesus responded to him *explaining he was wrong*. Truthful knowledge can only be known by a spiritual transformation. There is nothing wrong with knowledge of information. We have more knowledge today than any time in history.

L

Literary Criticism - A sub category of Biblical Criticism. The study of how, when, where, and why the books of the Bible were written. Usually divided into **Source Criticism, Tradition Criticism, Redaction Criticism**, and **Author Criticism**. See each division for definition.

M

Mark of the Beast - The identification or branding of unbelievers during the period of the Tribulation. The mark will be connected to the work of the Beast. See End Time Events in chapter Six.

Mediator - The role of one bringing reconciliation between two parties. Christ brings the reconcilement between a human being and God.

Mercy - The act of compassion upon another. God shows mercy toward human beings following repentance, even though not deserved or earned.

Mercy Seat - The slab of gold placed over the Ark of the Covenant, functioning as a cover or lid.

Millennium - A period of one thousand. The period in the future when the influence of Satan will be temporarily removed. Several "time frames" have been presented by various scholars. See End Time Events in chapter Six

Monotheism - The belief that there is only one God. See **Polytheism**.

N

Natural Theology - The branch of theology, which includes evidence, found in nature proving the existence of God.

Naturalism - The view that the "natural" universe, the universe of matter and energy, is all that there really is.

Neo-Orthodoxy - A movement in Protestant theology that began after the outbreak of the First World War. It was the most influential and creative theological movement of the first half of the twentieth century. It was a Protest against liberal theology.

New England Theology. Rooted in the Westminster Confession, culminated in the work of Jonathan Edwards. It wrestled with the questions of God's sovereignty, original sin, and the Atonement.

New Testament Theology. See Old Testament theology.

Nicaea, Council of (325 C.E.). The first ecumenical council in the history of the church.

O

Old Testament Theology - The conclusion on a topic using the Scriptures of the Old Testament books and using a historical theology method. This discipline, along with **New Testament Theology** and biblical theology, arrange their materials in the order found in the Bible.

Ordinances - Almost all denominations practice two ceremonies, baptism and the Lord's Supper. Both picture and commemorate the sacrifices of Jesus, and both were established by Christ. Other "ordinances" have been recognized by some groups, but only two are Scripture based.

P

P Document - One of the possible literary sources (J.E.D.P.) of the Pentateuch. P derives from the *Priestly History*, likely written in Babylon during the period of the Exile (597-538 BCE). This document surveys the history of Israel from the creation to the Exile, and was possibly used to form the framework of the Pentateuch.

Pantheism - A theory of the doctrine concerning God, which teaches everything, is God and God is everything. Seneca said, "What is God?—He is all that you see and all that you do not see"[2] Each of the different forms of pantheism center around the individual mind which is infinite. Life is in the mind.

Plenary Inspiration - The thought that God is the author of the Bible, in varied ways. Each author was inspired in all that they wrote, though in varied ways. Deals with matters of content, which could only have been known by divine revelation. See **Verbal Inspiration.**

Philosophical Theology - A study on the various topics using the method of reasoning and drawing conclusions based on observation of the universe and without the Scriptures.

Pneumatology - The study of the Holy Spirit, a Person of the Trinity.

Polytheism - The belief in a multitude of distinct and separate deities. It characterizes Hinduism, Buddhism, and Taoism. In the ancient world, Egyptians, Babylonians, Greeks, Romans, and Assyrians worshiped a plurality of deities.

Practical Theology - This type of theology attempts to apply Exegetical Theology, Natural Theology, Historical Theology, and Systematic Theology to practical life. To apply these types of theology to the practical life, Practical Theology utilizes Homiletics, Church Organization, Church Administration, Liturgics, Missions, and Christian Education. We identify this branch as theology, which relates to Christian ministry.

Predestination - God foreordains whatsoever comes to pass. He has chosen a body of believers to reside with Him forever. The choice remains with the individual.

Progressive Revelation - The recognition that God reveals His nature, word, plans, and purposes—over time.

Propitiation (Pro PISH ee ay shun) - The turning away of wrath by an offering.

Providence - From the Latin "to foresee." Only God brings about future events. He continues to govern the world and to direct it toward the ends that God has set for it.

Pseuderpigrapha - Jewish writing from a few centuries before and after Christ, which are not included in the Bible. A few examples are *The book of Enoch, The Book of Jubilees, The ladder of Jacob,* and *The life of Adam and Eve.*

Psychoheresy - Involves trusting, believing, practicing, and pursuing the psychological wisdom of man for the issues of life where God has already spoken in His Word.

Purification - See Sanctification.

R

---

[2] Chafer, *Systematic Theology*

Bible Theology Terminology

Rapture of the Church - The removal or uniting of God's body of believers with Christ See End Time Events in chapter Six.

Reconciliation - A belief usually ascribed to Paul of the restoration of unity. A right relationship with God is the heart of all religion. God, in Christ, reconciles.

Redaction Criticism - A sub category of Literary Criticism, which attempts to understand the contribution to the finished manuscript made by the person who finally committed the oral or written traditions to writing.

Redemption - The means by which salvation is achieved, namely, by the payment of a ransom.

Regeneration - An inner re-creating of fallen human nature by the sovereign action of the Holy Spirit. The new birth.

Religion - This is a misunderstood term. It is used to describe many practices around the world. Many, including this author, would prefer not to use the term when referring to Christian believers. Followers of images, idols, or various "gods" have a "religion." Our statements above are clarified as we look at the word. The etymology of the word is uncertain. Many scholars have attempted to trace the word back to its origin, with little conclusion. However, ancient words such as *religare* (which did not include the topic of sin and need for redemption) and *relegere* (to observe earnestly that which concerns a worship of gods) allow us to comprehend the word "religion." A broader conclusion would state that religion is the expression of attitudes and action resulting from the individual's belief system.

Remission - Release from sin, Acts 2:38; Heb 9:22. More than a passive act by God. Jesus took initiative to break the grip of sin and set people free.

Repentance - A meaning of "to turn back, away from, or toward." It is almost exclusively used in the sense of regretting and having remorse.

Resurrection - Being raised to life from the dead. Allusions are in Ps 49:14-15; Isa 26:19-20. Also, refer to Dan 12:2. The Scriptures clearly teach the body shall rise again, but will be like the glorified body of Christ. It will be a reward of the righteous.

Revelation - From the Greek word *apokalupsis*, meaning, "To unveil, reveal, and uncover." This is the unfolding of truths which man could not know himself. The Bible contains revelation only revealed by God. He alone has given revelation on the many topics we include in foundations.

Consider *that the mystery (secret) was made known to me and I was allowed to comprehend it by direct revelation, as I already briefly wrote you.* (Ephesians 3:3); *The mystery of which was hidden for ages and generations [from angels and men], but is now revealed to His holy people (the saints)* - (Colossians 1:26-27); *according to the revelation (the unveiling) - of the mystery of the plan of redemption which was kept in silence and secret for long ages, 26 But is now disclosed* (Romans 16:25b-26a). Revelation is revealed by the Spirit of God to satisfy man's moral and intellectual nature. Because God made man a spiritual being having intellect, He supplies the answers in the form of revelation. God discloses Himself or communicates truth to the spirit and mind of man. Thiessen states it like this, "The revelation may occur in a single, instantaneous act, or it may extend over a long period of time; and this communication of Himself and His truth may be perceived by the human mind in varying degrees of fullness."[3] His Word is revelation; He is revelation. We will explore this further, by looking at the methods of revelation, in Chapter Five, Who Is God?

Righteousness - Christ was sent by God to die for the sins of every human being. When one believes in Christ and His sacrifice on the cross, righteousness is imputed to that one. That one is given by grace the gift of Christ's right standing with God.

S

Salvation - See Salvation in chapter Six.

---

[3] *Introductory Lectures in Systematic Theology,* Henry Clarence Thiessen, Life Line, Philippines, p. 31.

Sanctification - To make holy. To be set apart from the world and unto God. Refer to Lev 11:44; 1 Pet 1:16; Heb 12:14.

Sanctify - The action of being set apart to Christ. Used many times in the Bible. Refer to 1 Cor 7:14.

Saved - The act of accepting Christ, His sacrifice, and His resurrection for one's self. See Salvation in chapter Six.

Second Coming See End Time Events in chapter Six -

Sin - The word's meaning clarifies the fact that all persons have come short of God's design. Hundreds of times, the Bible refers to "falling short" or "failing" in one's walk in life. We may use words such as "trespass," "transgression," "disobedience," and "iniquity," (each an individual Greek word), to describe sin. Sin separates from God, and deserves judgment. Refer to Rom 3:23, 5:12, 19; 1 John 1:9, 3:4; 1 Thess 4:14-18.

Sinaiticus, Codex - The manuscript comprising virtually the entire Bible, discovered in 1844 on Mount Sinai. It contains most of the biblical books plus some parts of the Old Testament Apocrypha.

Soteriology - The study of salvation.

Source Criticism - A sub category of Literary Criticism. The search for the original sources, which lie behind a given biblical text. An example of source criticism is the study of the three Synoptic Gospels, Matthew, Mark, and Luke. A student of the Bible will notice that the three are very similar, indeed, at times identical. The dominant theory to account for the duplication states what is called the "two-source hypothesis." This suggests that Mark was the first gospel to be written, and that it was probably based on a combination of early oral and written material. Matthew and Luke were written later, and relied primarily on two different sources: Mark and a written collection of Jesus' sayings, which has been given the name "Q" by scholars. This latter document has now been lost, but at least some of its material can be deduced indirectly, namely through the material that is common in Matthew and Luke but absent in Mark. In addition to Mark and Q, the writers of Matthew and Luke made some use of additional sources, which would account for the material that is unique to each of them.

A second example of the use of source criticism is the "four-sources of the Pentateuch authorship." The JEDP theory advocated by German scholar, Julius Welhausen (1844-1918) has been a controversial topic for many decades and demands the research of source criticism.

Sovereignty of God - The doctrine that God has unlimited power and authority over all creation. Refer to Rom 8-11. See Omnipotence in cp Four.

Spiritual gifts - the many spiritual gifts given by the grace of God to His people. They are given for the building up and edification of His church. Every believer has at least one gift. Refer to the gifts, listed in 1 Cor 12:8-10; Eph 4:7-13; Rom 12:3-8. Each gift comes by the Person of the Holy Spirit and will operate in love.

Systematic Theology - "The collecting, scientifically arranging, comparing, exhibiting, and defending of all facts from any and every source concerning God and His works."[4] As a science, the topic must include historical and natural considerations in addition to the Biblical record. The historical and Biblical records are organized in a methodical and logical order under the various topics of theological study. The word "systematic" comes from the Greek word *sunistano*, meaning, "to organize." It is the opposite of disorganized or unarranged. The topic is discussed in a systematic way. Systematic theology results in part from Exegetical, Natural, and Historical Theology. The conclusion offered on each topic is the result of the many Scriptures written by God. Scripture is the final authority on each topic and is the concluding statements on each topic considered.

T

---

[4] Lewis Sperry Chafer, *Systermatic Theology* (Dallas: Dallas Seminary Press, 1950).

Talmud - A vast and varied work geared toward an understanding of a Jew's legal and moral responsibilities as set forth in the Bible. Interpreted by rabbis over a period of about seven hundred years, 200 BCE – 500 CE.

Temptation - The carnal, sinful principle within man that is opposed to God. Generally are actions produced by the flesh. The flesh can not be "saved." It can however be brought under the Spirit of God. Refer to one list of sins in Gal 5:19-21.

Textual Criticism - A sub category of Biblical Criticism, describing the attempt to determine the wording of the text of the Bible as first written down under the inspiration of the Holy Spirit. It compares the early copies with each other and determines what the original wording most likely was. Considered the most important and fascinating branch of study.

Theism - The belief in one personal God. The term, unfortunately, is used in several different ways. The understanding adopted in this book, defines Theism as One personal God, both immanent and transcendent, Who exists in three Persons. I will hold to this interpretation since all other concepts have a false view of God.

Theocracy - From the Greek word meaning "the rule of God." A people ruled by God, as in ancient Israel. First used by Josephus, who contrasts it to monarchy or democracy, to describe the system of government at the time of Moses.

Theology - Derived from the two Greek words, *theos* and *logos* (defined earlier) - , it refers to a compilation of Christian beliefs. The name carries a sense of completion. It is defined by Wiley as "the systematic presentation of the doctrines of the Christian Faith."[5] It is God's revelation in Scripture with attention given to the particular cultural settings of the biblical writers. Theology is concerned with the most important issues of life (see specific DEFINITION) including God (Theology Proper), man (Anthropology), sin (Hamartiology), salvation (Soteriology), Christ (Christology), the Church (Ecclesiology), Holy Spirit (Pneumatology), angels (Angelology) and end time events (Eschatology). It is the result of thorough exegesis (see above definition). The broad field of theology is divided into sub-types, which are narrow in scope. Generally, theology consists of five branches: Exegetical, natural, historical, systematic, and practical (see definition of each).

Theology Proper - A category of study within systematic theology. It is the study of the nature and existence of God. The term *Proper* is used to

---

[5] *Introduction to Christian Theology*, H. Orton Wiley and Paul T. Culbertson, Beacon Hill Press of Kansas City, 1946, p. 16.

distinguish the study of God the Father (in contrast to the study of Jesus Christ or the study of the Holy Spirit).

Theophany - A visible or auditory manifestation of God emphasizing the message of God.

Torah - Scroll of the law and teaching read in the synagogue on the Jewish Sabbath, Mondays and Thursdays, and of Jewish holy days. Included are the five books of Moses, the Pentateuch, hand-lettered by a *sofer* (scribe).

Tribulation - A great trouble as recorded in Matt 13:21; Jo 16:33; Rom 5:3. See the Great Tribulation, End Time Events in cp Six.

Trinity -The theological term describing the three-in-one God of the universe. The word does not appear in the Bible. However, on several occasions all three are present together. Three persons, Father, Son, and Holy Spirit are God. They are not separate persons or Gods, not does one exist without the other. All attributes of God are present in each one's actions and presence. See author's book *The Essence of Christian Belief.*

U

Universalism - A belief, which affirms that a specific time, everyone will be released from any penalty for sin and restored to God. It denies the biblical doctrine of eternal punishment and may be associated with early Gnostic teachers.

Unpardonable Sin - The belief that there is a sin, which cannot be forgiven. Matt 12: 22-32 and Mk 3:22-30 describe blasphemy against the Holy Spirit as being unforgivable. The exact meaning is not known. We do know that the sin cannot be committed by accident. If one is concerned about it, their very concern shows that they need not be afraid.

V

Verbal Inspiration - All the words and all the verbal relationships are inspired by God. All are of significance in the totality of inspired Scriptures. Dictation is not involved; there is no violation of the personality of the writer. See **Plenary Inspiration.**

Virgin Birth - The doctrine, which teaches that the mother of Jesus Christ was a virgin when He was conceived and had no biological father. God, by the Holy Spirit placed His Son inside Mary.

SIX

Additional Detailed Descriptions of Key Old Testament Words and Helps to Aid in Study

Ai

Ai, "heap of ruins," was Located east of Bethel. It was small in size—Joshua needed only 3,000 to capture it. Archeology has revealed a gate of the fortress located on the north side. Abundant ash, burned pottery, and stones remain as evidences of destruction by fire. (Joshua 8:28).

Anointed

To anoint, to rub with oil, especially in order to consecrate someone or something. Appearing almost seventy times, *mashach* refers to the custom of rubbing or smearing with sacred oil to consecrate holy persons or holy things.

Priests and kings in particular were installed in their offices by anointing. The most important derivative of *mashach* is *mashiyach* (Messiah), "anointed one." Messiah was translated into Greek as *Christos*, thus His designation, "Jesus Christ."

Samuel is the first book to use the word *anointed,* the origin for the word *messiah*.

Apocalypsis

"Apocalypsis" is a Greek word meaning "revelation," "hidden." or "concealed." It is a special type of literature that arose among Jews--it reveals mysteries.

These writings were not named apocalyptic for several hundred years after the Old Testament prophets' times. There were many books classified apocalyptic in ancient days. Most of them never made it to the "canon" (see Canon) of scripture, which is our Bible.

Some of the names of those books are *Book of Jubilees, I and II Enoch,* and *War Scroll.*

Of course, we are looking at God's Word. The earliest apocalypse book we have is Daniel, and all the other similar books were written in imitation of it.

Aramaic Dialect

A Semitic dialect formerly inaccurately called Chaldee (Chaldaic) because it was spoken by the Chaldeans of the book of Daniel (Dan 2:4-7:28). However, the term Chaldee has been abandoned.

This Babylonish Aramaean dialect supplanted the Hebrew, and became by degrees the prevailing language of the people, until in its turn was in some measure, though not entirely, supplanted by the Greek. It is commonly accepted that Jesus spoke Aramaic.

This was the language of Babylonia, and was acquired by the Jews during the exile, and carried back with them on their return to their own land.

Both Hebrew and Aramaic used the same alphabet, the one borrowed from the Phoenicians. The precise date of the invention of the alphabet is unknown, but it surely ranks as one of the most influential inventions in the history of humanity. This script quickly became adopted throughout the ancient Near East. It even served as the precursor of Greek, which in turn served as the model for Latin, the same alphabet we use today.

The Old Testament was written entirely in Hebrew, except for Gen 31:47; Ezra 4:8-6:18; Jeremiah 10:11; and Daniel 2:4-7:28, which were written in Aramaic. Scholars do not always agree why these texts are written in Aramaic instead of Hebrew. The basic reason seems to lie primarily with the language spoken by the audience originally being addressed by the biblical author. The author was in captivity in Babylonia.

Spoken from at least c. 2000 BCE, Aramaic eventually replaced many of the languages of the ancient world in popularity and usage. Aramaic was the common language spoken in Palestine in the time of Jesus.

Armageddon

During the past fifty or more years, various writings have emerged attempting to understand *Armageddon*. This is but another writing on this oft-misunderstood term. The attempt is to explain the meaning in simple language.

The English term *Armageddon* comes from two Hebrew words, *Har* and *Megiddo*

Har means "hill" and *Megiddo* roughly means "a place of troops." The city of Megiddo was located at a very critical junction in Palestine. A valley is located just south and east of Megiddo called Valley of Megiddo. Perhaps there have been more wars fought in that area than any other spot on earth. For example:

One of the earliest battles involved an Egyptian Pharaoh (Refer to the chart of Pharaohs in Volume 1, Chapter TEN of author's book *Travel Through the Old Testament*, Thutmose III called "the Napoleon of Egypt," oppressor of God's people. He defied all his advisors and marched his army single file through a narrow pass and so surprised the Canaanites—they ran!

It was here that Deborah and Barak sang a song of praise to God (Judges 5) thanking Him for literally sweeping away the Canaanite army by swollen waters.

Gideon defeated the Midianites (Judges 7) in this valley or plane of Meggido. It also was here that the deaths of King Saul and King Josiah happened.

The Assyrian Empire made it the capital of an entire province in 740 BCE, because of its strategic location.

And of course, another powerful leader figures prominently in this location sometime in the future; for it's here that Satan will gather armies to make a final attack near Jerusalem in a futile attempt to usurp God.

Armies heading north or south used this location, really a hill. This was the most traveled trade route in those days making it a vital junction for all travel in the known world. The town of Megiddo overlooked the Valley of Jezreel and controlled the narrow pass leading from Egypt and Mesopotamia and from Phoenician cities to Jerusalem. In an article by the Israel Ministry of Foreign Affairs in 2000 CE, he remarks "Megiddo is mentioned many times in Egyptian royal inscriptions from the 15th to the 13th centuries BCE. They attest to the city's importance as the center of Egyptian administration in Canaan as a logistical base on the road north." It is little wonder why so much is written concerning the term *Armageddon*, with widely differing conclusions, some of them false.

Revelation chapter 16 tells the true story surrounding *Armageddon*. Let us set the records straight by using His Word to do so. Revelation 16 informs us that God will dry up the mighty Euphrates River so that the "the great armies of the East" can walk across it, verse 12 *The sixth angel poured out his bowl on the ⏵ great river, the Euphrates; and ⏵ its water was dried up, so that ⏵ the way would be prepared for the kings ⏵ from the ⏵east.*

They will head directly to the Valley of Jezreel and on to the hill of Megiddo. At the same time, the "king of the North" (Daniel 11:40) will have gathered his forces south of Megiddo. He is located there because of a sudden attack on the king of the South. This king of the North will have great "Beast power" and be composed of a confederation of nations in the European vicinity. (It should be noted that as of 2008 CE, the Lisbon Treaty has been presented to twenty-seven European Union member states asking for ratification of this "constitution." The Los Angeles Times on Jun 14, 2008, reported, "This treaty will turn the EU into a super state"). The king of the South likely will be a confederation of Islamic states and its leader.

Dan 11:40-45 *"At the end time the king of the South will collide with him, and the ⏵ king of the North will ⏵ storm against him with chariots, with horsemen and with many ships; and he will enter countries, ⏵ overflow them and pass through.*

41 "He will also enter the ⬚Beautiful Land, and many countries will fall; but these will be rescued out of his hand: Edom, ⬚ Moab and the foremost of the sons of ⬚ Ammon.
42 "Then he will stretch out his hand against other countries, and the land of Egypt will not escape.
43 "But he will ⬚gain control over the hidden treasures of gold and silver and over all the precious things of Egypt; and ⬚ Libyans Ethiopians will follow at his ⬚heels.
44 "But rumors from the East and from the North will disturb him, and he will go forth with great wrath to destroy and ⬚annihilate many.
45 "He will pitch the tents of his royal pavilion between the seas and the beautiful ⬚ Holy Mountain; yet he will come to his end, and no one will help him."

The final battle does NOT take place in this location! Read carefully Revelation 16:16 *And they ⬚ gathered them together to the place which in Hebrew is called ⬚ Har-Magedon.* Notice *gathered*. Just before this verse, in verse 14 we read *for they are ⬚ spirits of demons, ⬚ performing signs, which go out to the kings of the ⬚ whole ⬚world, to ⬚gather them together for the war of the ⬚ great day of God, the Almighty.* Lying spirits persuade the kings of the earth to move down to Jerusalem in the "Har-Megiddo" where they gather. In Zechariah 14, we read *For I will ⬚ gather all the nations against Jerusalem to battle.*

Christ will war on all these kings and destroy them and their armies. *Now this will be the plague with which the* LORD *will strike all the peoples who have gone to war against Jerusalem; their flesh will ⬚ rot while they stand on their feet, and their eyes will rot in their sockets, and their tongue will rot in their mouth.* (Zechariah 14:12)

Armageddon is the gathering or staging place where the kingdoms of armies are motivated to go *up* (located on a hill) to Jerusalem for the battle of the great "day of God." See End Time Events.

Ashdad

Located some twenty miles from Gaza (Josh 13:3; 1 Sam 5:1), it was one of five Philistine cities. One of the cities never taken by the Israelites (Josh 15:46-47). When the ark was captured by the Philistines, it was placed here in the temple of Dagon (1 Sam 5:1-8). Egypt besieged Ashdad for 29 years.

Baal

Found in 1 Kings: 16:31; 18:19, 21, 26, 40; 22:53. *Baal* The word has the literal meaning of "master." Baal was considered as the "son" of the god EL or "father bull" and the fertility goddess Asherah, who is mentioned in 2 Kings 21:7. Baal was the leader of all the Canaanites' gods. Terrible rituals were linked with this worship including prostitution and infant sacrifice. Several times God's people were punished for their worship of Baal and Asherah (Judges 2:11–15; Jeremiah 19:4–6).

Babel

The Tower of Babel was built on the plain of Shinar, a site probably in ancient Babylonia in southern Mesopotamia, after the flood of Noah's time. The structure was built to satisfy the people's vanity: *"Let us make a name"* (Gen 11:4). The pyramid-like tower was expected to reach heaven. These people were trying to approach God on their own self-serving terms. This tower was probably built of bricks and mortar since no stones were available in the flat plain of southern Mesopotamia. An example of one such tower, built in Ur, in southern Mesopotamia, about 2100 BCE, was a pyramid consisting of three terraces of diminishing size.

Babylon

The incredible splendors of the city, including its "hanging gardens," its famous Ishtar Gate, ziggurat, and temples, were defended behind a vast system of fortifications.

The wall was about eleven miles long and eighty-five feet thick and was protected by a moat filled with water from the Euphrates. Actually, the wall was double: the outer wall was twenty-five feet thick and the inner one twenty-three feet thick with an intervening space filled with rubble. Watchtowers stood sixty-five feet apart on the walls. Eight or nine gates pierced the wall. The population of greater Babylon (the walled city and its suburbs) in Nebuchadnezzar's day has been estimated at about a half million. Hebrew accounts represent the city as great in size, beauty, and strength.

The "hanging gardens," which to the Greeks were one of the Seven Wonders of the World, are described as the hanging gardens of Nebuchadnezzar, rising in terraces, which supported full-grown trees. Recent archeological discoveries have shed new light on its location and construction. An ingenious method of *raising* the irrigation to each of the levels was found. How well the words of Daniel 4:30 fit this ambitious builder: *"Is this not Babylon the great, which I myself have built as a royal residence by the might of my power and for the glory of my majesty?"* Refer to author's book *The Chronological History of the Bible Lands*.

Beast

This word *beast* misleads us. We immediately relate it to some incredible creature from the black lagoon! Noah had used this word to describe all the animals he gathered. He referred to "clean and unclean, beasts." So let us not get the wrong idea here.

Most of our more recent translations use "animal" for the translation. The translation is sometimes "[wild] animal."

The translation "beast" is used in apocalyptic literature simple to represent the enemies of God and His people

Daniel says, *"These four great beasts are four great kings, four world empires who shall arise out of the earth."* See End Time Events.

Bethel

Bethel was named by Jacob, meaning "House of God." It was directly north of Jerusalem in the area now called the West Bank, and played an important role in the lives of Abraham and Jacob (Israel). Abraham built an altar between Bethel and Ai (Genesis 12:8). During Israel's monarchy, it was transformed into a center of idolatrous worship. For example, Jeroboam I set up a shrine to serve as an alternative to Solomon's temple. Hosea later called it "house of wickedness."

Ben Sira

Ben Sira (2nd century BCE) was a Hellenistic Jewish scribe, sage, and allegorist from Jerusalem. Sira was a scholar and scribe thoroughly versed in the Law, and especially in the "Books of Wisdom." He is the author of the Book of Sirach also known as the Book of Ecclesiasticus. Also, a medieval text, the alphabet of Sirach, has been attributed to Ben Sira. Ben Sira is also known as Jesus Ben Sira. He wrote his work in Hebrew, possibly in Alexandria, Egypt, *c.* 180–175 BCE, where he is thought to have established a school. Some commentators—claim Ben Sira was a contemporary of Simon the Just although it is more likely that his contemporary was the High Priest Simon II (219–199 BCE). According to the Greek version, the author traveled extensively and was frequently in danger of death. In his writings, he speaks of the perils of all sorts from which God had delivered him. He was exposed to many false statements in the presence of a king of the Ptolemaic dynasty.

Birthright

The birthright was not something taken "lightly." Rather it was taken "highly." It is interesting to realize the ancient birthright concerned mostly the material inheritance. The inheritance was divided into the number of sons, plus one. The eldest son received a double share. So the "stew" or soup bought from Esau the extra share, not the entire inheritance.

Canaan, Canaanites

Canaan was a son of Ham and a grandson of Noah. His descendants settled in areas God promised to Abraham. Excavations suggest that there was no middle class in their society. Later the area was known as Palestine and Israel. The cities of Canaan in ancient days of the Bible were each fortified against chariots and ruled by a king. The most powerful city-states included Hazor, Shechem, Gezer, and Jerusalem.

Canon of Scripture

A measuring rod or standard for books included in the Bible. The thirty-nine books of the Old Testament are historically accepted as meeting the standard. (Note there are also twenty-seven books accepted in the New Testament).

Captain of the Guard

The NIV translates this as *captain of the guard*. This *guard* was an elite, courageous band of rugged men. The Jewish historian Alfred Edersheim describes that group by telling that Potiphar was the "chief of the executioners." Potiphar was nobody to fool around with; he was a man of seasoned military experience with power over life and death.

Cherubim

Cherubim are angelic beings who do God's bidding. They are protectors of God's majesty: they protected the Garden of Eden (Genesis 3:24), they flank or support God's throne (Psalms 80:1; 99:1; Isaiah 37:16; Ezekiel 1:4-28; 10:1-22). They were present in the Tabernacle and the Temple. In the Tabernacle, the Israelites wove cherubim into the curtains covering the inner walls of the Tabernacle tent as well as in the veil that separated the Holy Place from the Most Holy Place. In addition, God ordered two cherubim to be placed on the "mercy seat" which covered the Ark of the Covenant. The cherubim appear again in Revelation 4:6-9, where they surround God's throne protecting his majesty. See Angelology in chapter Four.

Coat of Many Colors

The Hebrew word carries a meaning of "wrists" or "ankles." One scholar describes this coat as being sleeved and extending to the ankles.[6] Only one other place in the Scriptures do we find such a garment, that which describes the rich garment of David's daughter.

Covenants

The Noah Covenant

The rainbow that appears after a rain shower is a sign of God's promise (covenant/agreement) to never again destroy the earth by flood.
Because of the violence on earth, God determined to save a righteous man, Noah and his family and make a covenant with them.

The Bible says Noah walked with God in the midst of all kinds of evil. His obedience to God is recorded five times in this story, (Genesis 6:22; 7:5, 9, 16; 8:17).

Noah followed God's instructions in building a large ark, which saved him and his family in the cleansing waters of a flood. Noah and his family (God's people) could then start a new generation. Indeed, God's covenant promised that until the end of the earth, there would be seasons of planting and harvest and day and night. It also included a promise to uphold the rhythms of the earth in order to sustain human life, even though humans had rebelled against their Creator.

Today all of us, Noah's descends, should remember God's mercy to us when we see the beauty of the rainbow.

The Abraham Covenant

God's covenant with Abraham began with the unconditional promise in Genesis 12:2 *And I will make you a great nation, And I will bless you.* God promised He would multiply Abram's descendants and give them a land of promise, Canaan (13:14-17). I love this: He swore by Himself that He would do it! (22:15-18). Nothing is surer than His Word.

As with all covenants, God made demands. He commanded Abram and Sarai to leave their home and family in Ur, and go to a new land (12:1). He commanded them to be a blessing to others (12:2), to walk before Him and be blameless (17:1), and to circumcise the males in their household as a sign of the covenant (17:10). God asked for obedience, and Abram withstood the test of believing and obeying (15:6; 22:1-19).

---

[6] V 31 *Then they took Joseph's (distinctive) long garment* (AMP)

The Moses Covenant
At a mountain called Mt. Sinai, for the first time, God made a covenant with the entire nation of Israel (Exodus cps 19-24).

In this covenant, God first reminded the Israelites of who He was and how He had acted on their behalf. He was their Savior (19:4). In addition, if they made a covenant with Him, He promised to make the Israelites *My own possession* (Exodus 19:5). He would pay special attention to them and make them *a kingdom of priests and a holy nation.* God demanded of them that they would become holy or separated from all other nations. By that separation, they were to be the means by which the other nations would learn of the living God. This nation of priests would lead others to a correct worship of the true God (Psalms 117).

In this covenant, God promised to instruct the Israelites on how they should live (cp 20). As a people who had a relationship with the living God, the Israelites had to act a certain way, His Way. His Law would instruct them on this way of life. He loved them so much He taught them how to live in His Kingdom, now being established on earth.

The New Covenant
Jeremiah is the only Old Testament prophet who speaks of the New Covenant, (which Jesus authored in Matthew 26:28). In reading "new" in the New Covenant, one might be tempted to think of the former covenant, the Moses Covenant, as something that was incorrect. The Law of Moses was never designed as a means to obtain salvation. Instead, forgiveness of sins has always been God's gracious gift to those who have humbled themselves before Him in faith (Genesis 15:16; Micah 6:6-8). The Law was God's way of showing the journey, which believers should follow. In actuality, Israel did not follow that Law which pointed to life. The Israelites continually broke that covenant. God had demands to be met; however repeatedly through priests and prophets, they would repent and then fall away from Him. Idols many times replaced God. The hearts of the people remained unchanged. Only God Himself could change hearts and minds—thus, a New Covenant was needed.

Think of what the Israelites must have thought considering this New Covenant, announced by Jeremiah. The old covenant had come from the very hand of God, written as His glory streamed from His finger, cutting out words on a tablet of stone. The New Covenant would be His glory burning in a new heart, which would lead to the changed life! In addition, now they would have a "helper" to guide them to the covenant (Jeremiah 31:34). No priest or prophet would be needed to stand between a human and God. That Spirit would teach the people the knowledge of God, a knowledge that would be evidence by faith, obedience, and devotion to a personal Lord.

Compassion

We read in 7:19 *He will again have compassion on us; He will tread our iniquities under foot. Yes, You will ▯cast all ▯their sins Into the depths of the sea.* The Hebrew word means, "to love from the womb." Several times, it is translated *mercy*. Isaiah 14:1 uses the same word, and the AMP and NKJV both translate it *mercy*.

We know this word expresses the deepest of emotion; "from the womb." God loves His people with a deep compassion that is beyond expression. The Lord expressed this same love to Moses when it's recorded Exodus 34:6 *Then the Lord passed by in front of him and proclaimed, "The Lord, the Lord God, compassionate and gracious, slow to anger, and abounding in loving-kindness and truth; 7 Who keeps loving-kindness for thousands, who forgives iniquity..."*

Create

A rare Hebrew word in the Old Testament, "bara." It is always used of an act of God, and implying the act was "out of nothing." No other individual in the Bible is said to "bara." The results of six days were accomplished only by *Elohim*. Another Hebrew word, used hundreds of times, meaning "made" could have been used, however He used *"bara."*

Cupbearer

The cupbearer was quite high in rank, Pharaoh's inner circle. We see the similar position of Nehemiah. Nehemiah said, *"now I was the cupbearer to the King"* (1:11b). He had the King's "ear." As a result, he King of Persia, Artaxerxes, heard Nehemiah and granted him his request to return and rebuild his home city. Without that action of a cupbearer, we possibly would not know of a restored Jerusalem.

David's Specific Psalms. We learn many things about David

Psalms 7	I Samuel 24:11-12	David Hides
Psalms 18	II Samuel 22:1-51	David Delivered
Psalms 30	II Samuel 24:25	David Builds
Psalms 34	I Samuel 21	David Delivered
Psalms 51	II Samuel 11:12	David Sins

Psalms 52	I Samuel 22:9	David Distressed
Psalms 54	I Samuel 23:19	David Distressed
Psalms 56	I Samuel 21:10-11	David Delivered
Psalms 57	I Samuel 24:3-10	David Hides
Psalms 59	I Samuel 19:11	David Watches
Psalms 60	II Samuel 8:13	David Celebrates
Psalms 63	I Samuel 23:14	David Runs
Psalms 142	II Samuel 22:1	David Visits

Day

The Hebrew word for day is *yom*, normally meaning a 24-hour day. Reckoned a day, from evening to evening, from the first appearance of the stars in the evening to the first appearance of stars next evening. We may refer to Gen 1:5, 8; Ex 12:18; and Lev 23:32. Days were numbered rather than being named, with the exception of the Sabbath. We read six times in Gen 1, *And there was evening and there was morning, one day.*
The Scriptures also uses the word "day" in a symbolic sense, as in "the day of the Lord" (Isa 2:12, 13:6, 9).

God's Kingdom of heaven was not complete in itself. He had an expanded plan!

Think with me for a moment. Think first of the original thirteen states, The United States of America. Our country existed, first as those thirteen states and then forty-eight states for a long time. However, there came time when our nation, peacefully added to its territory, to eventually include two more "extensions of America." These two "extensions" were given the same, full rights of the "mother" country, the USA. Same government, benefits, rights, and choices of the nation. Equal representation. States of the United States.

Also, consider England. When they expanded and extended their commonwealth, The British Empire called their extensions, colonies. Let us use this in our comments because most of us understand a colony of a nation.

God extended His Kingdom; He expanded, to include earth as a colony, and extension of His Home, Heaven. However this colony would include something different—beings made like Him.

These beings would have God's authority over the colony; totally in service to God as Father, but with His benefits and rights. Human beings created in the image and likeness of God would walk and talk with Him as His sons and daughters. They would fill the colony with generations of sons and daughters who would fill it and walk together in harmony and love for one another. Every one created with individual gifts to complement every other one.

That plan never changed. Interrupted yes, but never discarded.

Day of the Lord

One of the central themes of the Book of Joel is "the day of the Lord" (1:15; 2:1). This language describes a period of time in which God "comes down" in a dramatic way to bring wrath and judgment on the wicked *and* blessings *and* salvation to the righteous. God is Lord of time. Technically, there is no period that is not "the day of the Lord" in a general sense. However, at times God enters the space-time arena to assert in bold, dramatic ways that He is in control.

The day of the Lord is a major theme of Old Testament prophecy. Thirteen of the sixteen prophets address this subject. The concept of the day of the Lord probably originated with the conquest of Canaan—a conquest which was in fact the Lord's war (see Deut. 1:30; 3:22; Josh 5:13–15; 6:2); that is, a day of judgment for the wicked Canaanites (see Lev. 18:25; Deut 9:4, 5).

The day of the Lord is not an *isolated* phenomenon or a *single event* in human history. Periods in Israel's early history and latter history, the coming of Jesus, and His second advent are all called "the day of the Lord" in Scripture. The predictions of a coming day of the Lord can be fulfilled in a number of different events. The invasion of locusts in the historic events of the life of Joel was the day of the Lord (cp. 2). In addition, the day of wrath and deliverance that soon fell on Judah in the Babylonian invasion was also the day of the Lord.

While most references speak of *future events*, and this author prefers to examine the subject in this manner, four biblical texts describe the day of the Lord in terms of *past judgments* (see Is 22:1–14; Jer 46:2–12; Lam 1:1–2:22; Ezek13:1–9). These texts reflect circumstances of military defeat, tragedy, and judgment. Such events may have stimulated the development of the prophetic concept of a future "day" or time of judgment for the disobedient Israel and all of the nations (see Joel 1:15; Is 13:6, 9; Zeph 1:14–18).

However, the day of the Lord is not just a day of wrath and judgment on the disobedient. In some contexts, it *also* includes deliverance and restoration for the righteous, and indeed this author refers The Day in his summary below (and separate detailed manuscript. The day of the Lord speaks not only of future judgment, but also of future hope, prosperity, and blessing (see Is. 4:2–6; Hos 2:18–23; Amos 9:11–15; Mic 4:6–8). Joel reveals that this day is to be heralded by heavenly phenomena (2:30, 31) which will bring sudden darkness and gloom on the earth (2:2). It will be a day of divine destruction (1:15 on the nations that have persecuted Israel (3:12–14) and on the rebellious and disobedient of Israel (Amos 5:18–20). Yet it will also be a time of deliverance and unprecedented blessing for God's people (2:32; 3:16, 18–21; 1 Thess 5:2–5), a direct reference to a "catching away" of believers.

With that summary, note that the author has an extensive manuscript on "The Day of the Lord." A few additional statements will outline the main points. (1) As we approach the final days and **final** Day of the Lord, we should expect greater insight into the time of the rapture, the tribulation, including the days of Daniel's 70th week. His people will be informed by revelation knowledge of those times (2) Daniel's vision of the final seven years of God's plan for all Gentiles will include (chronologically), the first six seals of events brought about by anti-Christ upon all people, the rapture of His Church following the six seals when the righteous are taken away, the final "Day of the Lord" beginning with the seventh seal, bringing God's wrath on mankind including Israel and the nations, and the trumpets and bowls upon all the remaining unrighteous. (3) Seventy-five days of mourning and cleansing of the new Jerusalem Temple. (4) Eternal Kingdom age.

Dead or Alive

An excerpt from chapter seven of the author's book *Travel Through Ephesians* explains Paul's "Old Man." Before knowing Him personally, from Chapter two of Ephesians

#1 *You were dead.* Paul says the people (before accepting Christ) were spiritually dead in sin. They were lifeless towards God. One might have looked alive, but inside were cut off from life. Verse 1 *(you were dead) by [your] trespasses and sins* (AMP). In the Scriptures, death always means *separation*. That was a horrible place to be in…like a graveyard. The unbeliever isn't sick, he's dead; no appetite for food or drink. He doesn't have any pain; can't talk and complain. Dead. Every person (before accepting Christ) was dead.

#2 *You were defiant.* Notice as Paul continues, he uses next the words *you walked [habitually]*. Nicely translated in the AMP Bible because the Greek's compound of words means, "to walk around in one area all the time." This was the beginning of spiritual death, walking against the will of God. Three forces are at work to act as a magnet to attract the human being. The world-system, the devil, and his hierarchy of angels, and the human flesh with its desires for self-fulfillments.

#3 You were degenerated. V3 *obeying the impulses of the flesh and the thoughts of the mind [our cravings dictated by our senses and our dark imaginings]* (AMP, underlines added for emphasis). This unsaved person not *only* does evil (by defying God), but now has grown and is worse. So we add the word *degenerated*. The lost person lives to please the desires of the flesh and the mind. He is incapable of doing good. He is incapable of doing anything to be saved. However, always know the Spirit of God can break in to this degenerate person; however, it will take the constant prayers by others to do so.

#4 You were damned. The unsaved person has been condemned. The God-judge already passed the sentence, however in His mercy, is staying the execution. God loves a human because He sees *in* that person, the image He created. He loves that image. In fact, if we removed the results of sin from him, it would be hard to over-praise him. God's image, that man...would be perfect. So understand this—God will always welcome one back. There is this place of darkness; the one involved has no urging towards God; His love is available, just withdrawn from action in the life. Deuteronomy 31:17 *Then My anger will be kindled against them in that day, and I will forsake them and hide My face from them. 18 And I will surely hide My face in that day because of all the evil which they have done in turning to other gods.* Sin is like a cancer *in* every man, eating all it can get away with. God still reaches out to that sinner.

Every person alive should keep in mind; God will accept anyone into His Kingdom. God will never stop drawing him; patience, long suffering, not ever wanting a man to perish.

Division of The Promised Land

The people were divided into twelve territories, becoming twelve tribes. Each tribe represented the people descending from one of Jacob's twelve sons. Each of the sons had been at their father's deathbed and received his prophecy concerning their future.

Interesting to note, Joseph's two sons represented two of the tribes, Ephraim and Manasseh, while Levi received no land but was given 48 cities with land around them.

The apportionment of land in the Book of Joshua. We would note that Judah was honored of God in a very special way and had the first portion, being allotted land in the high country, south and west of Jerusalem. The other tribes' lands divided by casting of lots.

- To Judah, 15:1-63
- To Ephraim, 16:1-10

- To Manasseh, 17:1-18
- To Benjamin, 18:11-28
- To Simeon, 19:1-9
- To Zebulun, 19:10-16
- To Issachar, 19:17-23
- To Asher, 19:24-31
- To Naphtali, 19:32-39
- To Dan, 19:40-48

Reuben and Gad had received their land east of the Jordan before Joshua led them across. Also, Manasseh had received one-half of their total allotted land on the east side, before the crossing into Canaan.

Caleb, now eighty-five years of age, was given land inside Judah for his part in the conquest, 14:6-13. He took possession of the land, drove the Anakims out of the city, and changed its name to Hebron.

Edom

A nation located southeast of the Dead Sea. The mountainous region with many homes cut into the sides. Obadiah refers to "who live in the clefts of the rocks" v3. Edom was important because it controlled the trade routes. Edom was strongly involved in the economy of that entire area. The Edomites ancestry is traced back to Esau the brother of Jacob. Remember those twins? Edom descended from Esau; Judah descended from Jacob.

Descendants of Esau considered "brothers" by Israel. Edom was under Assyrian domination and prospered from the mining of iron and copper under them until the fall of Jerusalem. They participated in the 586 BCE destruction of Jerusalem, eventually *disappearing* from history.

Edomites

The people from Edom, southeast of the Dead Sea. Edom descended from Esau, the twin brother of Jacob. Their early rulers were called dukes (Gen 36:15-19), and kings (Gen 36:31-43). Many times Edom took advantage of a hatred relationship with Israel, even assisting other nations in attacking Israel and Judah. Because the Edomites were descendants of Abraham, the Israelites were not permitted to war against them.

Elohim

A Key Word in Genesis is the wonderful name we read as *God*, *"in the beginning God."*

It is the Hebrew *Elohim,* the most used Hebrew term for God. Many times it was translated "the almighty God," and rightfully so. It was the fullness of God—a plural word perhaps indicating the Trinity, His fullness—GOD.

Embalming

Found in our story Gen 50:1.[7] The Egyptian's extensive art of embalming became well known in other nations. Their idea was that the preservation of the body was essential to the life of the soul. As far as we know, it was not often practiced by Hebrews, with the exception of Jacob and Joseph. Jacob's sons carried his body back to Canaan at the close of Genesis.

End Time Events

The author has an extensive manuscript considering the entire End Time Events summarized below.

The next events in God's timetable will be the six seals of Revelation 6 followed by a "catching" or "snatching" away of all true believers, along with the bodies of all believers who have already died. The first four seals or events which take place during the first 3 ½ years, are the *beginning of sorrows,* and will reveal a leader who seemingly will step forth in a peace-negotiating place of world acceptance. Seals five and six are what we may refer to as the Great Tribulation which will take place at the mid-point of the seven-year period and end *much before* the end of the seventieth week (Daniel).

Mankind will initiate the first six seals and could be called "man's wrath" initiated through Antichrist. The seventh seal will open "God's wrath which will include the *trumpets and bowls.* The six seals are: (1) revealing of the Antichrist and his world religion, (2) war which brings about (3) famine and (4) pestilence, (5) martyr of a remnant of believers, and finally (6) the cosmic disturbance which *cuts short the Great Tribulation.* The seventh seal will open the *trumpets.* The body of Christ, the true Christ-serving believers, is removed following the sixth seal, on the very Day of the Lord (Luke 17:22-36), and prior to the Day of the Lord's Wrath (Trumpets and Bowls). The sign revealed in Matt 24:30 (Rev 6:12-13, *the sign of His coming*) is chaos, God's wrath, which will break out on earth at the opening of the seventh seal, following the rapture of the Church. We note that the word *wrath* in Revelation does not occur until verse 6:17, the Day of the Lord, informing us that the Lord's Wrath

---

[7] Gen 50:2-3 *Joseph commanded his servants the physicians to embalm his father. So the physicians embalmed Israel. 3 Now forty days were required for it, for such is the period required for embalming.*

begins following the rapture. The word *wrath* is found eight times in Revelation—all eight times follow the opening of the seventh seal. **His** wrath *does not* include the first six seals.

For our continuing consideration, a man will already have stepped forth, out of the Western Democracies (see below), the "little horn" of Daniel two, and brokered a peace covenant with Israel. Many nations will follow him, in particular, a European Federation of nations, a revived empire from the old Roman Empire territory. Perhaps this group of European nations is taking shape today.

This man will break that covenant with Israel exactly 3 ½ years from when it is signed. He gathers a large army, marches into Israel, and captures the rebuilt Temple in Jerusalem (which he allows the Jews to build on the Temple of the Mount before or during the 3 ½ years).

He enters the Temple's Holy of Holies and sets himself up as a god! He reveals a six-symbol numbering system, which he demands of all people. Perhaps it will include a set of numbers related to six, such as an expanded SS# of six numbers-six-numbers-six-numbers. If groceries (or other needs) are to be purchased, the mark must be present on the head or hand, perhaps utilizing "chip" implants or other technology.

Immediately, a tribulation will come upon the entire earth, like nothing ever seen before, which this author believes will take place before the rapture.

The four confederacies converge on Jerusalem after the great-tribulation on earth. They gather in the Jezreel Valley and march towards their real goal: Jerusalem. Jesus Christ then comes to earth in the actual "second coming," *with* His body of believers (already taken away in the rapture), the real Church, destroying the four confederacies.

Following will be His 1,000-year rule of full peace on earth, never before experienced since the entry of evil in the garden. The author of discord, evil, death, and suffering is placed in a pit for the 1,000 years, no influence on any person on earth. (I enjoy reading that it only takes a single angel to take hold of him, casting him in that pit!).

What a glorious period it will be on earth. The confederacies of all nations will be aligned during the seven-year period. The following is a pretty clear alignment:

The confederation of **northern nations**, which will include Russia. Daniel 11:40 represents a group of northern nations led by Russia. It is quite possible this federation will include Iran and the nations of central Asia.

The confederation of **southern nations** Daniel 11:40 represents the group consisting perhaps of Egypt and Islamic nations of North Africa and the Middle East.

The confederation of **eastern kings** Daniel 11:44; Revelation 16:12 representing nations east of the Euphrates River, possibly China, Afghanistan, India, Pakistan, Japan, and Korea.

The confederation of **western democracies**. Daniel 2:40-43 representing the old Roman Empire, perhaps now the European Federation of Nations. This is the 10-king led nations or territories, with one becoming the strong ruler we know as Antichrist. It also is possible that this will be the confederation that the United States will be joined with. Keep in mind that *all the nations of the earth* will gather against Israel in the final days; Zechariah 12:3; 14:2; Revelation 16:14.

At the end of the 1,000 years, Satan will be released from the pit "for a season." Again, he gathers a following, since many will be born during the 1,000 years of peace, and each person must make a decision of who to follow. He again builds a strong army and tries to destroy Jerusalem and Christ's people. A battle takes place with Christ quickly putting an end to Satan and all who choose to stand with him. All who have not chosen Christ from all the ages will stand in front of God in heaven, pronounced guilty, and cast away into a lake of eternal fire. This is the Great White Throne Judgment. A new heaven and an earth renovated by fire are revealed as the eternal location of all the righteous!

Egypt

Egypt handed down its history like no other country. Back to 3000 BCE, we can trace many details that confirm the Old Testament's writings.

Years of drought are well attested in record; a seven-year famine is detailed on a discovered rock; *"My heart is heavy over the calamitous failure of the Nile floods for the past seven years."* Several paragraphs of writing details the seven years. The story of Joseph in Egypt has astonishing confirmation.

At the time of the Exodus, Egypt was a strong and very advanced society/dynasty, already using papyrus and ink for hundreds of years; certainly a world leader. The pyramids had already been built some 1,500 years before.

The land was settled by Ham—and all nations can be traced back to one of the sons of Noah after the occurrence at Babel.

The Pharaoh during some of the years of oppression was perhaps Thutmose III, called "The Napoleon of Egypt"; he was on a mission to keep expanding Egypt's borders and influence to the Euphrates River. He marched many times through Palestine.

You might also recognize some other Pharaoh's names:

Tutankhamen or "Tut." Of course there was Rameses I and II. Refer to author's book *The Chronological History of the Bible Lands*.

Elijah's Cave

It is located near on the west side of the modern Israeli city of Haifa. In ancient times, what is now called the Cave of Elijah the Prophet was a place where believers practiced the cult of the pagan god Ba'al. The Cave of Elijah is a large natural cavern in a sloping rocky outcrop at the foot of Mount Carmel, 131 feet above the sea. Its limestone walls were carved in ancient times to suit its cultic purposes and smoothed by countless hands in the centuries since then, enlarging it to its current size, so that its floor is about 28.5 by 47.5 feet, and the ceiling is about 15–16 feet high

Ephraim

Following the division of the Promised Land into two separate nations, the Northern Kingdom (Israel), was also referred to as Ephraim.

Joseph's younger son was named Ephraim (fruitful). He was born after Joseph became prime minister of Egypt (Gen 41:45-52). Jacob placed his right hand upon Ephraim and prayed for him, saying he would become the ancestor of a multitude of peoples. The descendants of Joseph's two sons would be considered two of the tribes. The tribe of Ephraim was located north of Jerusalem and north of the tribe of Benjamin. Shiloh was located in this territory.

Exodus Pharaohs

Scholars disagree on the time period and kings (pharaohs). The following history of two periods, each of which could have been the oppression and exodus of the Israelites, should be considered. Of course, the question must be asked, "Why did Moses omit the name of the Pharaoh that he faced?" We should note that the Bible is not trying to answer the question, 'Who is the pharaoh of the exodus?' to satisfy the curiosity of modern historians; rather, it was seeking to clarify for Israel who was the God of the exodus."[8] The conclusion seems to be that the exodus-

---

[8] See 1 Kgs 11:40, 14:25; and 2 Chr 12:2, 5 (twice), 7, and 9. The fact that this new trend of identifying the name of a Pharaoh began during the reign of Shishak (Shoshenq I) should be of no surprise to the student of Biblical history, since Shishak's reign signaled both the beginning of a new ruling dynasty, the 22nd Dynasty of Egypt, and the beginning of foreign rule under pharaohs who hailed from Libya.

ALSO See 2 Kings 23:29, 33, 34, 35; 2 Chron 35:20, 21, 22; 36:4; and Jer 46:2. Pharaoh Hophra is named once as well, though his name appears only in a prophetic writing, where God calls him, "Pharaoh Hophra, King of Egypt" (Jer 44:30).

pharaoh's throne-name is absent for one reason alone: a skilled writer named Moses, born in Egypt and trained as a prince in all of the ways of the royal court of Egypt (Acts 7:22), followed the standard practice of his day by leaving unnamed the foreign monarch who assumed the role of a dreaded enemy of his own nation, in this case Israel.[9]

It is this author's opinion that Amenhotep II is the only legitimate candidate for the exodus-pharaoh. However, consider both the following two possible Exodus Pharaohs.

Amenhotep II ruled during the period following his father, Thutmose III. Amenhotep II, meaning "satisfied," was the seventh Pharaoh of the 18th dynasty of Egypt (see list of 18th and 19th dynasties in this volume). Amenhotep, who was not a firstborn son, inherited a vast kingdom from his father Thutmose III, holding it together by several military campaigns. His elder brother, Amenemhat was the intended heir; born of the chief wife, Satiah. However, Amenemhat died shortly after his father became Pharaoh. A Pharaoh generally had a chief wife, a "second favorite" as well as other "lower" wives.

Amenhotep II became Pharaoh at the age of eighteen, according to an inscription from his great Sphinx notation. It is concluded that the most accurate dates of his twenty-six year reign are *c.* 1453 to 1426 BCE. However, there are questions as to exact dates.

Egyptian records show that Amenemhat was the eldest son of Thutmose III, allowing Amenhotep II to have lived through the tenth plague, since he was not the firstborn.

The oldest son of Amenhotep II would have died during the tenth plague, which must be true of the exodus-pharaoh's son. In fact, none of Amenhotep II's sons claimed to be his firstborn. Even one prominent Egyptologist theorizes that the eldest son died inexplicably during childhood.

The 19th Dynasty in Egypt (see list of Pharaohs of the 18th and 19 Dynasties), began with Rameses I. Rameses I was a very old man when he was surprisingly appointed Pharaoh. The reason for his appointment was interesting. Pharaoh Horemheb (the last of the 18th dynasty) had no children, so actually chose his successor. Rameses, an older military man, had several children and grandchildren, who would assure a long succession of family rule. Rameses' son Seti I was followed by Seti II, known as Ramses the Great.

---

[9] ibid

Ramses the Great was groomed to be pharaoh from childhood and he would rule for 67 years, the longest rule in Egyptian history (1304-1237 BCE).

Ramses distinguished himself in two ways: as a military leader and as a builder.

He completed several halls and temples started by his father. However, Ramses the Great always carved his own name into the buildings. He also built his own structures, one of which was carved out of a mountain, the temple of Abu Simbel, designed to scare any boats sailing north. Four giant 67-foot tall statures of Ramses the Great seated on his throne greeted any visitor.

He organized the army into skill levels— infantry, archers, and charioteers. His army was 20,000 strong, divided into four divisions, each named after a god—Amun, Ra, Ptah, and Set. The army marched into Syria, where he met strong opposition of 40,000 Hittites. Ramses defeated the enemy almost by himself! "Follow me" was his cry to his 20,000. The fight was a standoff, but depicted as a great victory throughout Egypt.

About the 21st year of his reign, Ramses signed a peace treaty with the hated enemy of Egypt, the Hittites. This was perhaps the first peace treaty in history with the hated enemy of Egypt, the Hittites. Ramses continued to mellow. He married a Hittite woman, heaping many riches upon her. He took a 2nd Hittite bride a few years later, thus cementing the arrangement with the Hittites. Ramses had abandoned his military campaign and his first-born son died. Incredible but true, Ramses had over 100 children and dozens of wives. Surrounded by death, his attention turned to building tombs. A tomb built for his first and favorite wife, Nefertari, is the most beautiful in all Egypt.

It has been suggested that Ramses set the Israelites to work as slaves. It is also possible that some of the Israelites were originally hired to work for pharaoh to complete the city of Raamses, although the later Hebrew writers who reported this bondage are unlikely to have referred to "slaves."

It is possible that Ramses the Great was the pharaoh who had begun the oppression of the Israelites. His successor, Merneptah (1224-1211) would then have been the "the pharaoh who did not know Joseph." A large black granite stele, inscribed with a reference to "Israel is laid waste," referring to a people, not a nation.

Many Biblical scholars who affirm the historicity of the exodus now date it to the 13th century BCE, a step that requires a redefinition of concrete numbers in Biblical passages that, if taken literally, would indisputably place the exodus in the 15th century BCE, the period of Amenhotep II.

Gaza

Gaza was a major Philistine city (located in the territory given to Judah) from the time of the judges until its destruction by Alexander the Great following the close of The Old Testament. Located in the strip of land, which today is called Gaza Strip.

Gibeon

This was the only Canaanite city to make peace with Joshua. It was located a few miles northwest of Jerusalem and became an important place of worship. Solomon had come to offer sacrifices at this city when God spoke to him in a dream.

Today it is being excavated at the present time. It was a strategic city, ruling several other cities (Joshua 10:2). The Gibeonites came to Joshua at Gilgal and deceived him into an alliance (which he honored). Later, he made them servants because of it.

Gilgal

Gilgal was the site of the Israelites' first camp after crossing the Jordan River. There, Joshua set up stones as a memorial (Joshua 4:20-24). Gilgal remained the religious location in Israel until David brought the ark to Jerusalem. It was also the site of Saul's later confirmation as king, and the place where he disobeyed Samuel's instructions, resulting in his being rejected by God as king. Today there is remaining only a small cluster of mounds just northeast of Jericho.

God's Kingdom

God's Kingdom of heaven was not complete in itself. He had an expanded plan!

Think with me for a moment. Think first of the original thirteen states, The United States of America. Our country existed, first as those thirteen states and then forty-eight states for a long time. However, there came time when our nation, peacefully added to its territory, to eventually include two more "extensions of America." These two "extensions" were given the same, full rights of the "mother" country, the USA. Same government, benefits, rights, and choices of the nation. Equal representation. States of the United States.

Also, consider England. When they expanded and extended their commonwealth, The British Empire called their extensions, colonies. Let us use this in our comments because most of us understand a colony of a nation.

God extended His Kingdom; He expanded, to include earth as a colony, and extension of His Home, Heaven. However this colony would include something different, beings made like Him.

These beings would have God's authority over the colony; totally in service to God as Father, but with His benefits and rights. Human beings created in the image and likeness of God would walk and talk with Him as His sons and daughters. They would fill the colony with generations of sons and daughters who would fill it and walk together in harmony and love for one another. Every one created with individual gifts to complement every other one.

That plan never changed. Interrupted yes, but never discarded.

Grace

GRACE is favor or kindness shown without regard to the worth or merit of the one who receives it and in spite of what that same person deserves. Grace is one of the key attributes of God. The Lord God is "merciful and gracious, long-suffering, and abounding in goodness and truth" (Exodus 34:6).

Therefore, grace is usually associated with mercy, love, compassion, and patience as the source of help and with deliverance from distress. The grace of God is always free and unearned. I define His Grace as *"God lavishing on us ALL that He is, All of His benefits, even though we really deserve none of them."*

Greed

The characteristic word for "greed" or "covetousness" in the Old Testament is *betsa*, which means "unjust gain" or "to have an inordinate desire for what belongs to someone else." It is consistently denounced in the Bible, from the Ten Commandments (Exodus 20:17; Deuteronomy 5:21) and throughout the Bible:

Achan, the Israelite whose greed cost his nation a battle
Ecclesiastes blasts the emptiness of greed and materialism and exhorts the reader to "remember now thy Creator ..."
The sad story of **Gehazi's greed** serves as a contrast to the principled behavior of his master Elisha.
The first "woe" uttered by **Isaiah,** is against covetousness and greed. Isaiah encouraged the Jews to put away greed (56:9–11),

Nehemiah is quick to address the spirit of greed when it rose
Micah also is known as the champion of the oppressed. He condemns wealthy landowners for taking the land, attacks dishonest merchants for charging excessive interest rates, and even the priests and prophets who seemed to be caught up in the tidal wave of greed and dishonesty that swept his country.

Haran

City in Mesopotamia known for its worship of the moon god, Sin. Abram lived there to care for his ailing father, Terah, after leaving Ur in route to Canaan. He left for Canaan following his father's death. Haran flourished for the next 1,000 years based on its trade with other nations. Assyrian forces captured it in 763 BCE, made it its capital, and then saw it captured by the Babylonians in 609 BCE. Jacob also lived there for a short time. A son of Terah, one of the brothers of Abraham also had this name.

Hazor

The largest city/territory in Canaan during the second millennium BCE. Hazor is the largest archaeological site in Israel. It remained important even after the Israelite conquest. Remaining fortifications and residential buildings date from the tenth century BCE until its destruction in 732 BCE (2 Kings 15:29). It is located 8.5 miles northeast of the Sea of Galilee. It was heavily fortified with walls as wide as 24'. In 1962 CE, a clay tablet was found with its name on it (discovered by a tourist!).

"Hazor formerly was the head of all those kingdoms"—thus wrote the chronicler of the Book of Joshua (11:10), and the source before him was undoubtedly reliable and accurate. Of all the sites mentioned in the Book of Joshua as having been conquered by the Israelites, none is as important as the destruction of Hazor. As a result of this victory, *"Joshua took all this land ... the mountains of Israel and its lowlands from Mt. Halak and the ascent to Seir, even as far as Baal Gad in the Valley of Lebanon below Mt. Hermon"* (Josh 11:16-17).

During thirty excavation seasons conducted at the site of ancient Hazor, it became clear that this was the largest and most important city-state in the Land of Israel in the second millennium BCE. Hazor spanned 200 acres, 10 times the size of Jerusalem in the days of King David and King Solomon.

The magnificent find uncovered within the Ceremonial Palace of the Canaanite period point to extensive commercial, cultural and artistic ties with the centers of power in the region, from Babylon in the east, through the Hittite kingdom and Egypt, all the way to Cyprus and Greece in the west. Hazor's days of grandeur ended with its fall into the hands of the Israelite tribes that settled the land. As clearly shown by the famous Merneptah Stele, dated to the last decade of the 13th century BCE, the Israelites were present in Canaan. They are credited with having brought down the Canaanite Hazor.

The visitor to Israelite Hazor has the unique opportunity to witness the reliability of the Biblical historiography first-hand and to cast his eyes upon the structures attributed to the days of the monarchs of the Kingdom of Israel, from Solomon, through Ahab and Jeroboam II, until the days of Pekah son of Remaliah.

Evidence of the Joshua-destruction by fire has been discovered with a date of Joshua's time. Excavations have revealed its total destruction. Judges 4 records that Deborah and Barak continued, "Until they destroyed" Jabin (who ruled at Hazor).

Hebron

The word means *fellowship* or *communion*. A city located twenty miles southwest of Jerusalem. Abraham lived there for a short period and established his family burial at this location. David made this city his capital for the seven and one-half years he was king of the Southern Kingdom, Judah.

Hebrew

Exodus 2: 11-15 tells the story of an Egyptian beating a *Hebrew* slave. What is the meaning of the word Hebrew? A name derived from Eber, a descendant of Noah's son Shem, the line of the Hebrew race and used to refer to the people of God's nation. Shem was called *the father of all the children of Eber* (Genesis 10:21), which is perhaps the origin of Hebrew.

Today the term is often used to refer to the Jewish people or to their classical language, Hebrew, but it once had a much wider meaning.

In the Old Testament the term appears most frequently in the Joseph story (Gen. 39: 17; 40: 15; 41: 12), the Exodus story (Ex 1:16; 2:7; 3:18; 5:3; 7:16), and the story of the Philistine wars (1 Sam. 4:6, 13:19; 14:11).

The word is generally used by outsiders in speaking **of** the Israelites or by Israelites when speaking **to** outsiders. It does not express the sense of solidarity implied by the word "Israel," for there were Hebrews who were not members of the Israelite community.

Abraham is called a Jew for the first and only time in a peculiar tradition found in Genesis 14 about Abraham's wars with the kings of the east (Gen. 14: 13) According to Bible tradition, Abraham the Hebrew *('ihri)* was a descendant of Eber *C'eber).* In the genealogy found in Genesis 10

26-30, however, Eber was also the ancestor of other peoples. Arabs, Arameans, Moabites, Ammonites, and Edomites could trace their ancestry to him. All of this suggests that the term Hebrew" originally was more inclusive than it is in biblical texts, which refer specifically to the Hebrews who were slaves in Egypt and who eventually became the community known as Israel.

Later the term was restricted to the biblical Hebrews, the Jewish people, as in the Jonah story (Jon 1: 9) The Apostle Paul insisted that he was "a Hebrew born of Hebrews" (Phil. 3: 2).

Hezekiah's Tunnel

Hezekiah's Tunnel, discovered in 1880 CE was dug through solid rock from the Pool of Siloam to Jerusalem in order to ensure a supply of water for the city in anticipation of an Assyrian attack. It was cut through 1,750 feet of solid rock, with workers starting on opposite sides of the city and meeting in the middle, following an "S" shape. Had it followed a straight line, the length would have been 1,070 feet or 40% shorter.

The tunnel remains today and funnels water into the Pool of Siloam. Visitors from around the world visit the tunnel and view the markings on its walls.

High Places

Found in 2 Kings: 12:3; 14:4; 15:4; 23:8, 15, 20. This refers to a sacred area located on high ground such as a hill or ridge. There was nothing wrong with this in the early days of worship before the temple was built (1 Kings. 3:2–4). At a later time, the Israelites started worshiping pagan gods at these sacred sites. Because of that, this term high places in the Old Testament became associated with Israel's religious rebellion and apostasy (1 Kings. 14:23; Psalms 78:58; Jeremiah 19:5).

Hittites

The Hittites are mentioned fifty-four times in the Bible. Many well-known persons are mentioned in connection with Hittites. Abraham and Sarah, Isaac and Rebecca, and Jacob and Leah were all buried in the Cave of Machpelah, which Abraham had purchased from Ephron the Hittite (Genesis 49:29-32). Isaac's son Esau married Hittite women (Genesis 26:34; 36:2). Isaac's wife, Rebecca, feared that Esau's twin, Jacob, might marry a Hittite woman. She tells her husband, "I am disgusted with my life because of the Hittite women. If Jacob marries a Hittite woman what good will life be to me?" (Genesis 27:46). There were several references to Hittites during the Kingdoms of Israel and Judah (1 Kings 9:20; 10:29; 11:1; 2 Kings 7:6; 2 Chronicles 1:17; 8:7). Beautiful Bathsheba, whom King David desired when he spied her bathing, was married to a Hittite named Uriah. Refer to author's book   Refer to author's book *The Chronological History of the Bible Lands.*

Horeb

The second verse of cp 1 mentions they traveled from Horeb. Horeb (in the Pentateuch) is a name for Mt Sinai where the Israelites spent one year being taught. It had taken Israel about one year to reach Kadesh from Mount Horeb or Sinai and another year to reach the place where Moses was delivering the messages of Deuteronomy. The thirty-eight years between had been spent wandering. That is why in most of my information concerning dates; I refer to thirty-eight years of wandering.

Huldah

Huldah a prophetess lived during critical years in Judah's history. She foretells the destruction of Jerusalem, 2 Kings 22:14–20; 2 Chronicles 34:22–28▢. The name "Huldah" (Weasel) is derived from the Hebrew root *cheled,* which means, "to glide swiftly." Perhaps Huldah's name reflects her quickness of mind and her ability to swiftly and rightly discern the things of God.

Clearly, Huldah had established a reputation as God's spokes-person. We are even more impressed when we realize that the prophet Habakkuk, whose book is part of the Old Testament, was living at this time. Yet Huldah was clearly the king's first choice when seeking to know God's will.

Huldah had a word from God for the young king Josiah. God would indeed bring calamity on His sinning people. But because Josiah's heart was tender and he had responded when he heard God's Word, judgment would not fall during his reign.

Huldah experienced no conflict between the roles of prophetess and wife. Huldah's husband did not feel threatened by the fact that his wife had an important ministry.

Hyksos People

A multiracial people, infiltrated Canaan in the late eighteenth century on their way to Lower (Northern) Egypt, taking over and ending the 13th Dynasty in Egypt. They brought to Egypt music instruments and new breeds of animals. Their mighty chariots, drawn by horses were also brought to, and introduced to, Egypt. They remained in power from *c.*

1720 BCE until *c.* 1567, driven out by Ahmose, founder of the eighteenth Dynasty. This is the period when the Israelites went from royal favor, to reduced servants as a new king came to power. Refer to author's book *The Chronological History of the Bible Lands.*

Integrity and Character

Integrity relates to our behavior before other people, whether or not they are watching. Proverbs 20:7 *The righteous man walks in his integrity.* Psalm 26:1 *...for I have walked in my integrity.* Proverbs 10:9 *He who walks with integrity walks securely.*

By approaching every aspect of our lives with a concern for what God thinks, and a commitment to live with purity, we can develop confidence in our character. He is holy (Deuteronomy 7:6; 14:2), humble (Psalms 34:2), righteous (Isaiah 60:21), and upright (1 Kings 3:6). Someone said, *"We need to be known for our integrity as Tiffany's is known for jewelry."* God's people must be people of truth and unimpeachable integrity. How can that happen? Through fewer words and more deeds. That is the way to build consistent evidence of a new and credible lifestyle with lasting impact.

Psalms 15 lists ten marks of integrity. How does your life compare?
- Walks uprightly
- Works righteousness
- Speaks the truth
- Does not backbite
- Does no evil to a neighbor
- Does not take up a reproach against a friend
- Honors those who fear the Lord, not the ungodly
- Keeps his word, even when it is costly
- Does not practice usury
- Does not take bribes

There are many Old Testament examples of people with integrity. Two examples

Job's determination to hold fast his righteousness and integrity was remarkable. Though Job believed that God had taken away a fair trial, he would not put away his integrity. He persevered despite the discouraging words of his wife and friends.

Consider Joseph. He had no support system for his beliefs or values and no one to turn to for godly counsel as he made far-reaching decisions. In spite of the environment he was in, he walked with integrity:

He maintained his moral integrity when facing the advances of Potiphar's wife (Genesis 39:7–10).

He kept doing his best even when the situation was the worst when unjustly thrown into prison, (Genesis 39:22–23).

Indestructible Bible

The Bible has proven it is indestructible. The fact that the text of the Bible has survived throughout history is a wonderful testimony to the preserving power of God. The Scriptures have survived time, persecution, and criticism.

Satan does not question the importance and authority of the Bible. He has attempted to destroy it throughout history. Whether Romans in New Testament times, barbarians of the dark ages, Spanish Inquisitors in the Middle Ages, French radicals in the eighteenth century, Nazis in World War II, Soviet Communists or Chinese revolutionaries, all have tried to destroy the Bible. It is not unusual throughout history to read of gigantic fires where Bibles were burned.

Note with me its indestructibility: The first book of the Bible was composed some thirty-five hundred years ago; the last was completed nearly two thousand years ago. The original manuscripts were all written on perishable materials and have since disappeared. The thousands of copies we possess, however, accurately represent the originals. We investigated this in a paper printed in Volume 1 of this study course.

We also note the Bible has survived the persecution of its adherents. Consider the following examples of the tenacity of the followers of the Bible in preserving its text in the midst of persecution.

The mad tyrant Antiochus Epiphanes in 167 BCE decreed, "The books of the law (i.e. Jewish scripture) that they found they tore to pieces and burned with fire. Anyone found possessing the book of the covenant, or anyone who adhered to the law was condemned to death."

Note, in 303 CE, the Roman emperor Diocletian wrote an imperial letter ordering the destruction of all churches, the burning of all Scriptures, and the loss of civil liberties by all professing Christians. That did not stop the spread of Christianity or the proclamation of God's revelation in the Bible. Constantine, the Roman emperor who succeeded Diocletian, converted to Christianity and eventually ordered Eusebius to make fifty copies of the Scriptures, to be produced by the best scribes and at government expense.

Time passes, but the Bible remains a dramatic testimony to the keeping power of God for his revelation. Rulers come and go. The Bible remains. Critics come and go. The Bible remains.[10]

With the rise of Islam in the seventh century, the Bible has been consistently outlawed in strict Moslem countries. To this very day, distribution of Bibles is strictly forbidden in Moslem countries. Countless Christians have lost their lives for attempting to distribute the Bible and/or share its teachings to receptive Moslems.

In the year 1199 CE, Pope Innocent the First ordered that all French Bibles were to be burned and that people were forbidden to read it. In the year 1234 CE, Pope Gregory IX again ordered all people to surrender their Bibles for burning. In Spain, Ferdinand and Isabella, the very ones that sent Columbus out to find the new world, ordered the Bible to be turned in, and destroyed; and there are many other examples where people tried to destroy the Bible—and yet, it has survived!

In 1530, Henry VIII gave orders that all English Bibles were to be destroyed. People caught distributing the Tyndale Bible in England were burned at the stake. This attempt to destroy Tyndale's Bible was very successful, as only two copies have survived.

Voltaire, the noted French infidel who died in 1778, said that within one hundred years from his time, Christianity would be swept from existence and passed into history. But what has happened? Voltaire has passed into history, while the circulation of the Bible continues to increase in almost all parts of the world, carrying blessing wherever it goes. For example, the English Cathedral in Zanzibar is built on the site of the Old Slave Market, and the Communion Table stands on the very spot where the whipping-post once stood! The world abounds with such instances.[11]

There is a historical irony about the Voltaire matter. Fifty years after his death, the Geneva Bible Society used Voltaire's house and printing press to print hundreds of Bibles. Further, over two hundred years after Voltaire's death, Christianity is still not extinct!

In spite of persecution, perversion, criticism, abuse, and time, the Bible has survived virtually intact. An anvil has worn out many hammers. There is no ancient document, which has the manuscript support that even approximates that of the New Testament. The Scriptures are unique in the quantity, quality, and antiquity of their manuscripts. Many have sought to ban and destroy the Bible, but their efforts have been futile. The Bible is by far the most popular book in the world. Portions have been

---

[10] McDowell, Josh, *Josh McDowell's Handbook on Apologetics*, electronic ed., Nashville, Thomas Nelson, 1997
[11] Collett, Sidney, *All About the Bile*, Old Tappan, N.J., Revell, p. 63

translated into over one thousand seven hundred languages, and it has been copied and circulated more extensively than any other literature. Recent archaeological, historical, and linguistic evidence have refuted destructive critical theories in favor of the trustworthiness of Scripture.[12]

Then we add to our study, in Jeremiah, *God's Word was "destroyed," early in the sixth century* BCE (Jer Cps 11–26). The king should have been copying the Law for his self and heeding its message. Instead, he destroyed what Jeremiah had spoken and Baruch had written. King Jehoiakim dearly paid for his arrogance. You can try to destroy the Bible, but you will fail.

However, God's Word indeed is preserved (27–32). The king and his family are gone and would be forgotten were it not for the Book he tried to destroy! God's Word will endure: "Forever, O LORD, Your word is settled in heaven" (Psalms 119:89).

Jehoiakim listened as the scroll was read aloud; he did not appreciate this Word and tossed it into the fire. Read it in Jeremiah 36:23. Jehoiakim did not repent, later to be defeated by the Babylonians and dragged away in chains. He died in captivity. A lesson for all: "He who would attempt to destroy God's Word puts himself in great danger."

"The deathless Book has survived three great dangers: the negligence of its friends; the false systems built upon it; the warfare of those who have hated it." Isaac Taylor

In the past 100 years, Communist governments have attempted to discredit the Bible and to prevent its circulation in their countries. They have used both educational and legal measures.

Educationally, people have been taught that the Bible is a superstitious fairy tale book to be rejected by enlightened communist minds. Legally, many people have been arrested and imprisoned for attempting to smuggle Bibles into Communist countries.

The Bible will stand, even if all else were destroyed! Luke 21:33 makes it clear: *Heaven and earth will pass away, but My words will not pass away.*

Israel

The word "Israel" has undergone quite a change in its meaning over the years, so demands some detail. It makes for an interesting and educational study. I will trace the appearance of the word *Israel* in the Bible because the meaning has shifted over time.

---

[12] Wilkinson, Bruce; Boa, Kenneth: Talk Thru the Bible, Nashville

1. The word begins in the book of Genesis, where we find the famous story of Jacob wrestling with an angel. We will review his life in Four Great Men. In this story for now, we find Jacob, the founding ancestor of ancient Israel, made his journey across the Fertile Crescent moving back from an area called Aram-Naharim to his homeland in Canaan.

As he reaches the eastern side of the Jordan River, near Penuel and Succoth the Bible describes his confrontation with a man who wrestles with him throughout the night. In the end, the man could not prevail over Jacob; you can see from this, the great determination of Jacob, not his power, the angel even knocked Jacob's hip out of joint. As the day begins to break, Jacob holds on to the man and says: "I will not let you go unless you bless me." The man blesses him with a name. He says: "Your name shall no more be called Jacob, but Israel, for you have striven with God and with men and have prevailed." So we find that the name Israel is first used as *the name of a man*.

We learn that Jacob's opponent throughout the night was not a man, but God. In Jacob's struggle with his God, he receives a blessing, a new name, and an injury. Therefore, in our first encounter with the word Israel, we are talking about a person, a founding ancestor who is said to see God face to face, although we know God's face cannot be fully looked upon; it was shielded in some way.

2. Then, the patriarch, Jacob, had twelve sons whose descendents became the nation of Israel. This story is told to us in the books of Joshua and Judges. The book of Joshua opens with a promise that the twelve tribes of Israel, the descendents of Jacob, will together conquer the land of Canaan. It then narrates this divinely granted conquest with Joshua leading the twelve tribes of Israel to victory after victory. The book of Joshua closes with his call to all the tribes of Israel to gather at a place called Shechem and swear loyalty to their God. So, in our second encounter with the word Israel it designates *a people:* the twelve tribes of Israel.

So first a man, second a people. Later in the books of 1 and 2 Samuel, Israel is the name of **a** *monarchy* headed by King David and his son Solomon. This united monarchy unites and leads the twelve tribes of Israel so the word Israel then designated a kingdom made up of 12 tribes. However, after 75 years, the united monarchy divides and a rebellion within the twelve tribes' results in division, and Israel becomes the designation for the northern 10 tribes, under Jereboam. Judah is the designation for the tribes of Judah and Benjamin in the south under Rehoboam. (One tribe, Levi, is a priestly tribe that is not territorially bound). So Israel, during **this time** of the divided monarchy is still a kingdom, however, much smaller.

The northern kingdom, which has this name of Israel, falls to Assyria in 722 BCE. The southern kingdom of Judah falls to Babylonia in 586. Judah alone continues to exist as a people in exile from their land. As the sole remnant of the original twelve tribes of Israel, Judah becomes *the memory holder* for all Israel. By surviving as a people, Judah wins the right to tell the story of Israel. In that story, Judah sees itself as a remnant of Israel, the only remnant of Israel. In fact, when the Judean exiles return from Babylonia to their homeland in Judah, beginning in 538 BCE, this one remaining remnant tribe returns under the mantle of Israel.

It is interesting, as I was reviewing this history in my mind; David's rule started with only one tribe, Judah, and now again the nation of Israel consists mostly of one tribe, Judah, back in their homeland. Once there, the returning exiles from Babylonia find other Judeans living in the land. These Judeans had not gone into exile. In addition, conflicts immediately erupt between those who had experienced exile and those who had not. THE important factor here is that those Judeans who had experienced exile in Babylonia returned to Judah with a book, some form of the Torah.

It seems that their experience of conquest, deportation, and exile had led them to preserve their stories and their laws and to pass them down to their children in writing. In this written Torah, they preserved the story and the memory of their ancestor, Jacob. Jacob, they remembered, had also experienced exile in Mesopotamia and he had also returned to his homeland. As he returned he was met by God, wrestled with him throughout the night, and received the name Israel. So, the returning exiles who preserved this story saw themselves as the *new Israel*, the house of Jacob; the tribe who would bring the "Lion of Judah" the Messiah. Like their ancestor, they felt that in exile they **also** had wrestled with their God and come away both permanently marked with a limp, but also blessed, and with the name of Israel.

Through the centuries of history, the word Israel has changed. However, one aspect of the term remains consistent during each biblical period. In every period described in the Bible, Israel is of central importance. It is the chosen *person*, the chosen *nation*, the chosen *kingdom* and *remnant* of the Israelite God, and finally *a new-born Israel*. This remains a central theme today.

A man—A people—A kingdom—10 tribes—1 tribe, a memory holder—a captive remnant—a new Israel.

Israel Topography[13]

Travelling from the Mediterranean coast eastward, we note the land of Israel has four strips or geographical sections.

First is the *coastal plains* of Phllistia and Sharon, terminated at the north by the promontory of Mount Carmel. Further east, moving inland, rise the *central rugged plateau* (about the size of Long Island), dotted with unwelcoming thorns and scrub, seamed and broken by steep and narrow gorges, and occupied in historical times, from south to north, by the tribes of Judah, Ephraim and Manasseh (these last two forming the core of Samaria). Moving north again we cross into the land's most important inland plain of Jezreel, flanked by Mounts Carmel and Gilboa and merging, on Its northern side, into the slopes of Galilee.

Moving to the east, the country fell sharply into the *Jordan Valley*, which widened, at two points, into the Dead (or Salt) Sea and the Sea of Galilee

And finally, to the east, came *the hilly or mountainous fringe* tracts, not regarded, for millennia, as genuinely Israelite: Edom beyond Judah's Negeb wilderness, and Moab and Ammon across the Jordan.

The entire complex of small, varying, and often mutually hostile
Territories (Israel), extended for about a hundred and fifty miles from north to south, and less than seventy-five across.

"Ites" in the Promised Land

Hittites, located northwest (modern day Turkey). They had a few small settlements in the land.

Amorites, a general ethnic people located in portions of Babylon.

Girgashites, located east of the Sea of Galilee.

Canaanites, a term for the people of the Holy Land, specifically the inhabitants near the Jordan Valley.

Perizzites, near the hill country, which was eventually a part of the tribes of Judah, Ephraim, and Manasseh.

Hivites, located in the Lebanon region.

Jebusites, and independent clan near Jerusalem until David captured Jerusalem.

Jabesh

Jabesh was located in Gilead just east of the Jordan River and south of the Sea of Galilee. It was part of the half-tribe of Manasseh east of the Jordan.

---

[13] Summarized from Michael Grant, *The History of Ancient Israel,* Orion Publishing Group edition, 2002, p. 7

The city was named from its geographical characteristic "dry place." That was a common method of naming a person or city:
- Adam "soil"
- Abel "meadow"
- Bethlehem "location of Bread"
- Gath "wine press"
- Ramah "height"
- Zoar "small"

It was Jabesh that Saul rescued when the city was threatened by the Ammonites.

Jehovah[14]

The personal divine name YHWH has had an interesting history. In the Old Testament period, the Hebrew language was written only with consonants; vowels were not added until the Common Era, when Hebrew was no longer a living language. Based on Greek texts, which of course use both vowels and consonants, it is believed that the original pronunciation of the name was *Yah-WEH, Yahweh*. Notice the shortened form of the divine name in the exclamation, "Halleluyah-Praise Yah." However, because of its holy character, the name Yahweh was withdrawn from ordinary speech during the period of the Second Temple (*c.* 500 BCE and later) and the substitute Hebrew word, actually a title not a personal name-Adonai, or (The) Lord, was used, as is still the practice in synagogues. Scholars who translated the Hebrew Bible into Greek (the Septuagint) in the third century BCE adopted this synagogue convention and rendered YHWH as "(The) Lord." From this Greek translation, the practice was carried over into the New Testament.

The word Jehovah is an artificial form that arose from the *erroneous* combination of the consonants YHWH with the vowels of Adonai-written under or over the Hebrew consonants to indicate that the substitute is to be pronounced. The erroneous translation, Jehovah, is nowhere found in Hebrew Scripture. This hybrid form is often held to be the invention of Peter Galatin, confessor of Pope Leo X, in a publication dated 1518 CE, but in actuality, it can be traced back to a work by a certain Raymond Martin in 1270.

Jewish reverence for the Name has influenced numerous modern translations, which, like the Septuagint translators, follow the ancient synagogue practice and substitute Adonai, which translates as "The Lord" in English.

---

[14] Compiled using *Understanding the Old Testament*, Bernhard W. Anderson, Prentice-Hall, 1986, p. 61.

Jewish Calendar

Tishri	7th	September-October	30 days
Heshvan	8th	October-November	29 or 30 days
Chislev	9th	November-December	29 or 30 days
Tebeth	10th	December-January	29 days
Shebat	11th	January-February	30 days
Adar	12th	February-March	29 or 30 days
Nisan (Abib)	1st	March-April	30 days
Iyar	2nd	April-May	29 days
Sivan	3rd	May-June	30 days
Tammuz	4th	June-July	29 days
Ab	5th	July-August	30 days
Elul	6th	August-September	29 days

Jericho

Jericho, located twelve miles north of the Dead Sea was called "the city of palm trees" (Deut 34:3) and strategically positioned. The city controlled the vital water supply for the entire area. It was one of the largest urban centers in the land of Canaan. The economy of Jericho had advanced beyond food gathering to production of food during that period. Pottery was made by the year 4500 and records indicated massive walls enclosed a population of perhaps two thousand.

Archeology has revealed cobbled streets, shops, storerooms, and living quarters of a bustling economy. The stone wall surrounding Jericho was approximately fifteen feet tall. Archeologists have discovered a small portion of the city wall that did not fall when all else was destroyed.[15] The section that remained standing was nearly eight feet high, with a house built against it, still intact.[16]

Jerusalem

Jerusalem existed as far back as the eighteenth century BCE, before the arrival of the Israelites. During that Middle Bronze Age II to Iron Age I (archaeological terms), it was a tiny area south of the Temple Mount,

---

[15] Joseph P. Free, *Archaeology and Bible History*, rev. and exp. Howard F. Vos (Grand Rapids: Zondervan, 1992), 109

[16] Bryant Wood, *The Walls of Jericho, Creation*, March 1999, www.answersingenesis.org

known today as the City of David. However, it did include a massive fortification, recently excavated. It consisted of approximately 11 acres with a population of 500-700 persons.

The city grew in population to the time of Kings David and Solomon in the 1000-800 BCE period. Solomon expanded the city to forty acres, mostly by way of the temple and related buildings. The population reached 2000-3000 persons.

During the next period, the Western Hill was added to Jerusalem. More than a hundred acres became land in Jerusalem. Archeologists have well documented this addition of territory. The fall of the northern kingdom of Israel at least partly accounted for the great increase in population.

The city expanded outside the walls, north, with a total population exceeding 7500. Sennacherib laid siege upon Jerusalem in 701 BCE causing a reduction in population to around 6000. When Babylonia destroyed the city in 586 BCE, the population was further reduced. Shortly before the time of the destruction of the Temple by the Babylonians, the walled city of Jerusalem consisted of approximately 160 acres. Following the destruction, a few habitants remained in the original territory of the City of David. When the Persians took Jerusalem from the Babylonians, Jerusalem again was only a small territory, with a population reduced to around 400-700, living on the forty acres.

During the remainder of the BCE period, Jerusalem grew in population to approximately 8000 in a slightly expanded territory. But then came the next archeologically documented period slightly before the 70 CE destruction by the Romans. This is the time when Jesus was there. Estimates of the population vary, but the better number would be 20,000. The Christian city of Jerusalem gradually grew in size and population until it reached a peak as high as 100,000 in the fifth-sixth centuries and then steadily decreased to 15,000 by the seventh century.

In 637 CE, the Muslims besieged Jerusalem and the Islamic Jerusalem resulted. By the tenth century, the population was approximately 7000.

Jezebel

Jezebel is introduced in 1 Kings 16:31 in the listing of the evils of her husband's reign. Probably Ahab's marriage to her sealed an alliance between Israel and Tyre just as the powers of Syria were threatening the coastal states.

Jezebel induced her weak husband not only to introduce the worship of her native idols but eventually to become himself a worshipper of them. Jezebel was able to cut off the worship of God by killing the prophets of Yahweh (1 Kings 18:4,13). She is the first great instigator of persecution against the saints of God. At the same time, she was able to maintain the prophets of Baal. Notice her father's name: Eth**baal**; taught his daughter very well! He ought to be proud!

The New Testament was the first to say, "This is [a] Jezebel." She literally stamped her name on history as the representative of all that is *designing, crafty, malicious, revengeful, and cruel.*

Judges

The name "Judges" is a fitting name, referring to the unique leaders God sent to preserve them from enemies. The name means "deliverers" or even "saviors." The book is not a chronological book, rather it is thematic.

Samuel probably wrote both Judges and Ruth. 1 Sam 10:25 reads *Then Samuel told the people the ordinances of the kingdom, and wrote them in the book and placed it before the Lord.*

Judges spans a period from Joshua to immediately before Saul, approximately 1392 to 1050 BCE.

Judges is a sequel to Joshua, continuing the story of conquest and settlement. They also formed one book along with Ruth, in the Hebrew Bible.

Kadesh *(Numbers 13)*

Kadesh-barnea was an important location in Israelite history, between the Sinai desert and the southern boundary of Canaan. Moses sent twelve spies into Canaan from here. Perhaps Kadesh-barnea was regarded as a potential base for the invasion of Canaan. The place was an important crossroads, from which routes run in every direction. Today it is an obscure waterhole. Since 1905 CE, fortresses have been excavated at the location in northern Sinai. Today, it is an obscure waterhole. Since 1905 CE, fortresses have been excavated at the location in northern Sinai.

The Kings of Judah (Two Southern Tribes) and
The Kings of Israel (Ten Northern Tribes)

Judah		Israel	
1 Rehoboam	975-959 BCE	1 Jeroboam	975-954 BCE
2 Abijam (Abijah)	958-955		
3 Asa*	955-914	2 Nadab	954-953
		3 Baasha	953-930
		4 Elah	930-929

		5 Zimri	929
		6 Tibni	929-924
		7 Omri	929-917
		8 Ahab	918-897
4 Jehoshaphat*	914-889		
		9 Ahaziah	898-897
		10 Jehoram (Joram)	897-884
5 Joram (Jehoram)	898-884		
6 Ahaziah	884	11 Jehu	884-857
7 Athaliah**	884-878		
8 Jehoash (Joash)*	879-839		
		12 Jehoahaz	857-840
9 Amaziah*	839-811	13 Jehoash	840-826
10 Azziah (Azariah)*	810-758	14 Jeroboam II	826-785
		15 Zachariah	784-773
		16 Shallum	772
11 Jotham*	758-742	17 Menahem	772-762
12 Ahaziah	742-726	18 Pekahiah	761-760
		19 Pekah	759-739
13 Hezekiah*	726-697	20 Hoshea	730-720
14 Manasseh	697-642		
15 Amon	642-640		
16 Josiah*	640-609		
17 Jehoahaz (Shallum)	609-608		
18 Jehoiakim (Eliakim)	607-596		
19 Jehoiachin (Jeconiah)	597		
20 Zedekiah (Mattania)	597-586		

*Considered good kings
**Only female ruler (Queen)

Kirjath-jearim

A town of the Gibeonites (Josh 9:17) on the boundary line between Judah and Benjamin (Josh 15:9; 18:14 15). It fell to Judah (Josh 15:48, 60; Judg18:12). It was here the ark remained twenty years after the Philistines sent it back to the Israelites (1 Sam 6:19-7:2). It was also called Kirjath-baal (Josh 15:60; 18:14) and Baalah (Josh 15:9, 11).

Lachish

Lachish is generally regarded as the second most important city in the southern kingdom of Judah. Sennacherib invaded here, during his 701 BCE battle with Judah. More than 1,000 iron arrowheads were found in the ramp as well as a chain for catching the battering rams. The city was surrounded by two walls including a lower retaining wall.

Lamps, Pitchers, Trumpets

The sight of trumpets and torches, at first concealed in clay pitchers, when suddenly revealed, would be dramatic! Each light could indicate a legion behind it, indicating a large enemy may soon attack. Each of the 300 men had a trumpet in one hand, and an empty pitcher with a lamp burning inside it, in the other. Imagine...breaking the pitchers (which would have protected the torch from any breeze), holding the lamp in their left hands, and then crying *"The sword of the Lord and of Gideon."* 301 trumpets (including Gideon) blaring forth and a sudden cracking of pitchers revealing lamps were indeed startling. The Midianites fled!

Land of Ancient Israel

Jericho (see information on Jericho elsewhere in this volume), located twelve miles north of the Dead Sea and one mile from the modern city which bears the name, emerged as early as *c.* 7000 BCE according to the earliest of records. (Note that the author recognizes Ussher's chronology, which does not agree with this early date).

The area was surrounded by a semi-tropical oasis, which provided a clean, abundant water supply. Jericho, even at this early date, produced its own food and made unique pottery. A population of 2000 was protected by a massive wall.

The first group of "outsiders" spread into Jericho, Egypt, and Mesopotamia near the second half of the fourth century (3500 BCE). Many new villages were established, displaying technical and artistic advances. The use of copper appears in the historical records. Jericho was strengthened, and many other cities were built around defensible rock formations and near a water supply. The peoples spoke a Semitic tongue by this period. Also, see Three Lands.

Light

The author has done many hours of studying on "light." It's almost impossible to separate "I am light", from His Glory. Where He is, His glory is. It's pure light. Remember God said "I am light?" Don't forget He also said "YOU, are the light of the world." The source of everything is Light. Science is just now accepting this fact. They even measure distance by *light* years.

In studying the Glory of God, there seems to be two distinct divisions. First the actual Glory that God is, which is seldom seem, but many times experienced. This was/is God manifesting Himself in a powerful, and many time, visible form. I have concluded that there is a three stage progression of growth: (1) an absolute surrendering of self in worship (2) the manifesting of healings and miracles (3) a visable Glory of God. We have, to some extent, these today. However, the fullness of this Glory is a future experience.

Consider the following Scriptures:

Psalm 104:1-2
Lord my God, You are very great;
You are clothed with splendor and majesty,
Covering Yourself with light as with a cloak

Ezeiel 3:22-23
The hand of the Lord was on me there, and He said to me, "Get up, go out to the plain, and there I will speak to you." 23 So I got up and went out to the plain; and behold, the glory of the Lord was standing there....

Daniel 7:9
"I kept looking
Until thrones were set up,
And the Ancient of Days took His seat;
His vesture was like white snow
And the hair of His head like pure wool.
His throne was ablaze with flames,
Its wheels were a burning fire.

Matthew 17:2
And He was transfigured before them; and His face shone like the sun, and His garments became as white as light

And serveral other New Testament passages refer to this.

In addition, those tablets given to Moses... You think God just wrote them, or Moses wrote them? Listen to this: Habakkuk 3:4 *His radiance is like the sunlight;*

He has rays flashing from His hand, And there is the hiding of His power.

So it's no wonder Moses' face shown as he came down to the people. The reflection of God remained upon him for a long time.

Ladder

This *ladder* in Hebrew is a word describing the passing from one realm to another; a "passageway" from earth through the first heaven and second heaven, to God's heaven, the third heaven. The Lord does not have to use a stairway. He is pictured here as standing at the top; actually, the Hebrew has Him beside the ladder.

Leaven

Throughout Scripture, the word always refers to some form of evil. False doctrine (Matt 16:11) are compared to yeast (leaven), because like yeast once fermentation begins, eventual permeation of the entire substance takes place. During the Passover week, no leaven was allowed in the house.

Luz

Luz no longer appears on most maps; in fact, very few antiquity maps will have the name. Refer to these Scriptures: Gen 28:19 *He called the name of that place Bethel; however, previously the name of the city had been Luz;* Gen 35:5-6 6 *So Jacob came to Luz (that is, Bethel), which is in the land of Canaan;* Josh 18:13 *From there the border continued to Luz, to the side of Luz (that is, Bethel) southward; and the border went down to Ataroth-addar, near the hill which lies on the south of lower Beth-horon.* Luz was an important location North of Jerusalem on the cross roads of major traffic. Archeologists have shown that two distinct areas were populated together, sort of a main city and a suburb.

Maccabeans

Following the return from exile in Babylon in the sixth century BCE until the death of Alexander the Great in 323 BCE, the Hebrews continued under the direction of the high priest. However, the generals of Alexander divided the regions of his vast empire. By 198 BCE, the Syrian King had added Palestine to his territory. The Hebrews were allowed to live by their law, the Torah. Syria was so pressed by Rome, that they seized the silver and gold in safe keeping in the Temple at Jerusalem. This was the beginning of the revolt by the Jews. In 167 BCE, a Jewish priest, Mattathias organized the uprising against the Syrians but died in 165. Two of his five sons, Simon and Judah led the revolt. Judah was given the name "Maccabee" meaning "hammerhead." The Maccabeans, led by Judah's skills and courage, gained control of their land in 164 BCE and restored the worship of God in a rededicated Temple (now celebrated as Hanukkah).

Manna

A special food, which resembled white seeds or flakes and was sweet to the taste. God provided this to His people for the forty years in the desert. Manna explains who Jesus is.

It was *small*; which speaks of His humility; He became a baby, then a servant.

It was *round*; a circle of His eternity, the Son of God.

It was *white*; purity and sinlessness

It was *sweet*; "taste and see that the Lord is good." The Hebrews asked for onions and garlic of Egypt; we cannot improve on what God brings by His Word.

It was *nourishment*. A nation lived on it for 40 years; all that is needed for us, is to feast on the Bread that will always fill.

Note the place where the manna was found. Each morning, it came from heaven and was on the earth all around them. It was not high on the mountains where each family would have to climb to retrieve. It was not in some deep valley outside the camp where the people would have to search for it. It was not placed on hard rocks or in tree branches. The manna was outside every tent.

Mesopotamia

Located in modern Iraq, the word means, "land between the rivers." The Euphrates River marks the eastern boundary of the land promised to Abraham (Genesis 15:18). Only briefly did Israel's boundary extend that far (1 Chronicles 18:3). Most scholars have arrived at the conclusion that Genesis 2-11 is set in Mesopotamia, more specifically in southern Iraq and extending into south western Iran and northeastern Kuwait. In light of this, it is perhaps not surprising to learn that there is an area north of the Persian Gulf where the Tigris, Euphrates, and Karun Rivers converge that is called the "Garden of Eden. The government of Iraq has recently sought to protect it.

This area has a long, rich history. They witnessed the birth of the Sumerian culture. In the first millennium BCE, this area was called the Sealand, and later it came to be known as Chaldea. The Chaldeans resisted Assyrian domination; however, Sennacherib, the son of Sargon II, destroyed the city of Babylon in 689 BCE because of the ongoing rebel lion, and hunted the Chaldean rebels in the marshes. Refer to author's book *The Chronological History of the Bible Lands*.

Mishna (or Mishnah)

These *oral laws* or traditions are somewhat akin to judges interpreting the law of the land based on past interpretations by other judges.

This authority to rule and make judgments on God's will likely began when Moses accepted his father-in-law's advice to share the burden of leadership with 70 elders of the community *(Exodus 18:13–26)*.

The oral law itself is thought to originate with the instructions that Adonai gave Moses on Mount Sinai. These laws were passed down orally as well as through the written word.

The first Mishna (or Mishnah) (compilation of oral traditions), Tractate Avot states: "Moses received the Torah at Sinai and transmitted it to Joshua, Joshua transmitted it to the Elders, the Elders transmitted it to the Prophets, and the Prophets transmitted it to the men of the Great Assembly. They said three things: Be deliberate in judgment, raise many students, and make a protective fence for the Torah."

Pirkei Avot, a section of the Mishna (or Mishnah) (first major written redaction of the Oral Law) devoted to ethics, traces an unbroken span of teachings that originate at Sinai. Although those teachings began to be written down nearly 1,500 years after Sinai, it is believed they have been faithfully preserved.

Judaism traditionally believes that the Torah cannot be fully understood without the oral law.

If one rejects the oral law, such as the Karaites do, it is said that one will only end up creating a new oral law that does not originate from Sinai, but from subjective interpretations or the imagination.

The oral law deals with two main categories: Halakha — legal decisions regarding the precise way a commandment is to be performed; and Haggada — nonprescriptive elements meant to inspire and edify, such as rabbinic stories, sermons, and commentaries relating to the Tanakh [Old Covenant] and Jewish life.

The Babylonian Talmud contains much of the Halakha and Haggada and was compiled in written form by AD 600 with about 2.5 million words. Within these words are a wide variety of *traditions, folklore, and laws*.

Many are at odds with one another and with Scripture; yet, there is room for this in traditional Judaism, which by its nature is based on evolving traditions and ideas.

Moab

A land located east of the Jordan, 35 miles long, and 25 miles wide. To the south and west was Edom. To the north was Ammon. It was settled by the descendants of Lot's son, Ammon. They became a numerous people, expanding their land to include the area from the plain people of Heshbon to the wady Kurahi.

It was in this land that the Israelites had their last encampment. Eglon, king of Moab invaded Israel and oppressed the people until the Judge Ehud delivered them. Eventually, Moab became a Roman province. Prophecies about Moab are in Jeremiah 48, Amos 2, and Zephaniah 2.

Ruth was a Moabite.

Myrtle

Found in Isa 41:19; 55:13; Neh 8:15. A lovely indigenous shrub with dark green, scented leaves, star like flowers, and edible, dark-colored berries. Isaiah referred to the myrtle as one of the choice plants of the land during the future Kingdom.

Myrtle branches were used in constructing booths for the Feast of Tabernacles, the great feast remembering Israel's redemption out of Egypt (Lev 23:43).

The myrtle trees were seen in *the ravine* perhaps a display of Israel's "hidden condition" during the time of Gentiles and before the coming of Christ.

Names

Names were particularly important in the biblical world. The *New International Encyclopedia of Bible Words* reminds us "in biblical cultures a name did more than identify; it communicated something of the essence, the character, or the reputation of the person or thing named."

This fact helps us understand why the Bible is so filled with many and wonderful names of God. Each name reveals something about the essential nature and character of God. Moreover, no single name or title could possibly sum up who He is. It is fascinating as we survey the Old Testament names of God to note that some names emphasize His power and excellence, others His relationship with human beings and still other names are descriptive, providing special information about who He is.

The prophet Isaiah reports a vision in which he "saw the Lord sitting on a throne, high and lifted up, and the train of His robe filled the temple" (Isaiah 6:1). In Isaiah's vision, seraphim were positioned around the throne, together crying *"Holy, holy, holy is the LORD of hosts; the whole earth is full of His glory!"* (v 3).

Isaiah's reaction was one of awe and humility. Confronted by this revelation of God enthroned in heaven, the prophet cried, *"Woe is me, for I am undone! Because I am a man of unclean lips, and I dwell in the midst of a people of unclean lips"* (v 5).

Through his vision, a stunned Isaiah suddenly became fully aware of the vast gap that exists between any human being and God. We are made in the image of God, yet God remains unimaginably different from and greater than us. What theologians speak of as the transcendence of God was impressed upon the prophet, and Isaiah was immediately aware of how far he fell short of God's glory (Rom. 3:23).

Our God is high and lifted up. He is a God of power and excellence. He is so far above us that we can never truly fathom His greatness and majesty. Yet, through certain names in Scripture, we are invited to glimpse His greatness, and like Isaiah, we are called to bow down in wonder before Him. Here, then, are Scripture's exalted names of our God.

Nineveh

Located near the Tigris River in Mesopotamia, 200 miles east of Haran. Nineveh is first mentioned in the Bible in Genesis 10:11, which states that Nimrod, a mighty hunter before the Lord, came from the land of Shinar (Babylonia) to Assyria and there built Nineveh. A huge city, taking three days to walk from one side to the other. 2 Kings 19:36 simply states that Sennacherib after his aborted attack on Jerusalem (19:35) returned to Nineveh, where he had made his capital. Two contemporary prophets, Zephaniah (2:13-15) and Nahum, told of the fall of Nineveh (612 BCE). Nineveh became "*a desolation, a dry waste like a desert,*" and passed into oblivion for 2,500 years.

There is archeological evidence that the site of Nineveh was occupied as early as 5000 BCE (which would demand an early date for creation).

Oracle

The Hebrew word *massa* has a meaning of "to bear" or "to lift up." In our study, it appears as a heading above Zechariah 9:1 and 12:1 in several translations. The word is most likely used by the prophet to be an encouragement or "to lift up." It is used this way in Num 23:7; 24:3, 15-16. In the context of Zechariah, the two oracles are primarily promises of salvation. Some translations have "burden." (NKJV, NASU, ESV). The AMP uses both *THE BURDEN or oracle (the thing to be lifted up)*.

Ox goad

Found in Judges 3:31. A rod about eight feet long sharpened to a point and sometimes covered with iron. It was used in driving animals. Eccl 12:11 *The words of wise men are like goads, and masters of these collections are like well-driven nails.* An animal injuring itself by coming against the sharp point of the goad is the metaphor used by Christ to Saul in Acts 9:5.

Palestine

Palestine was a nation who occupied a territory along the southern coast of the Mediterranean Sea, (Gaza today). We may also refer to the Philistines/Philistia. It gradually was the name used when referring to the entire territory between Egypt and Syria.

Passover

Found in 2 Chronicles 30:1, 15; 35:1, 9, 11, 13, 18, 19. This word has a literal meaning of "to pass" or "to leap over." An important word to consider, the Passover celebration commemorated the day God spared the firstborn children of the Israelites from the death plague brought on Egypt. The Lord "passed over" those who sprinkled the blood from the Passover lamb on their doorposts (Exodus 12). It was the first of the three annual Hebrew festivals at which all the men must appear at the sanctuary (Exodus 13:3-10). Passover, as specified in the Law of Moses, reminds the Israelites of God's great mercy on them (Leviticus 23:5–8; Numbers 28:16–25; Deuteronomy 16:1–8). The Passover meal is a type of Christ, our "Passover Lamb," whose blood rescues us from death.

Patriarchs

The term Patriarchs is assigned to the period before Sinai. From Adam, Seth, Enoch, Methuselah, and Noah before the flood, to Shem, Terah and the four "major" patriarchs of Abraham, Isaac, Jacob, and Joseph, following the flood. Notice a genealogy of Patriarchs in 1 Chron 1:1-2:2. Many times we refer to only the Four Great Men of Abraham, Isaac, Jacob, and Joseph as the Patriarchs; however many men prior to Mt. Sinai are Patriarchs "the founders of a family."

Philistines

These were among the several groups of *sea people* occupying Philistia, the region along the southern coast of the Mediterranean Sea. The Philistines were the enemies of the Israelites, invading Canaan in the 12th century BCE, and well-attested, from Samson's slaying of a thousand

Philistines (Judges 15) and David's battle with the Philistine giant Goliath (1 Samuel 17).

The Philistines were traders and seafarers who lived in the area between what is now Gaza and Tel Aviv from 1200 to about 600 BCE. They spoke a language of Indo-European origin.

They were also said to have been experts in making wine and oil, certainly not lacking in culture. Described by Ramses III as tall, slim warriors wearing tasseled kelts and ribbed helmets, originating from Cyprus or Crete. The attempted to invade Egypt in 1177 BCE but were turned away. They retreated to Canaan and settled in previously conquered land, a fertile strip forty miles long and fifteen miles deep along the Mediterranean coastal plain. The Philistines were in competition with God's nation during most of the Old Testament period. Saul also fought "the Philistines" on Mt. Gilboa, another site in the north (1 Sam 41) where "the Philistines" hung the bodies of Saul and his three sons.

They were ahead of the Hebrews in technology because they mastered metallurgy, making use of metal to perfect spearheads and battle-axes. Sea Peoples' javelin heads found at several northern sites have an elongated blade, which very close parallels Aegean and Cypriot forms. They controlled much of Palestine and worshipped Canaanite gods. David conquered them, but they still had battles with both the Northern and Southern Kingdoms during the following centuries. Recent discoveries reveal they were a people who did not practice circumcision, ate pork and dog, and were experts in making wine and oil. They assimilated to the civilization of the Canaanites and intermarried with them. Even their language was eventually replaced by a local Canaanite dialect. Refer to author's book *The Chronological History of the Bible Lands*.

Philistine City-States

According to the Bible, the Philistines ruled the five city-states (the "Philistine Pentapolis") of Gaza, Askelon, Ashdod, Ekron, and Gath, from the Wadi Gaza in the south to the Yarqon River in the north, but with no fixed border to the east. The Bible paints them as the Kingdom of Israel's most dangerous enemy.

Phoenicia

Never organized as a nation, rather it consisted of a group of independent cities along the northern seacoast of Israel. The well-known cities of Sidon and Tyre have been located by archeologists.

They were a people of sea traders of lumber and purple dye. The Phoenician alphabet was borrowed by the Greeks. Solomon sought their help to build the temple. Their practice of human sacrifice influenced and penetrated Judah.

Plagues of Egypt

Following are the ten plagues, as recorded in Ex 7:14-12:30. The timing and severity of the plagues was under the direction and control of God. Some natural occurrences were used by God, at His calling.

1. *The Water of the Nile Turned into Blood* (Ex 7:14-25). This first plague probably was the pollution of the Nile River by large quantities of fine, red earth, brought down from the Sudan and Ethiopia by abnormal flooding. The pollution of the water provided a favorable environment for the growth of microorganisms and parasitic bacteria. Their presence could have led to the death of the fish in the river (Ex 7:21). In addition to depriving Egypt of water and fish-an important part of their diet-the plague also had a religious effect. The Nile River, god of the Egyptians, had been confronted by the power of the Redeemer God of the Hebrew people.
2. *Frogs Cover the Land* (Ex 8:1-15). Seven days after the first plague, frogs came out of the river and infested the land. The frogs would have been driven from the Nile and its canals and pools by the polluted water. When Moses prayed to God, the frogs died in the houses, courtyards, and fields. The frogs were symbols of the Egyptian goddess, Heqt, who was supposed to help women in childbirth. This plague was another demonstration of the superior power of God over the gods of Egypt.
3. *Lice Throughout the Land* (Ex 8:16-19). Insects of various kinds are common in Egypt. It is not easy to identify the exact pests involved in the third and fourth plagues. Various translations have lice (KJV, NKJV), gnats (NASB, RSV, and NIV), maggots (NEB), and sand flies and fleas (RSV).
4. *Swarms of Flies* (Ex 8:20-32). Many kinds of flies are common in Egypt. The mounds of decaying frogs would have provided an ideal breeding ground for these pests. Some scholars suggest that the swarms mentioned here were a species known as the stable-fly, a blood feeder that bites man as well as cattle. This fly is a carrier of anthrax, which is probably the disease brought on by the sixth plague.
5. *Pestilence of Livestock* (Ex 9:1-7). Either the frogs or the insects may have been the carriers of this infection. The livestock of the Israelites were

miraculously protected (Ex 9:6-7). This was the second time God had made a distinction between the Israelites and the Egyptians in the plagues, which He sent (Ex 8:22-23).

6. *Boils on Man and Beast* (Ex 9:8-12). This infection was probably anthrax, carried by the flies of the fourth plague. The festering boils broke into blisters and running sores.

7. *Heavy Hail, with Thunder and Lightning* (Ex 9:13-35). Egypt was essentially an agricultural country. By destroying the crops, this plague and the next struck at the heart of Egypt's economy. Moses' warning gave the Egyptians a chance to save their remaining livestock, and some acted upon it (Ex 9:19-20). The severe storm caused great destruction (Ex 9:24-25). The flax and barley were ruined, but not the wheat because it had not yet been planted (Ex 9:31-32). This would suggest early February as the time of this plague. Again, the Israelites received special protection. There was no hail in the land of Goshen, where the Hebrews lived (Ex 9:26).

8. *Swarm of Locusts* (Ex 10:1-20). The destruction from the previous plague was fresh in the minds of Pharaoh's advisors (Ex 10:7). The eighth plague must have followed the hail very closely. Heavy rainfall in July-September would have produced conditions favorable for locusts in March. These locusts, swarms of foliage-eating grasshoppers, probably were driven into the Egyptian delta by strong winds. They wiped out the vegetation, which had survived the earlier destruction. Again, as after the seventh plague, Pharaoh confessed, "I have sinned" (Ex 10:16). Again, after the plague was withdrawn, Pharaoh hardened his heart and would not let the children of Israel go (Ex 10:20).

9. *Three Days of Darkness* (Ex 10:21-29). This darkness could have been caused by a severe dust storm. For three days, darkness covered the land (Ex 10:23). This storm would have been intensified by fine earth deposited over the land by previous flooding. This plague probably occurred in March. Again, the Israelites were spared the effects (Ex 10:23). By showing God's power over the light of the sun-represented by one of Egypt's chief deities, the sun-god Ra-this plague was a further judgment on the idolatry of the Egyptians.

10. *Death of Egyptian Firstborn* (Ex 11:1-12:30). The tenth plague, although not considered as a "plague," was the most devastating of all—the death of the firstborn in Egyptian families. The Hebrews were spared because they followed God's command to sprinkle the blood of a lamb on the doorposts of their houses. The death angel "passed over" the houses where the blood was sprinkled-hence, the name PASSOVER for this

religious observance among the Jewish people. Only a supernatural explanation can account for the selective slaughter of the tenth plague.[17]

Positions in Prayer (Old Testament)

1. Kneeling
    a. Solomon 1 Kings 8:54
    b. Elijah 1 Kings 18:42
    c. Ezra 9:15
    d. Daniel 6:10
2. Standing 1 Kings 8:22
3. Lifting up Hands
    a. 1 Kings 8:22
    b. Psalms 141:2
4. Bowing
    a. Genesis 24:26
    b. Exodus 4:31; 3:8

Quail

A migrating bird that arrives in droves along the shores of the Mediterranean Sea. They have poor flying skills, but usually fly rapidly for only a short time because of their heavy body weight. They seem to just be exhausted after a flight and can be caught by hand. They give away their presence by a shrill whistle.

So when the Hebrew people longed for meat in the Sinai desert, God just directed thousands of quail to their camp, where they dropped in exhaustion and whistled their presence.

Ramoth Gilead

Ramoth Gilead was one of three cities of refuge in Trans-jordan (with Bezer Golan). In the Israel-Syrian wars, Ahab fought at Ramoth Gilead and was mortally wounded (1 Kings 22:1-40). Today, the ruins of Gilead may be viewed. Gilead died here.

Samaria

Built as a political capital of the Northern Kingdom about 880 BCE by Omri, the sixth king of Israel (1 Kings 16:24). Samaria occupied a 300-foot high hill about 42 miles north of Jerusalem.

Because of its hilltop location, Samaria could be defended easily. Several kings ruled from there, including Omri, Ahab, and Jehu.

---

[17] (Some of the above information is consolidated from Nelson's Illustrated Bible Dictionary, Copyright © 1986, Thomas Nelson Publishers)

During this period, it was the seat of idolatry (Isaiah 9:9; Jeremiah 23:13; Ezekiel 16:46-55; Amos 6:1; Micah 1:1). Ahab, Omri's son, built a temple to Baal here.

Archeologists have discovered that at the time of Ahab, the city may have been 20 acres in extent, enclosed by an outer wall 20 to 30 feet thick, with a more narrow inner stone wall about 5 feet thick. A two-story palace was constructed at the higher western end of the hill around some courtyards. In one of these courtyards, a pool about 17 by 33 feet has been discovered. This may have been the pool where the blood of Ahab was washed from his chariot after he was killed in a battle against the Syrians. Samaria finally fell to the Assyrians, in 722-21 BCE. Refer to author's book *The Chronological History of the Bible Lands*.

Scapegoat

In Leviticus 16, the term refers to the second of two goats. One was sacrificed, the second was released after praying and laying on of hands to signify the sins of the people being transferred and released into the desert. This was only done annually on the Day of Atonement. The word comes from an Arabic word meaning *remove*. This Day of Atonement is the spiritual "center" of this book of Leviticus.

Semite

The descendants of Shem, one of Noah's three sons. Many groups of people were known as "Semitic" or of a "Semitic Family" of languages. Broadly refers to groups of people from Mesopotamia or South Asia. Some of those were the Canaanites, Hebrews, Arabs, Assyrians, Babylonians, and Ethiopians.

Selah

This word appears seventy-one times in the Psalms and means "to lift up," possibly a musical sign, to pause. It also appears three times in the Book of Habakkuk. To guess at its exact meaning would only be conjecture.

Salvation

Found in Isaiah 12:2 *"Behold, God is my salvation, I will trust and not be afraid; For the Lord God is my strength and song, And He has become my salvation."*

Isaiah 25:9 *And it will be said in that day, "Behold, this is our God for whom we have waited that He might save us. This is the Lord for whom we have waited; Let us rejoice and be glad in His salvation."*

Isaiah 49:6 He says, *"It is too small a thing that You should be My Servant To raise up the tribes of Jacob and to restore the preserved ones of Israel. I will also make You a light of the nations. So that My salvation may reach to the end of the earth."* There are many other references in Isaiah of this same word, salvation.

This great word describes deliverance from distress as a result of victory. It's God's work on your behalf, carrying a meaning of the deliverance of a single individual...YOU...ME.

Then, always realize, this word is much, much more than a new birth. This word includes—deliverance from the power of sin, including forgiveness as well as wholeness for the whole personality.

In the Old Testament, the word salvation sometimes refers to deliverance from danger (Jeremiah 15:20), deliverance of the weak from an oppressor (Psalms 35:9-10), the healing of sickness (Isaiah 38:20), and deliverance from guilt and its consequences.

All this is in salvation.

Sheba

Sheba was the land of the Queen who visited Solomon. The Bible informs us that the Queen, having heard of King Solomon's wisdom, traveled to Jerusalem to test him. It is recorded (1 Kings 10:13) that she returned to her own land." The land probably was located at the southwest tip of the Arabian Peninsula, the Kingdom of Saba that was well known, (modern day Yemen). Another possible location was on the opposite shore of the Red Sea, Aksum, in Ethiopia (continent of Africa). The location allowed a strong sea trade with both Africa and India. In addition, a strong caravan trade which went through Israel. The Queen visited Solomon to negotiate a trade agreement (a clay script was located revealing this treaty).

Shechem

Located west of the Jordan River near Samaria, an important city, an ancient fortified city in central Palestine, long before the Israelites occupied Canaan. It was first mentioned in the Bible in connection with Abraham's journey into the land of Canaan. When Abraham eventually came to Shechem, the Lord appeared to him and announced this was the land He would give to Abraham's descendants.

After the Israelites conquered Canaan under the leadership of Joshua, an altar was built at Shechem. The significance of Shechem in Israel's history continued into the period of the Divided Kingdom. Rehoboam, the successor to King Solomon, went to Shechem to be crowned king over all Israel (1 Kings 12:1). Here, at this same place, the ten tribes renounced the house of David and transferred their allegiance to Jeroboam (ver. 16), under whom Shechem became the capital of his kingdom. Eventually, Samaria became the permanent political capital of the Northern Kingdom, but Shechem retained its religious importance. We note also that it apparently still was a sanctuary for the worship of God in Hosea's time.

Sheol

Found in Ps 9:17; 2 Sam 22:6; Isa 5:14; Jonah 2:2. One of five distinct areas of departments under the earth. They are Tartaros, Paradise, Sheol/Hades, Bottomless Pit, and Gehenna. Sheol (Heb, OT) /Hades (Greek, NT) is a place of the un-righteous until after the Millennium. We refer to it as Hell and is a literal place, one of the departments under the earth. It is referred to in the New Testament in Acts 2:27; Luke 10:15; Rev 1:18 etc.

Some scholars prefer to translate Hades as "grave." Job's description of Sheol as a place of darkness, dust, worms, and decay may refer to "grave." In many places, such as Pro 15:11 and 27:20, and Ps 9:17 would demand "hell" because of context.

Shepherd

Shepherds were responsible for the physical survival and welfare of the flock. In comparison with goats, which tended to fend for themselves, sheep depended on the shepherd to find pasture (Ezekiel 34:2, 9, 13), and they required "quiet" water (Psalm 23:3). Shepherds also had to provide shelter, medication, and provision for lameness and weariness. Without the shepherd, the sheep were helpless.

He entertained himself by making music on a readily made reed pipe (Judges 5:16). The shepherd would count his sheep twice a day, one by one, probably calling each by its own name. He would talk to his sheep until each one recognized his voice (John 10:4).

For the most part, the shepherd's long days and nights in the field made for a lonely life.

At night, the shepherd gathered his sheep into a group for protection against beasts, thieves, and the weather.

This selfless, caring attitude of the shepherd is attributed to Jesus throughout the New Testament. "We are the people of his [God's] pasture and the sheep of his hand"

Many of the best-known Old Testament persons, including the patriarchs and the prophets, had personal experience as successful herdsmen. Moses, who learned sheep tending from the seven daughters of Jethro and for a time tended the flock of the priest of Midian (Exodus 2:15-3:1); David, who when Samuel found him was "keeping the sheep" (1 Samuel 16:11); and Amos of Tekoa, an under shepherd whom "the Lord took from following the flock" and commanded to "prophesy to my people Israel" (Amos 7:15; 3:12).

David's experiences at Bethlehem were an ideal training for a future king and spiritual leader. His occupation developed prudence, promptitude, and prowess. His long night vigils allowed a solitude, which directed him to God.

Shiloh

Shiloh was located north of Jerusalem. Samuel was raised there, and mentored under Eli the high priest.

This also was where Joshua erected the tabernacle, making Shiloh Israel's religious center for the next 300 years. Shiloh was destroyed by the Philistines in the early 11th century BCE.

Excavations have revealed a large building complex prior to 1050 BCE.

Son of Man

A **KEY WORD** in Ezekiel was easy to pick. It is found in 2:1; 3:17; 12:18. Ezekiel uses this phrase *"son of man,"* over 90 times in referring to himself. He was chosen by God to be a spokesperson for God.

It simply means "human one." Only found two other times in the Old Testament. Daniel saw a heavenly being *"like the Son of Man"* (Daniel 7:13). Of course, Jesus later adopted the title "Son of Man," as He too was a living sign to all.

So Ezekiel was to be a living example, a representative of God to the captives.

Sons

Found in 1 Chronicles 1:43; 3:12; 4:25; 5:14; 9:4; 11:22; 26:28. This word has the literal meaning of "to build." The Hebrews considered their children to be "builders" of the future generations. The word may refer to a direct son or to a future descendant. (1 Kings 2:1; 1 Chronicles 7:14). Benjamin in the Old Testament means "Son of my Right Hand." In the plural, *ben* can be translated as "children" regardless of gender (see Exodus 12:37—"children of Israel"). Even God used this term to describe His relationship with Israel: *"Israel is My son, My firstborn"* (Exodus 4:22).

Satan

#1, He's not some imp with a red body and a pitchfork sitting on your shoulder whispering ugly thoughts in your ear.

#2 He is the most attractive, brilliant, powerful archangel that God ever created; not a popular thought, but one you should not forget.

#3 Job never knew what was going on in heaven. Satan still loves to work in the background; however being invisible—does not mean he is unreal. Not heard does not mean he is silent. Not being flashy does not indicate he's asleep.

#4, As I read through the first 2 cps of Job, I found some interesting things about our enemy that I wrote down. You may be surprised to realize:

- He is alive
- Has access to heaven
- Accuser of believers
- Goes from place to place
- Associates with angels
- Appears before God
- Roams the earth
- Carries on conversations with God
- Singles out individuals hoping to destroy them
- Hates good men
- Envies the blessing of God upon others
- Seeks to destroy fellowship between God and His children
- Seeks to cause men to curse God
- Limited by God in touching His children
- Can destroy riches of men
- Has agents on earth who do his bidding
- Can send fire from heaven
- Would like to destroy good men
- Propagator of sickness and disease in the bodies of men.

Saul's Five-Step Failure

1. His presumption at the altar of God

    1 Samuel 13:8-9 Now *he waited seven days, according to the appointed time set by Samuel, but Samuel did not come to Gilgal; and the people were scattering from him. 9 So Saul said, "Bring to me the burnt offering and the peace offerings."*

2. His cruelty to his son

    1 Samuel 14:44 Saul said, *"May God do this to me and more also, for you shall surely die, Jonathan."*

3. His disobedience concerning Amalek
   1 Samuel 15:20-23 *Then Saul said to Samuel...I did obey the voice of the Lord,* "But the people took some of the spoil," Samuel said..." *For rebellion is as the sin of divination And insubordination is as iniquity and idolatry. Because you have rejected the word of the Lord, He has also rejected you from being king.*"
4. His jealousy and hatred of David
   1 Samuel 18:29 *then Saul was even more afraid of David. Thus Saul was David's enemy continually.*
5. His appeal to a witch
   1 Samuel 28:7 *Then Saul said to his servants, "Seek for me a woman who is a medium that I may go to her and inquire of her."*

Semitic Languages

These include Arabic, Hebrew, and Aramaic (including the Moabites and Edomites, the kindred of the Hebrews, along with the Canaanites, and the Phoenicians). Generally speaking, Semitic is used especially of or pertaining to the Jews. The choice of name was derived from Shem, one of the three sons of Noah in the genealogical accounts of the Book of Genesis. In Europe, they have also been known as Oriental languages. In the 19th century, *Semitic* became the conventional name. The Semitic languages covered what are today the modern states and regions of Iraq, Syria, Israel, Jordan, Lebanon, Palestine, Saudi Arabia, Kuwait, Oman, Yemen, United Arab Emirates and the Sinai Peninsula and Malta. The earliest historic (written) evidences of them are found in the Fertile Crescent (Mesopotamia) an area encompassing the Akkadian, Babylonian and Assyrian civilizations along the Tigris and Euphrates rivers (modern Iraq).

Septuagint

The Septuagint, the standard Greek translation of the Old Testament, was composed to meet the needs of Greek-speaking Jews in Egypt during the Hellenistic period. This large Jewish community was concentrated in the city of Alexandria. The Jewish leaders located there began to translate the Old Testament into Greek in the third century BCE, completing their labor of love approximately in 132 BCE.

The standardized Greek text became known as the Septuagint (Greek for "seventy"). The Septuagint is often abbreviated LXX, the Roman-numeral notation for seventy. According to tradition, the Septuagint was prepared by seventy-two learned Jews during a seventy-day period, each working separately. The Lord so honored their effort, tradition goes, that when the scholars met, their translations were identical in every respect.

However, in reality, the LXX took several centuries to complete, and as a translation, it varies in quality. Some parts are faithful renderings of the Hebrew, other parts are less so. In places, it seems to diverge from the Masoretic text. *The Masoretic Text* is the authoritative Hebrew and Aramaic text of the Tanakh or Jewish three-fold structure of the Scriptures. The entire work included the thirty-nine books, plus the books known in English as Deuterocanonical ("second canon"). Deuterocanonical is used to describe books not included in the Jewish Canon.

The importance of the LXX is that it is an ancient witness to the text of the Old Testament. Even in those places where the text differs from the Masoretic text, the percentage of difference is not great, and the differences do not represent significant changes in meaning.

Shittim (A city, Numbers 25)

This was the Israelite's final wilderness encampment before they crossed the Jordan River. Shittim was located just east of Jericho (actual full name was *Abel Shittim*). This is where Moses ascended Mount Nebo, as well as where Joshua dispatched the spies to Jericho. It was here also that Israel fell in to Baal worship. This city has been located showing ruins of houses, a fortress with towers and surrounded by 4' thick walls. Moses gave three addresses to the nation. Note that Jesus, in the wilderness, used these three speeches to rebuke Satan as He began His ministry.[18]

Sinai Topography

It is difficult to describe 24,000 square miles of nothingness, poised between Africa and Asia. Indeed, it was a land of "wandering." A wilderness where a new nation of people could easily become disoriented and move in circles. Even today, it would be quite easy to get lost. With this in mind, along with the knowledge that the land has had little change over the past 3000 years, we might understand the difficulties of the Israelites' journey.

As mentioned previously, the most probable route the Israelites followed was the southern. The Sinai is divided into three distinct inhospitable regions. (1) The northern could be called classical desert, mostly flat, mounds of sand formed by winds, and a few oases. Most of the inhabitants would live in this area, as it remains the most temperate. (2) The middle layer of the Sinai is one of sandy hills and multi-colored

---

[18] Matt 4

canyons. This is perhaps the area, which we would identify with the Israelites' wandering. It is a land of constant change; atmosphere, soil, and color of hills. Little is desired of its lackluster mountains. It could be considered as the least hospitable part of the peninsula. The lack of water can be noticed by the absence of dew in the morning. **(3)** The southern region (which has already been stated, is the most obvious route of the exodus). There are several oases along the Gulf of Suez.

Six Related Old Testament Books
Put your thinking caps on.

The six books, 1 and 2 Samuel, 1 and 2 Kings, and 1 and 2 Chronicles are related directly to each other. Together, these six books are the recordings of the history of God's chosen people.

1 and 2 Kings were originally a single book called "Kings" in the Hebrew text, named from the very first verse which begins *"King David..."* When we studied 1 and 2 Samuel in Volume One, we noted that those two books were a single volume called "Samuel."

The important and widely used Greek Septuagint and the later Latin Vulgate both divided Kings into two books, probably because of the immense length. There was no ideal place to make the division; it was pretty much divided half-way.

The Vulgate further defined these six books. The Vulgate used the names 1 and 2 Kings for what we have as 1 and 2 Samuel. They then named what we have as 1 and 2 Kings, as 3 and 4 Kings, to keep them in their continuous history.

So, their books of 1st, 2nd, 3rd and 4th Kings, which we have as 1 and 2 Samuel and 1 and 2 Kings, were the complete history of Judah and Israel's Kingdoms. Are you with me so far?

I think it was clearer to have those earlier names. You would immediately realize their relationship and continuity.

Then we add to this study, 1 and 2 Chronicles—a similar pattern was used. Originally they were a single book in the Hebrew text, named "The annals (or events) of the days." It became the name Chronicles when the Hebrew was translated into the Latin in approximately 400 CE.

Those original books of Samuel and Kings were a history of both Israel and Judah both in their united state and also after they were divided. The Annals (our two books of Chronicles) only reviews the line of David, emphasizing only the kingdom of Judah.

Now, concerning the authors of Kings and Chronicles, similar to the books called Samuel, not a great amount of detail is known. Most likely Kings was authored by some unnamed prophet who lived with Israel in

Babylon and wrote the history of the nation. Whoever the author was, it was written during the period of 561 and 450 BCE.

It is believed that the author of Chronicles was Ezra the priest known as "The Chronicler." It was probably written a little later, around 450 BCE. We will look more at Ezra in the final Section of our study. The author used many non-Biblical sources to pen the books (refer to the list in Volume One). This does not change the fact that God inspired the Books and made sure that the sources used were accurate.

Sumerians

The first people to migrate to Mesopotamia, the "land between the rivers" probably earlier than 4000 BCE. They created a great civilization along the rivers and made many advances in technology. The wheel, plow, and writing (a system that we call cuneiform) are examples of their achievements. The farmers in Sumer created levees to hold back the floods from their fields and cut canals to channel river water to the fields.

There were seven great city-states, each with its own king and a building called a ziggurat, a large pyramid-shaped building with a temple at the top, and having an army to protect itself from its neighbors.

Around 2300 BCE, the independent coalition of Sumer, considered the very beginning of civilization, was conquered by Sargon the Great of Akkad. Sargon was an Akkadian, a Semitic group of desert nomads who eventually settled in Mesopotamia just north of Sumer. Eventually, the Akkadian Empire fell, and was replaced by the Old Babylonian Empire, possibly the first empire in existence.

a. The Sumerians were a non-Semitic people who established the highest standard civilization in existence (see above). They had a form of language, using Pictographs by 3500 BCE. As stated in the above Depth detail, Mesopotamia was invaded from the north by the Akkadians and overrun by Sargon, forming what was perhaps the first empire, including Syria and Palestine. However, only a few years later, the kingdom of Egypt, under pharaoh Pepi (c. 2325-2275) invaded Sargon's empire.

b. Recent discoveries of fifteen hundred tablets near Ebla in northern Syria provide us with a rich store of information. Ebla, a town of many three-storied buildings, attained political power over this new empire of Sargon's. Its third king, Ebrum descended from one of Abraham's ancestors. The Ebla tablets include references to Sinai, Jerusalem, Hazor, Megiddo, and Lachish. The tablets also include the names of Esau,

Ishmael, David, Saul, and Israel. The name Yahweh has also been detected in these documents.

Refer to author's book *The Chronological History of the Bible Lands*.

Sun, Stand Still

Many explanations have been offered. I agree with what Spurgeon said: *"How He did it is no question for us, it is not ours to try and soften miracles, but to glorify God in them."* (From Spurgeon's Devotional Bible.)

Perhaps the next verse, 14, helps us.[19]

What is amazing is that God did not initiate this miracle as He usually did/does. A man did! God did as Joshua asked!

The earth actually stopped revolving (or the earth and sun revolved together). This allowed Joshua to complete the battle with total victory.

Also note what a Yale professor, (Totten, *Our Race*), in addition to reports from Egyptian and Chinese research and several other prominent scholars, have calculated that one full day is missing in the astronomical calendar.

An interesting and quite likely explanation of this story may be presented. To understand this, we must first become familiar with the physical features of the land. We realize that Joshua was responding to the agreement he made with the Gibeonites.[20] He and his military force-marched during the entire night, thus arriving at Gibeon in the dark just before dawn. This cover of darkness allowed an element of surprise upon the five kings. We then understand that Gibeon sits east of the Aijaolon Valley.[21] In relationship to their location, the sun was east, the moon was west, and the only time of day for this arrangement, was sunrise. Because Joshua came towards Gibeon form Gilgal, it means at the time of attack, the sun was in the eyes of those he attacked. As he pursued them to the west, the enemy looked back towards Joshua with the sun in their eyes. Fighting would have been almost impossible as they retreated west. Joshua requested that the sun remain in the east at dawn keeping the sun remaining in their eyes. So it was more likely that Joshua commanded the sun from rising, rather than the common thought of commanding the sun from going down.

Susa

---

[19] Josh 10:14 *There was no day like that before it or after it, when the Lord listened to the voice of a man*

[20] Josh 9:14-15 *So the men of Israel took some of their provisions, and did not ask for the counsel of the Lord. 15 Joshua made peace with them and made a covenant with them, to let them live; and the leaders of the congregation swore an oath to them.*

[21] Josh 10:12 *"O sun, stand still at Gibeon, And O moon in the valley of Aijalon."*

Shushan or called Susa ("a lily"), the ancient capital of Elam inhabited by the Babylonians; later a royal residence and capital of the Persian Empire. The site is modern Shush in Iran on the Ulai River, about 250 miles east-southeast of
Babylon.

Long before the time of Abraham in the Old Testament, Shushan was the center of Elamite civilization. Some scholars believe it was a cult city centering upon the worship of one of the chief Elamite gods.

Ahasuerus the king of Persia, who married Esther, held court in Shushan (Susa), one of three principal capital cities in Persia. In addition, Darius I built his palace here, which was restored by Artaxerxes. Many of the events in the Book of Esther occurred here.

Theophany

Theophany was the direct, visual manifestation or apparent incarnation of the presence of God in the Old Testament. The key word is visual, since God makes His presence and power known throughout the Bible in a variety of ways. However, even in a Theophany a person does not actually see God Himself.

Theophanies proper are limited to the Old Testament, mostly common in Genesis and Exodus. The most frequent visible manifestation of God's presence in the Old Testament is the "Angel of the Lord." Other appearances that would be considered a Theophany are the burning bush (Exodus 3:1-6), the pillar of cloud and the pillar of fire (Exodus 13:21-22), the cloud and fire of Sinai (Exodus 24:16-18), and the cloud of the glory of the Lord (Exodus 40:34-38). Theophanies are never given for their own sake or to satisfy a curiosity about God; rather to convey some revelation or truth about Him.

Tirzah

Became the capital city of the northern kingdom, located a few miles northeast of *Shechem*. During Tirzah's glory days, Song of Solomon was written. It was the capital of the northern kingdom for forty years while Baasha and his son Elah were in rule. Then a short rule of Zimri ended as Omri, the army general, seized the country. A scared Zimri burned down the citadel while inside it, (a 3' tall area of burned debris has been located). It was re-built for a short period while the permanent capital was being constructed in Samaria. Song of Solomon mentions *Tirzah* as one of the two great cities of Israel. The location seems to be forgotten after the fall of the Northern Kingdom.

Tower

Many remains of ancient towers have been unearthed in Babylonia. Most cities were built around it with a temple on top to worship a god. The towers were built with many stories, each in a color. The record of the destruction of one of them reads, "The building of this temple offended the gods. In a night, they threw down what had been built. They scattered them abroad and made strange their speech." Many of these towers fell into the hands of later peoples and became forerunners of the Mohammedan mosque.

Theophany

Theophany was the direct, visual manifestation or apparent incarnation of the presence of God in the Old Testament. The key word is visual, since God makes His presence and power known throughout the Bible in a variety of ways. However, even in a Theophany a person does not actually see God Himself.

Theophanies proper are limited to the Old Testament, mostly common in Genesis and Exodus. The most frequent visible manifestation of God's presence in the Old Testament is the "Angel of the Lord." Other appearances that would be considered a Theophany are the burning bush (Exodus 3:1-6), the pillar of cloud and the pillar of fire (Exodus 13:21-22), the cloud and fire of Sinai (Exodus 24:16-18), and the cloud of the glory of the Lord (Exodus 40:34-38). Theophanies are never given for their own sake or to satisfy a curiosity about God; rather to convey some revelation or truth about Him.

Tyre

A fortified Phoenician city located on the Mediterranean coast. It sent its ships all over the world, founding the city of Carthage in northern Africa. Jezebel was from here. Assyria conquered the city, later came under the domination of Persia. Ezekiel wrote his prophecy against Tyre (Ezekiel 26). Nebuchadnezzar turned against the city following his destruction of Jerusalem. Alexander the Great invaded the Persian Empire in 332 BCE, destroying the fleet of ships of Persia. He almost destroyed the city along with the mainland section and the island offshore, ½ mile away.

Ur

We ask the question "Where is this place of Abraham, called Ur?" It was the place in which Abraham lived before moving to Canaan (Gen 11:28, 31; 15:7; Ne 9:7).

Scholars have suggested two sites. One is in southern Mesopotamia, a second in northern Mesopotamia. We do not know with absolute certainty, which is the city mentioned in the Biblical account (Gen 11:31).

The southern city was located one hundred miles southeast of Babylon near the Euphrates River, in what is now known as Iraq. It was a Sumerian city, a major metropolis in the early world. The Sumerians were the first literate people in Mesopotamia and probably the first literate people in the world. They created a great civilization with major, metropolitan centers, urban centers, of which Ur is probably the most famous.

The city was not known until an archeologist discovered it in the early part of the 20th century. Sir Leonard Woolley found many pieces of gold along with remarkable architecture. Also uncovered were thousands of cuneiform documents telling us about the history, culture, and economics of the city. His 1920 book, *Ur of Chaldees, was published, however, contained* little evidence that this was indeed the birthplace of Abraham. His idea and discovery led to many accepting the southern location of Abraham's Ur.

Today, this southern location is a railway station near the Persian Gulf. Copies of mathematical tables discovered, including square and cube roots, were in their society.

A second possible site, this one in northern Mesopotamia is the city of Urfa, still called that to this day, and located in southern Turkey. As you drive into the city of Urfa, there is a sign "Welcome to Urfa, birthplace of Abraham." There is a lot of biblical evidence for this location. The author accepts the location of Ur in northern Mesopotamia.

Joshua chapter 24, states that Abraham came from *beyond* the Euphrates. Actually, the southern city of Ur is on the Euphrates River, on the western shore. When following God's instructions to travel from Ur to Canaan, using the southern route would not cross the Euphrates. The northern route (from Ur in the south) would not travel from *beyond* the Euphrates. Urfa would be in agreement with Joshua 24. Every time I taught on this journey of Abraham, I questioned the conclusion that Abraham, listening to God's instructions, travelled from a southern Ur, many miles north, when his destination was directly west. A statement in Genesis 11 informs us that when Terah, Abram, Sarai, and Lot set off on their journey from Ur to Canaan, they stopped in the city of Haran where Terah died. Abraham continued onward from Haran towards the land of Canaan. Again, I ask, why did Abraham travelling from (southern) Ur to Canaan, journey north to Haran, when Canaan was west. The northern location of Ur makes more sense, as it is directly east of Haran.

This would also allow a more clear understanding of Gen chapters 24 and 29. When Abraham's grandson Jacob and others returned to the *family homeland*, they went to the region of Aram in northern Mesopotamia, not to southern Mesopotamia. After the Chaldeans came into Babylonia, Ur was placed under their control and called "Ur of the Chaldeans." Refer to author's book   Refer to author's book *The Chronological History of the Bible Lands.*

Yahweh

Our English word for the Hebrew word for God. Also translated incorrectly "Jehovah." See previous Names of God for more information concerning His names; also refer to the following Expanded Help Paper, Jehovah.

Ziklag

Listed as one of the 29 towns in Negev and was assigned to the tribe of Simeon (Joshua 15:31; 19:5). It was apparently controlled by the Philistines during King Saul's rule, and was given by King Achish of Gath to David when he was running from Saul. David used it for a home base for raids against various groups who threatened the southern borders of Judah (1 Samuel 27). After being away one time, he returned to find it ransacked by the Amalekites.

INDEX

INDEX

INDEX

Aaron 26, 27, 29, 30, 37, 147
Aaron's Rod 209
Abana River 190
Abarim 190
Abdon 147
Abednego 147
Abel 147, 277, 300
Abel-meholah 190
Abel-shittim 190
Abiathar 147
Abib 209
Abide 209
Abiel 147
Abiezer 147
Abigail 147
Abihail 147
Abihu 147
Abijah 147, 281
Abijam 147
Abimelech 41, 147
Abinadab 148
Abishai 148
Abner 148
Abomination 209, 225
Abomination of Desolation ... 209
Abraham 148
Abraham Covenant 250
Abram 148, 266, 307
Absalom 52, 148
Absolution 225
Abstain, ... 209
Abstinence 209
Accad 190
Accountability 209
Achan 148, 265
Achish 148
Achor 190
Acsah 148
Adadah 190
Adaiah 148
Adam 148

Addan 190
Adjuration 209
Adna 148
Adnah 148
Adonai 148, 277, 278
Adonijah 148
Adonikam 148
Adoniram 149
Adoni-zezek 148
Adoption 225
Adoraim 190
Adoration 209
Adversary 149
Advocate 209
Affliction 209
Africa 259, 305
Agag 149
Age of Accountability 225
Agnosticism 225
Ahab 149, 280, 281, 294
Ahasuerus 77, 149, 304
Ahava 190
Ahaz 149
Ahaziah 149, 281
Ahiezer 149
Ahijah 149
Ahimaaz 149
Ahimelech 149
Ahinoam 149
Ahithophel 149
Ahitub 149
Ahlab 190
Ai 37, 190, 243
Aijalon 190
Akkad 190
Akkadians 302
Akkub 149
Aleph 209
Alexander 285, 306
Alexander the Great 149
Alexandria 248

INDEX

Alexandria Egypt 190
Alien 149
Allegory 209, 225
Almighty 225
Alphabet of Sirach 248
Alush 190
Amalek 149, 299
Amalekites 149, 307
Amariah 150
Amarna 190
Amasa 150
Amasai 150
Amaziah 119, 150, 281
Ambassador 150, 209
Amen 209
Amenemhet 262
Amenhotep 262, 264
Amenhotep II 262, 264
Ammiel 150
Ammon 150, 276, 287
Ammonites 150
Amnon 150
Amon 150, 281
Amorites 276
Amos 113, 119, 150, 254, 287, 294
Amram 150
Amraphel 150
Amulet 209
Anak 150
Anathema 209
Anathoth 191
Ancient of Days 209
Angel 304, 305
Angel of the Lord ... 209, 304, 305
Angelology 225, 240, 249
Angels 255, 298
Annunciation 210
Anoint 210
Anointed 29, 243
Anthropology 225, 240
Anthropomorphism 225
Anthropopathism 225
Antichrist 225, 258, 260
Antiochene Theology 225
Antiochus 150
Anti-Semitism 226
Antitype 210
Aphek 191
Apocalypsis 243
Apocalyptic 226
Apocalyptic Literature 210
Apocrypha 210, 226
Apologetics 226
Apostasy 210, 226
Ar 191
Arab 191
Arabah 191
Arad 191
Aram 150
Aramaic 69, 70, 109, 181, 243, 244, 299, 300
Arameans 150
Aranunah 150
Ararat, Mount 191
Araunah 151
Archangel 210, 298
Archeologists 278, 279, 284
Argob 191
Arioch 151
Ark 249
Ark of the Covenant 210, 249
Armageddon 191, 210, 226, 244, 245, 246
Arminianism 226
Armor of God 210
Arnon River 191
Arphaxad 151
Artaxerxes 72, 74, 75, 151, 252, 304
Artaxerxes II 151
Artaxerxes III 151

INDEX

Articles of Faith 226
Arumah 191
Asa 151, 281
Asahel 151
Asaph 151
Ascension of Christ 210, 226
Ascents, Song of 210
Ashdad 246
Ashdod 191
Asher 151
Asher, Tribe of 151
Asherah 55, 247
Ashkelon 191
Ashtaroth 191
Ashurbanipal 151
Asia Minor 191
Asshur 151
Assurance 226
Assyria 151, 191, 288, 305
Assyrian Empire 59, 245
Assyrians 130, 151, 294
Astrologers 151
Athaliah 151, 281
Atheism 226
Atonement 25, 210, 226, 235, 294
Atonement, Day of 210
Attai 151
Attempts to Destroy the Bible
    271
Author Criticism 227
Authority 227
Ava 191
Avenger of Blood 210
Azarel 152
Azariah 111, 152, 281
Azmaveth 152
Azzur 152
Baal .. 55, 152, 246, 247, 280, 294
Baale 192
Baal-Hazor 192
Baal-perazim 192

Baanah 152
Baasha 152
Babel 15, 192, 247, 260
Babylon 70, 71, 72, 95, 102, 110, 111, 121, 192, 247, 285, 302, 304
Babylonia 192, 247, 275, 279, 305, 307
Babylonish Aramaean Dialect
    243
Backslide 210, 227
Balaam 152
Balak 152
Balm of Gilead - 211
Bani 152
Barak 152, 267
Barren 211
Baruch 102, 152, 273
Barzillai 152
Basemath 152
Bashan 192
Bathsheba 152
Bealiah 152
Beast 248
Bedan 152
Beer 192
Beersheba 192
Begotten, Only 211
Bela 153
Belshazzar 153
Belteshazzar 153
Ben Sira 248
Benaiah 153
Ben-hadad 153
Ben-Hur 153
Benjamin 153, 257, 282
Benjamin, tribe of 153
Ben-Oni 153
Berechiah 153
Berekiah 153
Beriah 153
Beth 211

313

INDEX

Beth anath 192
Beth Car 192
Beth-diblathaim 192
Bethel 192, 243, 248, 284
Beth-horon 192
Bethlehem 192
Beth-peor 192
Beth-shan 193
Beth-shemesh 193
Bethuel 153
Beth-zur 193
Betrothal 211
Beulah 193
Bezer 193
Biblical Criticism 227, 232
Biblical Hermeneutics 232
Biblical Theology 227
Bildad 153
Bilhah 153
Bilshan 153
Binding and Loosing 211
Birsha 153
Birthright 211, 249
Bitter Herbs 211
Biztha 153
Blasphemy 211
Blood 26, 291
Boaz 153
Bondage 211
Book of Ecclesiasticus 248
Book of Jubilees 243
Book of Life 211
Book of Sirach 248
Book of the Law 219
Books of Moses 211
Born Again 227
Bozrah 193
Branch 96, 99, 100, 106, 140, 153, 211
Branch, Jesus as the 153
Brass Serpent 211
Breastplate 211
Breath of God 211
Brimstone 211
Bukki 154
Bul 211
Bulrush 211
Burning Bush 212
Buz 154
Buzi 154
Cain 154
Cainan 154
Caleb 30, 154, 257
Calf, Golden 212
Calneh 193
Calvinism 228
Cambyses 154
Canaan 17, 18, 30, 35, 36, 154, 249, 257, 258, 266, 267, 270, 274, 278, 280, 284, 290, 306
Canaan, Land of 193
Canaanites 37, 154, 249, 276, 290, 294, 299
Cankerworm 212
Canon 77, 100, 158, 212, 226, 231, 243, 300
Canon of Scripture 249
Capstone 212
Captain 154
Captain of the Guard 249
Carchemish 193
Carmel ... 118, 174, 193, 261, 276
Carmel, Mount 193
Carnal 212
Catching Away 258
Cave of Machpelah 269
Chaldea 193
Chaldean 154
Chaldeans 17, 131, 133, 154, 243, 286, 307
Chaldee 243

INDEX

Chariot Cities 193
Chariot of Fire 212
Chebar 193
Cherith 193
Cherub 212
Cherubim 212, 249
Chilion 154
Chinnereth 193
Chosen People 154, 212
Christian Ethics 228
Christology 228, 240
Chronology of Ezra and
  Nehemiah 70, 74
Church 228
Circumcision 212
Cistern 212
Cities of Refuge 193
City of David 193
Clay Tablets 212
Coat of Many Colors 250
Codex 212
Communion 228
Compassion 252
Concubine 154, 212
Concupiscence 212
Condemnation 212, 228
Confess 228
Conscience 228
Consecration 212
Constantine 271
Constructive Theology 228
Contrite 212
Conversion 228
Convict of sin 228
Corban 212
Covenant 26, 28, 31, 33, 46, 50,
  51, 63, 83, 191, 213, 218,
  228, 233, 249, 250, 251, 287
Covenant People 213
Covenant, Book of the 213
Covenant, New 213
Covetousness 213
Covetousness in the Old
  Testament 265
Create 252
Crown of Thorns 213
Cuneiform 213
Cupbearer 154, 213
Cush 154, 194
Cuth 194
Cyrus 70, 71
Cyrus, King of Persia 154
D Document 229
Dagon 154
Damascus 194
Dan 155, 194, 257
Dan, Tribe 155
Daniel 70, 107, 109, 110, 111,
  155, 243, 244, 245, 247, 248,
  259, 260, 297
Darius I the Great 155
Darius the Mede 155
Darius, King of Persia 155
David 37, 45, 48, 49, 51, 52, 55,
  56, 61, 63, 64, 66, 85, 86, 98,
  138, 139, 155, 250, 252, 253,
  264, 267, 269, 275, 277, 279,
  290, 296, 297, 299, 301, 302,
  303, 307
David, city of 194
David's Specific Psalms 252
Day 253
Day of Atonement ... 24, 213, 294
Day of the Lord 115, 116, 118,
  121, 134, 213, 255, 258
Dayspring 213
Dead or Alive 255
Dead Sea 194, 257, 278, 282
Debauchery 213
Debir 155
Deborah 40, 155, 267
Decree 213
Dedan 155
Defiled 213

INDEX

Degrees, Songs of 213
Deism 229
Delilah 155
Den of Lions 194
Depravity 229
Depression 214
Deuterocanonical................300
Deuteronomy ..33, 256, 269, 270
Diadem.................................214
Diaspora...............................214
Diblaim.................................155
Dinah....................................155
Diocletian.............................271
Discern 214, 229
Discerning of spirits 214
Discipleship..........................214
Dispensation 214, 229
Dispersion of the nations......214
Divination.............................214
Division of Land...................256
Doctrine 214, 229
Dodo 155
Doeg.....................................155
Dogmatic Theology 229
Dor 194
Dothan 194
Doxology 214
Dumah 155
Dura 194
E Document. 229
Ebal, Mount 194
Ebenezer 194
Eber......................................155
Ecclesiastes 90, 265
Ecclesiology..................229, 240
Eden, Garden of 194
Edom 121, 194, 246, 257, 276, 287
Edomites 121, 136, 257, 268, 299
Eglon 156, 194
Egypt 18, 19, 20, 22, 29, 30, 67, 118, 194, 244, 245, 246, 248, 259, 260, 261, 262, 263, 267, 268, 270, 282, 285, 287, 289, 290, 291, 292, 293, 299, 303
Ehud.....................................156
Ekron............................194, 291
Elah 156
Elah Valley............................194
Elam 156, 195, 304
Elath.....................................195
Eldad 156
Eleazar 156
Elect 214
Elhanan 156
Eli 48, 156, 297
Eliab 156
Eliakim..........................156, 281
Eliam 156
Eliasaph................................156
Eliashib.................................156
Eliel 156
Eliezer 156
Elihu.....................................156
Elijah....................145, 156, 261
Elimelech.......................44, 156
Eliphaz..................................157
Eliphelet...............................157
Elisha............................157, 266
Elisheba................................157
Elkanah 157
Elkosh...................................195
Elnathan...............................157
Elohim 18, 252, 257
Eloth.....................................195
Elul 214
Eluzai....................................157
Embalming 258
Empirical Theology..............229
End Time Events..................258
Endor 195

INDEX

En-gedi 195
Enmity 214
Enoch 157, 289
Enoch, I and II 243
Enosh 157
Epher 157
Ephes Dammin 195
Ephod 214
Ephraim 114, 157, 195, 256, 261, 276, 277
Ephraim, tribe of 157
Ephraim, Tribe of 195
Ephrath 195
Ephron 157
Epistemology 229
eremoth 166
Eridu 195
Esarhaddon 157
Esau 157, 249, 257, 269, 303
Eschatology 214, 229, 240
Esek 195
Eshbaal 157
Eshcol 195
Eshtaol 195
Essenes 157
Esther 8, 76, 77, 78, 157, 304
Eternal life 214
Eternal Life 230
Eternity 230
Ethan 157
Ethanim 215
Ethics, Biblical 230
Ethiopia 195
etribution 220
Eunuch 157, 215
Euphrates River 195, 245, 260
Eve 157
Everlasting Life 230
Evil one 215
Evil-Merodach 158
excavation 266
Exegesis 230

Exegetical 230, 236, 239, 240
Existentialism 230
Exodus 29, 30, 40, 260, 261, 262, 265, 267, 293, 297, 304, 305
Ezekiel 87, 106, 107, 108, 110, 158, 294, 297, 305
Ezer 158
Ezion-gaber 195
Ezra 8, 69, 70, 71, 72, 75, 77, 104, 118, 158, 244, 302
Faith 230
Fall 15, 230
Familiar Spirit 215
famine 260
Fatalism 230
Fate 230
Feast of Booths 215
Feast of Harvest 215
Feast of Ingathering 215
Feast of Lights 215
Feast of Unleavened Bread ...215
Feast of Weeks 215
Ferdinand and Isabella 272
Fertile Crescent 195
Fetters 215
First six seals 258
Firstborn 215
Firstfruits 215
Fish Gate 196
Foreknowledge 215, 231
Forgiveness 231
Form Criticism 227, 231
Former Rain 215
Four Covenants 250
Frontlet 215
Fullness of time 215, 231
Fundamental Theology 231
Gaash, Mount 196
Gabriel 158
Gad 158
Gad, Tribe of 158

317

INDEX

Gallows 216
Gamaliel 158
Garrison 196
Gatam 158
Gate, East 216
Gate, Fish 216
Gate, Fountain 216
Gate, Sheep 216
Gates of Jerusalem 216
Gath 196
Gath-hepher 196
Gaza 196, 264, 291
Geber 158
Gedaliah 158
Gehazi 158
Gehazi's Greed 266
Gehenna 196
Gemariah 158
Genesis 26, 248, 249, 257, 258, 267, 268, 269, 271, 274, 285, 293, 299, 304, 305, 307
Gennesaret 193
Gentiles 158
Gerar 196
Gerizim, Mount 196
Gershom 158
Gershon 158
Gerzites 196
Geshem 158
Gezer 196
Gibeah 196
Gibeath Elohim 196
Gibeon 196, 264, 303
Gibeonites 264, 282, 303
Gideon 40, 41, 159, 282
Gihon 196
Gilalai 159
Gilboa 276
Gilboa, Mount 196
Gilead 159, 196
Gilgal 196, 264, 299, 303
Ginnethon 159
Girgashites 159, 276
Glorification 231
Glory 29, 63, 77, 97, 106, 107, 120, 137, 138, 214, 231, 247, 251, 283, 288, 304, 305
Glory of God 283
Gnosticism 231
God's Kingdom 264
God's Wrath 255, 258
Gog 159
Golan 197
Goliath 159
Gomer 114, 159
Gomorrah 197
Goshen 197
Gospel 231
Gozan 197
Grace 265
Graveclothes 216
Greed 265
Guni 159
Habakkuk 110, 131, 133, 159, 269, 295
Hadad 159
Hadassah 159
Hades 197
Hagar 159
Haggai 70, 72, 138, 139, 159
Haggith 159
Halah 197
Ham 159
Haman 76, 77, 78, 159
Hamartiology 231, 240
Hamath 197
Hammedatha 159
Hammurapi 159
Hammurapi, Code of 216
Hanan 160
Hanani 160

INDEX

Hananiah 160, 181
Handbreadth 216
Hannah 160
Hanukkah 215, 285
Har 244, 246
Hara 197
Haran 160, 197, 266, 288, 307
Hardness of Heart 216
Harhaiah 160
Harim 160
Hariph 160
Harlot 160
Harod, Spring of 197
Hasadiah 160
Hashabiah 160
Hashem 160
Hashubah 160
Hathach 160
Hazael 160
Hazeroth 197
Hazor 197, 249, 266, 267, 303
Heal 231
Heaven 231
Heber 160
Hebrew 15, 18, 21, 22, 33, 43, 250, 252, 253, 257, 263, 267, 268, 277, 280, 284, 291, 293, 299, 300, 307
Hebrew poetry 93
Hebrews .. 63, 113, 160, 285, 298
Hebron 197, 257, 267
Heldai 160
Helem 161
Helez 161
Hell 197, 232
Heman 161
Hena 197
Henry VIII 272
Hephzibah 161
Hermeneutic 232
Hermeneutics 231
Hermon, Mount 197

Heth 161
Hexateuch 216
Hezekiah 86, 161, 268, 281
Hezron 161
Hiddekel 197
Hiel 161
High Places 216, 268
High Priest 161
Higher Criticism 232
Hilkiah 161
Hinnom, Valley of 197
Hiram 161
Historical Criticism 227, 232
Historical Theology 232
Hittites 161, 263, 268, 276
Hivites 161, 277
Hobab 161
Hodaviah 161
Holy of Holies .. 51, 216, 218, 259
Holy of Holies) 218
Holy Spirit 232
Hophni 161
Hor, Mount 198
Horam 161
Horeb 198, 269
Horse Gate 198
Hosea 113, 114, 161, 296
Hoshaiah 161
Hoshea 162, 281
Host of Heaven 216
Huldah 162, 269
Humble 67, 270
Hur 162
Hushai 162
Hyksos 162, 270
Hypocrite 232
Ibhar 162
Ibzan 162
Ichabod 162
Iddo 162
Idolatry 90, 108, 145, 216, 294
Idumea 198

INDEX

Igal 162
Illumination 232
Image of God 216
Immer 162
Imminence 232
Immoratlity 216
Immortality 216, 233
Immutability 217, 233
Imputation 217
Incarnation 217, 233
Indestructible Bible 271
Inerrancy 233
Infallibility 233
Infinity 217, 233
Innocence 217
Inquire of the Lord 217
Inspiration 233
Integrity and Character 270
Intercession 217
Ira 162
Irad 162
Iru 162
Isaac 15, 16, 17, 18, 19, 33, 162, 269, 289
Isaiah 78, 87, 93, 97, 98, 110, 113, 118, 126, 132, 162, 252, 266, 287, 294, 295
ISH bee beh NOB 163
Ishbi-Benob 162
Ish-bosheth 162
Ishmael 162
Ishmaiah 163
Ishvi 163
Islam 272
Israel 198
Israel (the man) 163
Israel, its meaning 274
Issachar 163
Issachar, Tribe of 163
"Ites" in the Promised Land .276
Ithamar 163
Ittai 163
Iye-abarim 198
J Document 234
Jaaziel 163
Jabal 163
Jabbok River 198
Jabesh 163, 277
Jabesh-Gilead 198
Jabez 163
Jabin 163
Jabneel 198
Jachin 163
Jacob 15, 16, 17, 18, 19, 33, 163, 248, 256, 257, 258, 266, 269, 274, 275, 284, 289, 307
Jacob's Well 198
Jadah 163
Jaddua 163
Jael 163
Jahaz 198
Jahaziel 163
Jair 164
Jakin 164
Jalam 164
Jalon 164
Jambres 164
Jamin 164
Jannes and Jambres 164
Japheth 164
Japhia 164
Jared 164
Jarib 164
Jashen 164
Jashobeam 164
Jashub 164
Jason 164
Javan 164
Jazer 198
Jearim, Mount 198
Jebus 198
Jebusites 198, 277

INDEX

Jedaiah 164
Jediael 164
Jeduthun 164
Jehiel 165
Jehoahaz 101, 165, 281
Jehoash 119, 165, 281
Jehohanan 165
Jehoiachin 102, 165, 281
Jehoiada 165
Jehoiakim 102, 165, 273, 281
Jehoram 165, 281
Jehoshaphat 68, 165, 281
Jehoshaphat, Valley of 198
Jehosheba 165
Jehovah 277, 307
Jehovah-Shammah 198
Jehozabad 165
Jehu 165
Jeiel 165
Jemimah 165
Jemuel 165
Jephthah 41, 166
Jephunneh 166
Jerahmeel 166
Jeremiah 55, 59, 88, 90, 97, 99, 101, 102, 103, 105, 110, 121, 166, 244, 247, 251, 268, 273, 287, 294, 295
Jericho 37, 198, 264, 278, 279, 282, 300
Jerimoth 166
Jeroboam 59, 119, 166, 281, 296
Jeroboam II 166
Jeroham 166
Jerubbaal 166
Jerusalem 51, 59, 63, 70, 71, 72, 73, 74, 75, 77, 94, 95, 99, 103, 104, 105, 142, 198, 245, 246, 248, 249, 252, 256, 257, 259, 260, 261, 264, 267, 268, 269, 277, 279, 284, 285, 288, 294, 295, 297, 303, 306

Jerusalem (a short history of) 279
Jeshaiah 166
Jeshua 166
Jesse 166
Jether 166
Jethro 166
Jetur 166
Jeuel 167
Jeush 167
Jewish Calendar 278
Jews 71, 77, 78, 139, 142, 167, 243, 244, 259, 266, 285, 299, 300
Jezebel 167, 280, 305
Jeziel 167
Jezrahiah 167
Jezreel 167, 199
Jezreel Valley 199
Joab 51, 167
Joah 167
Joash 60, 116, 119, 167, 281
Job .22, 79, 81, 82, 167, 271, 298
Job's comforters 167
Jobab 167
Jochebed 167
Joel 116, 167, 254
Joelah 168
Joezer 168
Johanan 168
Johoahaz 168
Joiada 168
Joiakim 168
Joiarib 168
Jokmeam 199
Jokneam 199
Jokshan 168
Joktheel 199
Jonadab 168
Jonah 113, 123, 124, 168, 296
Jonathan 48, 168, 299
Joppa 199

INDEX

Joram 168, 281
Jordan River 199, 264, 274, 277, 300
Joseph 16, 17, 18, 19, 168, 250, 256, 258, 260, 263, 267, 271, 278, 289
Joshaphat 168
Joshua 23, 30, 35, 36, 37, 40, 168, 243, 256, 257, 264, 266, 267, 274, 280, 297, 300, 303, 306, 307
Josiah 68, 101, 102, 136, 168, 245, 269, 281
Jotham 168, 281
Jozabad 169
Jubal 169
Judah 49, 53, 56, 57, 59, 60, 65, 68, 71, 95, 98, 99, 101, 102, 104, 105, 106, 115, 116, 119, 133, 135, 136, 139, 142, 145, 169, 254, 256, 257, 264, 267, 269, 275, 276, 277, 281, 282, 285, 291, 301, 302, 307
Judah (JOO duh), tribe of 169
Judea 199
Judges 38, 40, 267, 274, 280, 289, 296
Judith 169
Jush-Hesed 169
Justification 217, 234
Kadesh 27, 269, 280
Kadesh-Barnea 199
Kadmiel 169
Kassites 169
Kedar 169
Kedorlaomer 169
Keilah 199
Kemuel 169
Kenan 169
Kenosis 217, 234
Keren-Happuch 169
Kerioth 199
Keturah 169
Keziah 169
Kidron Valley 199
Kileab 169
Kilion 169
King of the North 245
King of the South 245
Kingdom of God 217
Kings of Judah and Israel, side by side 281
Kinsman-Redeemer 217
Kirjath Jearim 199
Kirjath-jearim 282
Kish 169, 199
Kishon River 199
Knowledge 234
Kohath 170
Korah 170
Laban 170
Lachish 200, 282
Ladan 170
Ladder 284
Laish 200
Lamb of God 217
Lamech 170
Lamps, Pitchers, Trumpets ... 282
Land of Ancient Israel 282
Latin Vulgate 301
Leah 170
Leaven 217, 284
Lebanon 200
Lehi 200
Lemuel 170
Leper 217
Levi 170, 256, 275
Levites 170
Levitical Cities 200
Lewdness 217
Libya 200
Licentiousness 217

INDEX

Light 283
Literary Criticism 227, 234, 237, 238
Living Creatures 217
Lo Debar 200
Lo-Ammi 170
Locusts in Joel 254
Loincloth 217
Longsuffering 218
Lord God 265
Lot 170
Lot's wife 170
Lots, Casting of 218
Lowland 200
Lucifer 170
Lud 170
Lukewarm 218
Luz 200, 284
LXX 300
Lydia 200
Maacah 170
Maasai 170
Maaseiah 171
Maaziah 171
Maccabeans 284, 285
Maccabees 171
Machir 171
Machpelah 200
Madai 171
Magicians 171
Magog 200
Mahalath 171
Mahanaim 200
Maharai 171
Maher-Shalel-Hash-Baz 171
Mahlon 171
Mahol 171
Makir 171
Malachi 144, 145, 171
Malkijah 171
Malkishua 171
Mamre 200

Manasseh 68, 171, 256, 257, 276, 277, 281
Manasseh, Tribe of 171
Manna 218, 285
Manoah 171
Mara 171
Marah 200
Mareshah 172
Mark of the Beast 234
marks of integrity 270
Masada 200
Mash 172
Masoretic Text 300
Massa 172
Mattaniah 172
Mattathias 285
Mebab 172
Medes 172
Mediator 234
Mediterranean Sea 201
Meggido 245
Megiddo 168, 175, 191, 201, 244, 245, 246, 303
Melatiah 172
Melchizedek 172
Melech 172
Memphis, Egypt 201
Menahem 172, 281
Mene Mene 218
Mephibosheth 172
Meraioth 172
Mercy 234
Mercy Seat 218, 234
Meribah 201
Merib-baal 172
Merneptah 263, 267
Merneptah Stele 267
Merodach-baladan 172
Mesha 172, 201
Meshach 172
Meshech 172
Meshullam 173

INDEX

Meshullemeth 173
Mesopotamia 162, 180, 192, 193, 194, 195, 197, 199, 201, 203, 207, 212, 213, 216, 245, 247, 266, 275, 282, 285, 288, 294, 299, 302, 306, 307
Messiah 106
Methuselah 173
Mibsam 173
Micah 173, 251, 266, 294
Michael 173
Michaiah 173
Michal 173
Michmash 201
Midian 173, 201
Midianites 173, 245, 282
Midwife 218
Migdol 201
Mighty Men 173
Mijamin 173
Milalai 173
Milcah 173
Millennium 218, 234
Millo 201
Millstone 218
Miriam 23, 27, 30, 173
Mishael 173
Mishma 174
Mishmannah 174
Mishna 218, 286
Mithredath 174
Mizpah 201
Moab 174, 201, 246, 276, 287
Moabite 44
Moadiah 174
Modin 201
Molech 174
Monotheism 218, 235
Mordecai 76, 77, 78, 174
Moreh 201
Moriah 201

Mosera 201
Moses 22, 23, 26, 27, 29, 30, 33, 34, 36, 37, 51, 174, 261, 269, 280, 284, 291, 292, 297, 300
Moses Covenant 251
Most Holy Place 218
Mount Carmel 276
Moza 174
Mt. Sinai 290
Myrtle 287
Naamah 174
Naaman 174
Nabal 174
Naboth 174
Nachon 174
Nadab 174
Nahamani 174
Nahash 175
Nahor 175
Nahum 175, 288
Naioth 201
Names, Biblical meaning of ... 287
Naomi 175
Naphish 175
Naphtali 175
Napoleon of Egypt 244
Nathan 52, 64, 175
Nathan-melech 175
Natural Theology 235
Naturalism 235
Nazarite 175
Nazirite 218
Nebaioth 175
Nebo 202, 300
Nebuchadnezzar 102, 111, 175, 247, 306
Necho, King of Egypt 175
Negeb wilderness 276
Negev 202
Nehemiah 8, 70, 73, 74, 75, 175, 266

INDEX

Neo-Orthodoxy 235
Nephilim........................175, 218
Ner 175
Neriah 176
Nethanel 176
Nethinim 176
Netophah 202
New Covenant 251
New England Theology 235
New Testament Theology.....235
Nicaea, Council of 235
Nile River..............................202
Nimrod 176
Nimshi 176
Nineveh 124, 130, 202, 288
No (Thebes).........................202
Noah19, 176, 247, 249, 260, 267, 289, 294, 299
Nob 202
Nod 202
Nogah...................................176
Northern Kingdom218, 261, 294, 296, 305
Northern Kingdom of Israel ..202
Numbers............22, 29, 280, 300
Nun 176
Obadiah........................176, 257
Obed 176
Obed-edom..........................176
Obelisk 218
Og 176
Ohad 176
Oholah and Oholibah............176
Oholiab 176
Oholibamah 177
Old Testament 219
Old Testament Positions in Prayer...................293
Old Testament Theology.......235
Olives, Mount of 202
Omar 177
Omnipotence 219
Omnipresence......................219
Omniscience 219
Omri......................................177
Onan 177
Ophir 202
Oracle............................219, 288
Oral Laws or Traditions 286
Ordinance 219
Ordinances 235
Orontes 202
Orpah 177
Othniel 40, 177
Ox Goad 219, 289
P Document 235
Paarai 177
Padan-Aram 202
Pagan 219
Pahath-moab 177
Palal 177
Palestine202, 249, 260, 289, 290, 299, 303
Pallu 177
Palmerworm 219
Palti 177
Pantheism 235
Papyrus..211, 212, 219, 221, 260
Parable 219
Paran 202
Parchment 219
Parosh 177
Parousia 219
Parshandatha.......................177
Pas Dammin 203
Pashhur................................177
Passover 21, 219, 289
Pathros.................................203
Patriarch 219
Patriarchs 18, 289
Pedaiah 177
Pekah 177, 281
Pekahiah 177, 281
Pelaiah 177

325

INDEX

Peleg 177
Pelet 177
Peniel 203
Pentateuch 23, 219, 269
Pentecost 219
Peor 203
Perdition 219
Perez 177
Perizzites 178, 277
Persia 78, 203, 304, 305
Persian Empire 304, 306
Persians 279
Pethahiah 178
Pethor 203
Pethuel 178
Petra 203
Pharaoh 178
Pharaoh Horemheb 262
Pharaohs 261
Phenice 203
Phicol 178
Philistia 203
Philistine 51, 63, 290, 291
Philistine City-States 290
Philistines 41, 178, 246, 282, 289, 290, 291, 297, 307
Philosophical 212
Philosophical Theology 236
Phinehas 178
Phoenicia 203, 291
Phylacteries 215, 219
Pildash 178
Pillar 220
Pillar of cloud 304, 305
Pillar of fire 304, 305
Pillar of Fire and Cloud 220
Pisgah, Mount 203
Pison 203
Pithom 203
Plenary Inspiration 236, 241
Pneumatology 232, 236, 240
Polytheism. 235, 236
Pool of Siloam 268
Pope Gregory IX 272
Pope Innocent 272
Poratha 178
Potiphar 178, 249, 271
Potiphar's wife 178
Potsherd 220
Practical Theology 236
Predestination 236
Priests 23, 56
Principality 220
Prison 271
Profane 220
Progressive Revelation 236
Promised Land 22, 23, 30, 34, 37, 203
Propitiation 220, 236
Proselyte 178
Proverbs 8, 86, 87, 88, 121
Providence 220, 236
Provocation 220
Psalms 8, 75, 85, 101, 118, 123, 251, 295
Pseudepigrapha 220, 236
Psychoheresy 236
Puah 178
Pul 178
Purification 236
Purin 220
Put 178
Putiel 178
Q - Document 220
Quail 293
Qumran 203
Raamah 178
Raamses 263
Rabbah 203
Rachel 17, 178
Raddai 178
Rahab 37, 179

326

INDEX

Ram 179
Ramah 203, 277
Rameses 290
Rameses, Pharaoh 179
Ramoth 293
Ramoth Gilead 204, 293
Ramses 261, 262, 263
Ramses the Great 263
Rapture 220
Rapture of the Church 237
Rebekah 17, 19, 179
Reconciliation 220, 237
Red Sea 204
Redaction Criticism 237
Redeemer 43, 44, 291
Redemption 220, 237
Refuge, Cities of 204
Regemmelech 179
Regeneration 220, 237
Rehoboam 56, 68, 179, 275, 281, 296
Rehoboth 204
Rehum 179
Religion 237
Remaliah 179
Remission 220, 237
Remnant 275, 276
Repentance 220, 237
Rephaiah 179
Rephaim 179
Reprobate 220
Resurrection 220, 237
Reuben 179
Reuben, Tribe of 179
Revelation 237
Rhesa 179
Riblah 204
Righteousness 220, 238
Rizpah 179
Rome 204
Rosh 179
Ruth 40, 42, 43, 44, 280, 287

Sabbath 220
Sabtah 180
Sabteca 180
Sacar 180
Sackcloth 221
Salem 198, 204
Sallai 180
Salmon 180
Salt Sea 204
Salt, City of 204
Salt, Valley of 204
Salvation 238, 295
Samaria ... 75, 204, 294, 296, 305
Samaritans 180
Samson 180
Samuel 40, 45, 47, 48, 51, 56, 64, 180, 243, 252, 253, 264, 275, 280, 297, 299
Sanballat 180
Sanctification 221, 238
Sanctify 238
Saph 180
Sarah 17, 19, 180, 268
Sarai 180, 307
Sargon 59, 172, 180, 181, 190, 286, 302, 303
Sargon II, King of Assyria 180
Satan 16, 245, 260, 271, 298, 300
Saul 40, 43, 45, 48, 61, 264, 277, 280, 289, 299, 303, 307
Saul (King) 181
Saul's Five-Step Failure 299
Saved 238
Scapegoat 221, 294
Scepter 221
Scribe 181
Scripture 221
Scroll 221
Sea People 290
Seal 221
Second Coming 221, 238
Security of the Believer 238

INDEX

Seir 181
Seir, Mount 204
Sela 204
Selah 294
Semite 294
Semites 181
Semitic Languages 299
Sennacherib 181, 279, 282, 286, 288
Sepharvaim 204
Septuagint 221, 299, 301
Sepulchre 221
Serah 181
Seraphim 181, 221
Seth 181, 289
Seti II 263
Shaaph 181
Shabbethai 181
Shadrach 181
Shallum 181, 281
Shalmaneser 181
Shamgar 181
Shammah 182
Shammua 182
Shaphan 182
Shaphat 182
Sharezer 182
Shaul 182
Shavsha 182
Shealtiel 182
Shear-jashub 182
Sheba 182, 204, 295
Shebaniah 182
Sheber 182
Shecaniah 182
Shechem 182, 204, 249, 274, 295
Sheep Gate 221
Sheerah 182
Shelemiah 182
Shelomith 182
Shem 183
Shemaiah 183
Shemariah 183
Shemer 183
Sheol 197, 205, 296
Shephatiah 183
Shepherd 296
Sherebiah 183
Sheshbazzar 183
Shethar-bozenai 183
Sheva 183
Shewbread 221
Shiloh 205, 297
Shimea 183
Shimei 183
Shimron 183
Shinar 205
Shishak 183
Shitrai 184
Shittim 205, 300
Shobal 184
Shuah 184
Shual 205
Shunem 205
Shuni 184
Shur 205
Shushan 205, 304
Shuthelah 184
Sidon 184, 205
Sihon 184
Siloam Pool 205
Simon the Just 248
Sin 238
Sin, Wilderness of 205
Sinai 205
Sinaiticus, Codex 238
Siphmoth 205
Sisera 184
Six Related Old Testament Books 301
Snatching Away 258

INDEX

Sodom and Gomorrah 205
Solomon 51, 53, 55, 56, 57, 63, 64, 66, 67, 68, 86, 88, 89, 90, 91, 94, 184, 248, 264, 267, 275, 279, 291, 293, 295, 296, 305
Son of Man 297
Song of Solomon 93, 305
Sons 297
Soothsayer 184
Sorek 205
Soteriology 238, 240
Source Criticism 239
South Ramoth 206
Southern Kingdom 101, 102, 221, 267
Southern Kingdom of Judah .. 206
Sovereignty of God 239
Spirit of God 116
Spiritual Gifts 221, 239
Standard 221
Store City 221
Storehouse 221
Stumblingblock 221
Submission 239
Succoth 206
Sumer 206, 302
Sumerians 302
Sun, Stand Still 303
Supplication 221
Susa 206, 304
Swaddling Clothes 222
Syria 206, 280, 285
Systematic Theology 239
Tabor, Mount 206
Tadmor 206
Tahan 184
Tahpanhes 206
Tahpenes 184
Tahrea 184
Talent 222
Talmud 240

Tamar 184
Tanakh 300
Tapestry 222
Taphath 184
Tappuah 184
Tarshish 206
Taskmaster 222
Tebah 184
Tekel 218
Tekoa 206
Telem 184
Tell 222
Tema 184
Teman 185
Temple 55, 66, 70, 137, 259, 285
Temptation 240
Ten marks of integrity 270
Tent of Meeting 222
Terah 185
Teraphim 222
Terrestrial 222
Testament 222
Textual Criticism 227, 240
The Aramaic Dialect 243
The Day of the Lord 254
The Plagues of Egypt 291
The Septuagint 299, 300
Thebes 206
Theism 240
Theocracy 222, 240
Theology 240
Theology Proper 241
Theophany 222, 241, 304, 305
Thummin 222
Thutmose III 244, 260, 262
Tibni 185
Tiglath-pileser 185
Tiglath-pileser II 185
Tiglath-pileser III 185
Tigris River 206
Timnah 206
Timnath serah 206

INDEX

Tirhakah 185
Tirzah 304
Tithe 222
Tobadonijah 185
Tobiah 185
Tobijah 185
Togarmah 185
Tola 185
Topography of Israel 276
Topography of the Sinai 300
Torah 219, 222, 241, 275, 285, 286
Tower 305
Transjordan 207
Tree of Knowledge of Good and Evil 222
Tree of Life 222
Tribulation 222, 241
Tribulation, The Great 222
Trinity 223, 241
Triumphal Entry 223
Trumpets 282
Tubal 185
Tubal-cain 185
Twelve spies 185
twelve tribes ...19, 256, 274, 275
Tyre 207, 280, 305
Universalism 241
Unpardonable Sin 241
Upharsin 218
Ur 17, 207, 247, 266, 306, 307
Uri 185
Uriah 185
Uriel 186
Urik 207
Urim 223
Ussher 282
Usury 223
Uthai 186
Uz 186, 207
Uzza 186

Uzzah 186
Uzzi 186
Uzzia 186
Uzziah 186, 281
Uzziel 186
Vajezatha 186
Valley of Dry Bones 207
Vashti 76, 77, 78, 186
Verbal Inspiration 241
Virgin Birth 241
Voltaire 272
Vophsi 186
War Scroll 243
Watchman 223
Watchtower 223
Wilderness 22, 223
Wisdom Literature 223
Wormwood 223
Xerxes 78
Xerxes of Persia 186
Yahweh 277, 303, 307
Year of Jubilee 223
Yoke 223
Zabad 186
Zabbai 186
Zabdi 186
Zaccur 187
Zachariah 187
Zadok 187
Zalmon 187
Zarephath 207
Zebadiah 187
Zebidah 187
Zeboim 207
Zebulun 187
Zechariah 72, 140, 142, 187, 246, 260, 289
Zedekiah 102, 187, 281
Zephaniah 110, 135, 187, 287, 288

INDEX

Zerubbabel 69, 72, 138, 139, 142, 187
Ziba 187
Ziggurat 302
Ziklag 207, 307
Zilpah 187
Zimri 187
Zin, Wilderness of 207
Zion 207
Zipporah 187
Ziv 223
Zoar 207
Zophar 188
Zorah 207